FRESH LEAVES

BY

FANNY FERN

FANNY FERN

PREFACE.

Every writer has his parish. To mine, I need offer no apology for presenting,

First, a new story which has never before appeared in print;

Secondly, the "hundred-dollar-a-column story," respecting the remuneration of which, skeptical paragraphists have afforded me so much amusement. (N. B.—My banker and I can afford to laugh!) This story having been published when "The New York Ledger" was in the dawn of its present unprecedented circulation, and never having appeared elsewhere, will, of course, be new to many of my readers;

Thirdly, I offer them my late fugitive pieces, which have often been requested, and which, with the other contents of this volume, I hope will cement still stronger our friendly relations.

FANNY FERN.

A BUSINESS MAN'S HOME;
OR, A STORY FOR HUSBANDS.

CHAPTER I.

"There's your father, children."

The piano was immediately closed by the young performer, and the music-stool put carefully away, that the new-comer might have an unrestricted choice of seats; a wide space was immediately cleared before the grate which had been carefully replenished with coal but half an hour before; a stray cricket was hastily picked up and pushed beneath the sofa, and an anxious glance was thrown around the room by Mrs. Wade as her husband entered the room.

"Too much light here," said the latter, as he turned down the gas burner. "I hate such a glare. Waste of coal, too; fire enough to roast an ox, and coal seven dollars a ton;" and Mr. Wade seized the poker and gave the grate a vindictive poke.

Mrs. Wade sighed—she had too long been accustomed to such scenes to do any thing else. It was not the first time, nor the second, nor the hundredth, that her unwearied endeavors to make home cheerful had been met with a similar repulse; the young people, so gay but a moment before, skipped, one by one, out of the room, closing the door noiselessly behind them as culprit-like they glided away.

"Heigh-ho," muttered Mr. Wade, as he threw himself down, boots and all, on the sofa, "heigh-ho."

"Does your head ache?" asked his patient wife.

"I want my tea," growled Mr. Wade, without deigning a reply.

Mrs. Wade might have answered—most women would—that it had been ready this half-hour. She might also have said that she had just come up from the kitchen, where she had been to see that his favorite dish of toast was prepared to his liking. She might also have said that she did not like to order tea till he had signified his wish for it—but as I said before, Mrs. Wade had been too long in school not to have learned her lesson well. So she merely touched her forefinger to the bell, for Betty to bring in the tea.

It was strong and hot—Mr. Wade could not deny it;—the milk was sweet; so was the butter, the toast was unexceptionable, and enough of it; the cake light, and the sweetmeats unfermented. Poor, ill-used Mr. Wade —he was in that most provoking of all dilemmas to a petulant temper, there was nothing to fret about.

"There's the door bell," he exclaimed, inwardly relieved at the idea of an escape-valve; "now I suppose I shall be talked deaf by that silly Mrs. Jones and her daughter, or bored by that stupid Mr. Forney; it's very strange that a man can not enjoy his family one evening free from interruption."

No such thing—Mr. Wade was cheated out of a fresh growl; the new arrival being a carpet-bag, and its accessory, Mr. John Doe, a brother-growler, whom Mr. Wade would rather have seen, if possible, than a new gold dollar. Mr. John Doe, as sallow as a badly-preserved pickle, and about as sweet—a man all nerves and frowns—a walking thunder-cloud, muttering vengeance against any thing animate, or inanimate, which had the temerity to bask in the sunshine. Mr. John Doe, a worse drug than any in his apothecary's shop, who believed in the eternal destruction of little dead babies; turned the world into one vast charnel-house, and reversed the verdict of Him who pronounced it "very good."

"Ah—how d'ye do—how dy'e do?" said Mr. Wade, with an impromptu lugubrious whine, as Mr. Doe ran his fingers through his grizzled locks, and deposited his time-worn carpet-bag in the corner; "it is pleasant to see a friend."

"Thank you, thank you," replied Mr. Doe, lowering himself as carefully into his chair as if he was afraid his joints would become unriveted; "there's no knowing how many more times you may have to say that; these sudden changes of weather are dreadful underminers of a man's constitution. Traveling, too, racks me to pieces; I can't sleep in a strange bed, nor get any thing I can eat when I wake, my appetite is so delicate; —sometimes I think it don't make much difference—we are poor creatures—begin to die as soon as we are born—how do you do, Mr. Wade? You look to me like a man who is going to have the jaundice, eye-balls yellow, etc.—any appetite?"

"Not much," said Mr. Wade, unbuttoning his lower vest button, under which were snugly stowed away a pile of buttered toast, three cups of tea, and preserved peaches enough to make a farmer sick—"not much;— a man who works as hard as I do, gets too exhausted to eat when it comes night, or if he does, his food does not digest; how's your family?"

"So, so," muttered Doe, with an expressive shrug; "children are a great care, Mr. Wade, a great care—my John don't take that interest in the drug business that I wish he did; he always has some book or other on hand, reading; I am afraid he never will be good for any thing; your book-worms always go through the world, knocking their heads against facts. I shouldn't wonder, after all my care, if he turned out a poor miserable author; sometimes I think what is to be, will be, and there's no use trying."

"Is not that fatalism?" quietly interposed Mrs. Wade, blushing the next moment that she had so far departed from "The Married Woman's Guide," as to question an opinion which her husband had indorsed by his silence. "Children are a great care, 'tis true, but it always seemed to me that the care brought its own sweet reward."

Mr. Doe wheeled round to look in the face this meek wife, whose disappointed heart, turning to her children for that comfort which she had in vain looked for from her husband, could ill brook that the value of this coveted treasure should have such depreciating mention.

"Pshaw! what signify words?" said her husband. "I hate argument; besides, women can't argue—every body knows that; and every body knows that if a man wants his children to do, or be, one thing, they are sure to do, or be, just the opposite. I've no doubt it will turn out just so with ours; there is no counting on 'em. In my day, if a man was a farmer, his son was a farmer after him, and never thought of being any thing else. Nowadays, children have to be consulted as to 'their bent.' Fudge— fiddlestick; their bent is for mischief and dodging work, and a tight rein and a good smart rod is the best cure for it."

Just at this point Mr. Doe gave a dismal groan, and doubled himself up like a jack-knife. "A touch of my old complaint," said he, holding on to his waist-band. "Rheumatism—it will carry me off some day. Mrs. Wade, if you will be so good as to look in my carpet-bag, you will find a plaster which I never travel without; and I will trouble you, Mrs. Wade, to have my bed warmed, and a fire in the room where you intend I should sleep; and if there should be any cracks in the windows, will you have the goodness to nail up a blanket over them? and I would like a very warm comforter, if you please, and a jug of hot water at my feet, if it would not be too much trouble."

"Of course not," said Mr. Wade, settling himself very comfortably down into his ample easy-chair; "of course not; Mrs. Wade, won't you attend to it?"

"And, Mrs. Wade, if you'd be so kind as to put the feather bed uppermost, and give me cotton sheets instead of linen; I should also prefer a hair to a feather pillow: I consider feathers too heating for my head; I am obliged to be careful of my head."

"Certainly," repeated Mr. Wade. "Mrs. Wade will see to it." And as she moved out of the room to execute these orders, these two despondent Siamese drew their chairs closer together, to bemoan the short-comings of two of the most long-suffering wives who ever wore themselves to skeletons, trying to please husbands who were foreordained not to be pleased.

CHAPTER II.

Mother's room! How we look back to it in after years, when she who sanctified it is herself among the sanctified. How well we remember the ample cushioned chair, with its all-embracing arms, none the worse in our eyes for having rocked to sleep so many little forms now scattered far and wide, divided from us, perhaps, by barriers more impassable than the cold, blue sea. Mother's room—where the sun shone in so cheerily upon the flowering plants in the low, old-fashioned window-seats, which seemed to bud and blossom at the least touch of her caressing fingers; on which no blight or mildew ever came; no more than on the love which outlived all our childish waywardness—all our childish folly. The cozy sofa upon which childish feet were never forbidden to climb; upon which curly heads could dream, unchidden, the fairy dreams of childhood. The closet which garnered tops, and dolls, and kites, and whips, and toys, and upon whose upper shelf was that infallible old-fashioned panacea for infancy's aches and pains—brimstone and molasses! The basket, too, where was always the very string we wanted; the light-stand round which we gathered, and threaded needles (would we had threaded thousands more) for eyes dimmed in our service; and the cheerful face that smiled across it such loving thanks.

Mother's room! where our matronly feet returned when we were mothers; where we lifted our little ones to kiss the wrinkled face, beautiful with its halo of goodness; where we looked on well pleased to see the golden locks we worshiped, mingling lovingly with the silver hairs; where, as the fond grand-mamma produced, in alarming profusion, cakes and candies for the little pets, we laughingly reminded her of our baby days, when she wisely told us such things were "unwholesome;" where ourbaby caps, yellow with time, ferreted from some odd bag or closet, were tried on our own babies' heads, and we sat, wondering where the months and years had flown between then and now; and looking forward, half-sighing, to just such a picture, when we should play what seemed to us now, with our smooth skins, round limbs, and glossy locks, such an impossible part.

Mother's room! where we watched beside her patient sick-bed through the long night, gazing hopelessly at the flickering taper, listening to the pain-extorted groan, which no human skill, no human love, could avert or relieve; waiting with her the dawning of that eternal day, seen through a mist of tears, bounded by no night.

Mother's room! where the mocking light strayed in through the half-opened shutters, upon her who, for the first time, was blind to our tears, and deaf to our cries; where busy memory could bring back to us no look, no word, no tone, no act of hers, not freighted with God-like love. Alas!—alas for us then, if, turning the tablets, they showed us this long debt of love unappreciated—unpaid!

No blossoming plants luxuriated in the windows of Mr. Wade's house; no picture attracted attention upon the walls; with the exception of a huge map of the United States in the hall, their blank whiteness was pitilessly unrelieved. The whole house seemed to be hopelessly given up to the household god—utility. If Mrs. Wade ever had any womanish leaning toward the ornamental, she had long since learned to suppress it; and what woman, how poor soever she may be, does not make some feeble attempt to brighten up the little spot she calls home? Beautiful to me, for this reason, is the crude picture, the cheap plaster-cast, or the china mug with its dried grass, or the blue ribbon which ties back the coarse but clean white curtain under humble roofs. Who shall say that such things have not a moral influence—a moral significance? Who shall say that there is not more hope of that young man on the walls of whose bachelor attic hangs a landscape, or a sweet female head, though not "by an old master?" Who that has been so unfortunate as to sojourn in that mockery of a home, called a boarding-house, has not, when passing through the halls, and by the open doors of rooms, formed favorable or unfavorable opinions of its occupants from these mute indications of taste and character? Let no one, particularly if he has children, wait till he can command the most costly adornments; have one picture, have one statue, have one vase, if no more, for little eyes to look at, for little tongues to prattle about.

If Mr. Wade had but understood this! If he had but brushed from his heart the cobwebs of his counting-room—for he had a heart, buried as it was under the world's rubbish; if he had not circumscribed his thoughts, wishes, hopes, aims, by the narrow horizon of his ledger. If—If! Dying lips falter out that word regretfully;—alas! that we should learn to live only when we come to die!

I have said Mr. Wade had a heart, ossified as it now was by the all-absorbing love of gain. At the age of seven years, he was left, with a younger brother, the only legacy to a heart-broken, invalid mother, who found herself suddenly thrown upon the world for that charity that she had been accustomed to bestow. To say that she found none, would be false; the world is not all bad; but there were months in which Mr. Wade, then a bright, handsome lad, was glad to carry home to her and his little brother, the refuse food of the neighbors' kitchens. They who have felt in early youth the griping hand of poverty, unfortunately learn to attach undue value to the possession of money. Day after day, as the boy witnessed his feeble mother struggling vainly with her fate—day after day the thought, for her sake to become rich, haunted his waking dreams and his boyish pillow. With his arms about her neck, he would picture the blessings and comforts of a future home, which his more hopeful eyes saw in the distance. The road to it, to be sure, was rough and thorny, but still it was there; no cloud of adversity could wholly obscure it to the boy's vision; and even in the darkest night, when he woke, in fancy the lamps gleamed brightly from its curtained windows; and so the boy smothered down his swelling heart, when the refuse food was tossed carelessly into his beggar's basket, and was thankful for the little job which brought him even a penny to place in her hand, as an earnest of what should come—God willing; and at night, when the younger brother shivered with cold, John would chafe his chilled feet, and, taking him in his arms, soothe him to blissful slumbers. That the world should ever chill such a heart! That the armor buckled over it in so righteous a cause, should contract around it and prove but its shroud!

Nobly the boy struggled: they who are not fastidious as to the means, seldom fail of securing the result they aim at. John Wade's pride never stood like a lion in his path; he heeded not the supercilious glance or careless tone of his employers, so that he received the hard-earned reward of his toil. At length, from loving money for what it would bring, he learned to love it for its own sake; and when death removed from him those for whom he toiled, he toiled on for love of the shining dross. Pity that gold should always bring with it the canker—covetousness.

CHAPTER III.

"I have a great mind to go to bed," said Susy Wade, yawning; "I'm not sleepy, either, but I don't know what do do with myself; there's that tiresome Mr. Doe down stairs—he croaks, and croaks, and croaks, till I feel almost as sick as he pretends to. Now he will keep mother nursing up his rheumatism, as he calls it, till ten o'clock, when he is no more sick than she is, nor half so much; mother never complains when any thing ails her; but I am not like mother; I am not patient a bit. Were it not for mother, Neddy, I should like to sail way off across the ocean, and never come back; I get so tired here at home, and I know she does, too, though she never says any thing; sometimes she sighs such a long sigh, when she thinks nobody hears her; I should rather she would cry outright; it always makes me feel better to have a good cry. I wish that our father was like Carey Hunt's father."

"So do I," said Neddy, fixing his humming-top—"so do I—they have such fun there. Tom told me that his father played games with them evenings, and showed them how to make kites, and brought them home story-books, and read them aloud, and sometimes the whole family go out together to some place of amusement. I wonder what makes our father so different from Tom Hunt's father? Tommy always runs down street to meet his father when he comes home, and tells him what has happened on the play-ground; I wonder why our father never talks to us about such things? I wonder how father felt when he was a boy—don't you suppose he ever played?"

"I don't know," said Susy, mournfully; "I'm only fifteen, but I mean to get married just as soon as I can, and then I won't have such a gloomy house, and you shall come and live with me, Neddy."

"But mother—" said Neddy.

"O, mother shall come to see us all the time," said Susy; "won't we have fun?"

"But perhaps your husband will be a sober man, like father, and won't want company, only people like Mr. Doe."

"But my husband will be young, you little goose," said Susy.

"Well—wasn't father young when mother married him?" said the persistent Neddy, whirling off his top.

"I suppose so," said Susy, with a sigh, "but it don't seem as if he ever was. Where's the Arabian Nights, Neddy, that you borrowed of Tom Hunt? let's read a story."

"Father made me carry it back," said Neddy; "he said it was nonsense, and I shouldn't read it."

"That's just why I like it," said Susy; "of course, nobody believes it true —and I'm so tired of sense! Isn't there any thing up in the book-rack there, Neddy?"

"I'll see," said Neddy, stretching his neck up out of his clean white collar —"I'll see—here's Moral Philosophy, Key to Daboll's Arithmetic, Sermons by Rev. John Pyne, Essays by Calvin Croaker, Guide to Young Wives, Rules for Eating, Walking and Talking, Complete Letter Writer, Treatise on Pneumatics, Buchan's Domestic Medicine. Which will you have?" asked Neddy, with a comical whine.

"Hush!" said Susy, "there's father's step."

Mr. Wade had come up to get his soft lamb's-wool slippers for Mr. Doe, that gentleman having experienced a chill in his left toe joint.

"Playing top," said he, contemptuously, looking at Neddy; "at your age, sir, I was wheeling stone for a mason, in the day-time, and studying arithmetic evenings. Where's your Daboll, sir? Study your pound and pence table; that's what's to be the making of you; how do you expect to become a man of business without that? You'll never drive a good bargain—you'll be cheated out of your eye-teeth. Get your Daboll, sir, and Susy, do you hear him say it. Tops are for babies, sir; a boy of your age ought to be almost as much a man as his father. How should I look playing top? God didn't make the world to play in." And Mr. Wade and his lamb's-wool slippers slipped down stairs.

"He didn't make it for a work-shop either," thought Susy, as she took down the offensive Daboll.

They to whom the word father comprises all that is reverent, tender, companionable and sweet, may refuse to recognize the features of this portrait as a true likeness of the relation for which it stands; they may well doubt—they whose every childish hope and fear was freely confided to a pitying, loving, sympathizing heart—they whose generous impulses were never chilled by the undeserved breath of suspicion and distrust—they whose overflowing love was never turned back in a lava tide to devastate their fresh young hearts—happy they for whom memory daguerreotypes no such mournful picture! Still, let them not for that reason doubt, that through the length and breadth of the land, are men and women who look back sorrowing on what they might have been, but for their blighted childhood!

"Blessed night!" the words often fell from Mrs. Wade's lips, as she closed her chamber-door, and, laying her weary head upon her pillow, sought oblivion in sleep.

"Blessed night;" the children did not hear it, for whose sakes she often repressed the rising sigh, and sent back to their fountain the scalding tears, and whose future, as her health and strength declined, she would have trembled to contemplate, but for her faith in God.

He did not hear it—one kind word from whom, one look, or smile, to say that he appreciated all her untiring efforts, would have brought back the roses of health to that faded cheek. He did not hear it, as he sat there over the midnight-fire, with groaning Mr. Doe, ringing the changes on dollars and cents, dollars and cents, which had come between him and the priceless love of those warm hearts.

Ay—Blessed night!

CHAPTER IV.

"I think it must be time for Henry to come home," and the speaker glanced at a little gold watch on the mantel. "What a noise those children are making. I told them to keep still, but after all, I'm glad that they didn't mind me; the most pitiful sight on earth to me, is a child with a feeble body and a large head, who never plays. Let them romp—broken chairs are easier mended than broken spines; who would be a slave to an upholstery shop, or a set of porcelain; who would keep awake at night to watch the key which locks up a set of gold or silver? Who would mew children up in the nursery for fear of a parlor carpet? My parlor is not too good for my children to play in, and I hope it never will be. Now I will go down and take out some cake for tea; how glad I am Henry loves cake, because I know so well how to make it; who would have thought I should have had such a good husband, and such a happy home—poor mamma—and she deserves it so much better than I. Sometimes I think I ought never to have left home while she lived, but have staid to comfort her. Oh my children must be very—very happy; childhood comes but once—but once."

So said Mary Hereford, Mr. Wade's married daughter, as she picked up the toys, and picture-books, and strings, and marbles, with which her romping children had strewed her chamber floor.

Mary Hereford was no beauty. She had neither golden brown, nor raven hair; her skin was not transparently white, nor her eyes dazzlingly bright, nor her foot and hand miraculously small. She was simply a plump, healthy, rosy, cheerful little cricket of a woman—singing ever at her own hearth-stone—proud of her husband—proud of her children, knowing no weariness in their service. Many a beautiful woman has wrung her white hands in vain for the love which lent wings to this unhandsome, but still lovely little wife, dignified even the most common-place employment, and made her heart a temple for sweet and holy thoughts to gather.

"Yes, there comes Henry now," said Mary, and before the words were well out of her mouth, her husband held her at arm's length, and looked into her face.

"You have been sewing too steadily, little wife," said he; "I must take you out for a walk after tea. I shall get a sempstress to help you if these children out-grow their clothes so fast."

Mary laughed a merry little laugh; "No such thing—I am not tired a bit —at least not now you are here; beside, don't you work hard down in that close counting-room, your poor head bothered with figures all day? Do you suppose a wife is to fold her hands idly, that her husband may get gray hairs? No—you and I will grow old together, but that is a long way off yet, you know," and Mary shook her brown hair about her face. "Come—now for tea. I have such nice cakes for you; the children have been so good and affectionate; to be sure they tear their aprons occasionally, and perhaps break a cup or plate, but what is that, if we are only kind and happy? Oh, it is blessed to be happy!" And Mary would have thrown her arms around her husband's neck, but unfortunately she was too short.

The smoking tea and savory cakes were set upon the table—Followed the children, bouncing and rosy—fairly brightening up the room like a gay bouquet. With one on either knee, Henry Hereford listened, well pleased, to tales of soaring kites, and sympathized with disastrous shipwrecks of mimic boats, nor thought his dignity compromised in discussing the question, whether black, blue, or striped marbles were prettiest, or whether a doll whose eyes were not made to open and shut, could, by any stretch of imagination, be supposed by its youthful mamma to go to sleep. How priceless is the balm of sympathy to childhood! The certainty that no joy is too minute, no grief too trivial to find an echo in the parental heart. Blessed they—who, like little children, are neither too wise, nor too old to lean thus on the Almighty Father!

"Where's my umbrella, Susan?" said Mr. Wade, "it is raining, and I am in a hurry to go to my business."

"It is Sunday, Mr. Wade; did you forget it was Sunday?"

"Sunday!" ejaculated Mr. Wade, in well-feigned surprise, "we didn't have salt fish, I believe, for dinner yesterday."

"No," replied his wife, penitently, "but I believe it is the first time it has been omitted since our marriage."

"It was an omission," said Mr. Wade, solemnly, as he laid aside his hat and coat. "Sunday, is it, Mrs. Wade, I wish I hadn't got up so early—I suppose you are going to take the children off to church, are you not? I'd like to be quiet, and go to sleep till dinner time."

"Perhaps you would step over to Mary's some part of the day," suggested his wife. "She came here yesterday to leave some nice jelly that she had been making for me, and said you had not been there for nearly two months."

"No," replied Mr. Wade, "I had as lief encounter a hornet's nest as those children of Mary's; they are just like eels, slipping up and slipping down; slipping in, and slipping out; never still. Mary is spoiling them. The last time I was there I found her playing puss in the corner with them; puss in the corner, Mrs. Wade!—how does she expect to keep them at a proper distance, and make them reverence her, as your Bible calls it, if she is going to frolic with them that way? and Henry is not a whit better; they are neither fit to bring up a family. Mary used to be a sedate, steady girl, before she was married; I don't know that I remember having ever heard her laugh in her life, while she was at home; I can't think what has changed her so."

His wife drooped her head, but made no answer.

The cold, hard man before her had no key with which to unlock the buried sorrows of those long weary years which Susan Wade was at that moment passing in review.

"Yes; I can't think what has changed her so," resumed Mr. Wade; "I think it must be Henry's fault—she was brought up so carefully; but after all, a great deal depends upon the sort of man a woman marries. I dare say," added he, complacently, "you would have been a very different woman had you married any body but me."

"Very likely," answered his wife, mournfully.

"To be sure, you would; I am glad you have the good sense to see it; I consider that a woman is but a cipher up to the time she is married—her husband then invests her with a certain importance, always subservient to his, of course. Then a great deal depends, too, on the way a man begins with his wife. Now I always had a great respect for Dr. Johnson, for the sensible manner in which he settled matters on his wedding day; it seems that he and his wife were to ride horseback to the church where they were to be married. Soon after starting his bride told him, first, that they rode too fast, then, too slow. 'This won't do,' said he to himself; 'I must begin with this woman as I mean to go on; she must keep my pace, not I hers:' and so, putting spurs to his horse, he galloped out of sight; when she rejoined him at the church-door, she was in tears—in a proper state of submission—he never had any trouble with her afterward; it was more necessary as she was a widow; they need an uncommon tight rein. Sensible old fellow, that Johnson. I don't know that I ever enjoyed any thing more than his answer to a lady who was going into ecstasies at some performance she had seen, and wondered that the doctor did not agree with her; 'My dear,' said he, 'you must remember that you are a dunce, and, therefore, very easily pleased.' Very good, upon my word—ha—ha—very good; 'Doctor Johnson's Life' is the only book I ever had patience to read; he understood the sex; ha—ha—upon my word, very good"—and Mr. Wade rubbed his spectacles with such animation that he rubbed out one of the glasses.

"Two and sixpence for getting excited!" said he, as he picked up the fragments; "well—it is a little luxury I don't often indulge in; but really that old Johnson was such a fine old fellow—I like him. Now take the children off to church, Susan; I want to go sleep."

"I hope he may never be sorry for sending that pale, sickly woman out in such a driving rain as this," muttered Betty, as her mistress walked over the wet pavements to church. "If there's a selfisher man than Mr. Wade, I'd like to know it; well, he won't have her long, and then maybe he'll think of it. I would have left here long ago if it had not been for her; it's work—work—work—with him, and no thanks, and that's what is fretting the soul out of her; she can't please him with all her trying. And Miss Susan and Neddy—cooped up here like birds in a cage, and never allowed to speak above their breath; they'll fly through the bars sometime, if he don't open the door wider; and Miss Susan getting to be a young lady, too—looking as solemn as a sexton, when she ought to be frisking and frolicking about like all other innocent young creturs. I used to get her down here, and make molasses candy for her, but she has out-grown candy, now—well, I don't know what will come of it all. At her age I was going to husking and quilting frolics, and singing-school; bless me—what a time I used to have coming through the snow-drifts. I really believe Isaiah Pettibone used to upset the sleigh on purpose. I suppose I might have married him if I had been as forrard as some girls—leastways I know he gave me a paper heart, with a dart stuck through it; but when I look at Mr. Wade, I say it is all right—ten to one he might have turned out just such a cranky curmudgeon. People say that for every bad husband in the world, there's a bad wife somewhere to balance it; I don't believe it—but, anyhow, if there is, I wish they'd each torment their own kind, and not be killing off such patient creturs as Mrs. Wade. I'll go up stairs and put her slippers to the fire, and then get something nice and hot for her to take when she comes back. I used to think that a poor servant-girl was not of much account in the world—I don't think so since I came here to live; I know it is a comfort to Mrs. Wade to feel that somebody in the house is caring for her, who is always doing for other people; and though she never says a word about her troubles, and I am not the girl to let her know that I see them, yet the way in which she says, 'Thank you, Betty; you are always kind and thoughtful,' shows me that, humble as I am, she leans on me, and pays me a hundred times over for any little thing I do for her. I think, after all, that God made nobody of so little account that he could not at some time or other help somebody else. There's the bell, now! Mercy on us! there's that croaking raven, Mr. Doe, coming here to dinner; he will be sure to eat up every thing good that I make for Mrs. Wade. I wonder how a man who is eternally grumbling and growling at every thing the Lord has made, can have the face to gormandize His good things, as Mr. Doe does. I'd either let 'em alone, or say Thank you—he don't do nary one."

CHAPTER V.

The bleak winds of March were abroad, causing even the healthy and rugged to shrink from their piercing breath, and fold more closely around their shivering limbs the warm garments of winter; while the delicate invalid, warned by his irritated lungs, ventured not beyond the equable temperature of his closely-curtained chamber.

Mrs. Wade's accustomed place at the table was vacant; her busy fingers no longer kept the domestic treadmill in motion. Ah! how seldom we feel till the "mother" is stricken down, how never-ceasing is the vigilance, how tireless the patience that ministers to our daily wants;—dropping noiseless, like the gentle dew, too common and unobtrusive a blessing to be noticed—till absence teaches us its value.

Death had no terrors for Mrs. Wade. It was only when looking upon the children whom she must leave behind, that she prayed, with quivering lips—"Lord, I believe; help Thou mine unbelief!"

If in the thorny path her woman's feet had trod, her daughter's trembling feet must walk! What human arm would sustain her? what human voice whisper words of cheer? And Neddy—the impulsive, generous, warm-hearted Neddy; quick to err—as quick to repent—what human hand would weigh justly in the scales of praise and blame, his daily deeds? What hand, save a mother's, in uprooting the weeds, would crush not the tender flowers? Oh, what mother, while pondering these things in her heart, and looking round upon the dear faces, in the near or distant prospect of dissolution, has not felt her heart-tendrils tighten around them, with a vice-like clasp that almost defied separation? Nature's voice is clamorous; but over, and above, and through its importunate pleadings, comes there to the Christian mother, the still, small whisper, "My grace is sufficient for thee!"

Mr. Wade at first refused to believe in the reality of his wife's sickness. Women, he said, were always ailing, and fancying themselves dying. But, as the parlor was vacated for the chamber, and the easy-chair for the bed, and the doctor's chaise stopped twice a day before the door, and

Mrs. Hereford left her own little family to sit beside her mother, and Betty wiped her eyes with her apron every time she left the chamber door —and, more than all, when Mr. Wade's toast was not browned as sheused to brown it, and his favorite pudding was wanting, and the lamp burned dimly on the lonely tea-table, and his slippers were not always in the right place—he resigned himself to what seemed inevitable, with the air of a deeply-injured man; and slept as soundly at night, in the room next his wife's, as if death's shadow had not even then fallen across the threshold.

At breakfast he drove Betty distracted with orders and counter-orders about egg-boiling and toast-making, after eating which, he drew on a pair of creaking boots and an overcoat, and mounted to his wife's room, to go through the ceremony of inquiring "how she was," holding the door open for the cold wind to blow upon the invalid, while he received the faint "Easy, thank you," from lips that contracted with pain, as the door closed after him in no gentle manner.

No thought of his children disturbed Mr. Wade's equanimity. He did not see, day by day, the sorrowful face of his daughter lifted to his, as if in search of sympathy; nor notice the tip-toe steps of the playful little Neddy, as he passed to and fro, with messages from Mrs. Hereford to Betty.

"It's infamous!" said the latter, slamming herself down in one of the kitchen chairs. "Is that man made of flesh and blood, or is he not? All last night, Mrs. Wade sat up in bed, with that dreadful distress for breath, tossing her arms up over her head, and that man snoring away like the seven sleepers. It's infamous! Now, I'm no eaves-dropper: I scorn it; but I was in the kitchen this morning, and the slide was open through the closet into the basement, and I heard Mrs. Hereford say to her husband, who had called to inquire after Mrs. Wade: 'Oh, James, James, how can I love or respect my father?' and she sobbed as if her heart would break; and then she told him that the doctor had ordered some kind of drugs to be burned in Mrs. Wade's room to help her breathing—something expensive—I don't remember the name, and Mr. Wade said the doctor was an old granny, and it was a useless expense, and wouldn't give his daughter the money for it. When Mrs. Hereford had finished telling, I heard her husband say a word I never expected to hear out of his mouth, and he kissed his wife, and handing her his pocket-book, told her to get whatever was necessary. Oh, dear; the Bible says, 'Honor your parents;' but whether such a man as that is a parent? that's the question. Some of the ministers must settle it; I can't. But it never will be clear to me that bringing a child into the world makes a parent. I don't care what they say; it's clear as day-light that the Lord meant that after that they should see 'em safe through it, no matter how much trouble turns up for 'em. When I'm married, if I ever am, I'll say this to my young ones: 'Now look here; tell me every thing. If you are sorry, tell me; if you are glad, tell me; if you are wicked, tell me; and I never, never, will turn away from you, no more than I want God to turn away from me. And if you break God's laws and man's laws, as I hope you won't—if you love Him and me—still, I never will shut my door in your face, no matter what you do, no more than I want my Maker to shut heaven's door in mine.' Now, that's my notion of a parent. Whether I shall ever have a chance to carry it out or not—that's another thing; but as sure as I do, there's where you'll find me; and it's my belief that many a man has swung on a gibbet, and many a woman has cursed God and man with her last breath, for want of just that. As if food, and drink, and clothes was all a child wanted, or a wife either, for that matter; as if that was all a husband or a father was bound to furnish; as if that was all the Lord would hold him accountable for; as if that was—gracious Gradgrind, there's my toast burnt all to a crisp."

Thanks to Mrs. Hereford, who procured the herbs ordered by the doctor, the poor sufferer was temporarily relieved.

"Who is that, Mary?" she asked, as she distinguished a strange footstep in the hall.

"It is Miss Alsop," replied Mary.

No reply from the invalid, but a weary turning of the pale face toward the pillow, and a gathering moisture in the eyes.

"Come here, Mary—nearer—nearer"—Mrs. Hereford bent her head so low that her brown curls swept her mother's pillow.

"That—woman—will—be—your—father's—wife   when—I—am—scarcely—cold."

"God forbid—don't, mother—don't;" and poor Mary's tears and kisses covered the emaciated face before her.

"You have a home—and a husband—and a kind one, Mary, but Susan and Neddy—it is hard to leave my children to her keeping. If I could but take them with me."

As she said this, Betty beckoned Mrs. Hereford out of the room, saying "that Miss Alsop wished to see her, to inquire how dear Mrs. Wade had passed the night."

"Tell her," said Mary, "that she is very ill, and that I can not leave her to receive visitors."

"If you please," said Betty, returning, "Miss Alsop says she is so weary that she will sit and rest for half an hour."

"Just half an hour before father comes home; then, of course, he will invite her to partake his solitary dinner; that's just what she came for; mother is right; how strange that I never should have thought of all this before!" and a thousand little things now flashed upon her mind in confirmation of what her mother had just said.

Miss Alsop was an unmarried woman of forty, and presented that strange anomaly, a fat old maid. Her teeth were good, her hair thick and glossy, and her voice softer than the cooing of a dove; one of those voices which are the never-failing herald of deceit and hypocrisy to the keen observer of human nature. For years she had had her eye upon Mr. Alsop, and actually claimed a sort of cousinly relationship, which she never had been able very clearly to establish, but upon the strength of which she had come, self-invited, twice a month, to spend the day. The first moment Mrs. Wade saw her, she was conscious of an instinctive aversion to her; but as she was never in the habit of consulting her own tastes or inclinations, she endured the infliction with her own gentle sweetness. No one who witnessed her offering Miss Alsop the easiest chair, or helping her to the daintiest bit on the table, would have supposed that she read the wily woman's secret heart. Not a look, not a word, not a tone betrayed it; but when the weary day was over, and Miss Alsop had exhausted all her vapid nothings, and, tying on her bonnet, regretted that she must trouble Mr. Wade to wait upon her home, Mrs. Wade, as they passed through the door, and out into the darkness, would lean her cheek upon her hand, while tears, which no human eye had ever seen, fell thick and fast.

Not that Mr. Wade had any affection for Miss Alsop—not at all—he was incapable of affection for any thing but himself and his money; but Miss Alsop had a way of saying little complimentary things to which the most sensible man alive never yet was insensible, from the stupidest and silliest of women. What wonder that the profound Mr. Wade walked into the trap with his betters? and though he would not, for one of his money-bags, have owned it, he always left her doubly impressed with the value of his own consequence. Then—Miss Alsop knew how to be an excellent listener when occasion required, and Mr. Wade was, like all egregious stupidities, fond of hearing himself talk; and occasionally Miss Alsop would ask him to repeat some remark he had made, as if peculiarly struck with its acuteness, or its adaptation to her single-blessed-needs, upon which Mr. Wade would afterward pleasantly reflect, with the mental exclamation, "Sensible woman, that Miss Alsop!" Let it not be supposed that this depth of cunning was at all incompatible with obtuseness of intellect—not at all—there is no cunning like the cunning of a fool. Yes—Miss Alsop knew her man. She knew she could afford to bide her time; besides, were personal charms insufficient, had she not a most potent auxiliary in her bank-book, which placed to her spinster credit twenty thousand dollars in the "People's Bank?"

CHAPTER VI.

Mrs. Wade sat propped up in bed by pillows, for the nature of her disease rendered repose impossible; dreadful spasms—the forerunners of dissolution—at intervals convulsed her frame. Pale, but firm, the gentle Mary Hereford glided about her, now supporting the worn-out frame—now holding to her lips the cup meant for healing—now opening a door, or slightly raising a window, to facilitate the invalid's labored breathing.

The fire had burned low in the grate, and when the gray light of morning stole in through the half open shutter, and the invalid would have replenished it, Mrs. Wade's low whispered, "I shall not need it, Mary," gave expression to the fearful certainty which her own heart had silently throbbed out through the long watches of that agonized night. Not a murmur escaped the sufferer's lips—there was no request for the presence of the absent sleeper, who had promised "to cherish through sickness and health;" no mention was made of the children, who had been trustingly placed in the hands of Him who doeth all things well, and who wearily slumbered on, unconscious that the brightness of their childhood's sky was fading out forever. The thin arms were wound around the neck of the first-born, about whom such happy hopes had once so thickly clustered, and peacefully as an infant drops asleep. Susan Wade closed her eyes forever; so peacefully that the daughter knew not the moment in which the desolate word—"motherless"—was written over against her name.

Motherless!—that in that little word should be compressed such weary weight of woe! It were sad to be written fatherless—but God and his ministering angels only know how dark this earth may be, when she who was never weary of us with all our frailties—she, to whom our very weaknesses clamored more loudly for love, lies careless of our tears.

"Henry!" said Mr. Wade to Mr. Hereford, "I had no idea, in fact—I didn't think"—and the embarrassed man tried to rub open his still sleepy eyes—"I didn't suppose, really, that Mrs. Wade would die yet; women are so notional, and that doctor seemed to be encouraging Mrs. Wade to be sick, as doctors always do—really I am quite taken by surprise, as one may say; I don't know any thing about these things—I should like to have you do what is necessary. I suppose it will not be considered the thing for me to go to the store to-day," and he looked for encouragement to do so in the face of his disgusted son-in-law.

"I should think not, decidedly," said Mr. Hereford, dryly.

"Of course it would not be my wish," said Mr. Wade, "when poor Susan lies dead; but one's duty, you know, sometimes runs a different way from one's inclination."

And vice versâ, thought Henry, but he merely remarked that he would take any message for him to his place of business.

Mr. Wade could do no less than accept his offer, so, after eating his usual breakfast with his usual appetite, he paced up and down the parlor; got up and sat down; and looked out at the window, and tried in various ways to stifle certain uncomfortable feelings which began to disturb his digestion. It was uncomfortable—very. The awe-struck face of Betty as she stole in and out, the swollen eyes of the children, the pallid face of Mrs. Hereford, who was trying to give them the consolation she so much needed herself, and the heavy step of the undertaker over-head performing his repulsive office. And so the day wore away; and the form, that a child might have lifted, was laid in the coffin, and no trace of pain or sorrow lay upon the face upon which the death-angel had written Peace!

Why did he fear to look upon its placid sweetness? No reproach ever came from the living lips—did he fear it from the dead?

How still lay the once busy fingers! What a mockery seemed the usual signs and sounds of domestic life! How empty, purposeless, aimless, seemed life's petty cares and needs. How chilling this total eclipse of light, and love, and warmth! Blessed they, who can ease their pained hearts by sobbing all this out to the listening ear of sympathy. But what if the great agony be pent up within the swelling heart till it is nigh bursting? What if it be pent up thus in the gushing heart of childhood? What if no father's arms be outstretched to enfold the motherless? What if the paternal hand never rests lovingly on the bowed young head? What if the moistening eye must send back to its source the welling tear? What if the choking sob be an offense? What if childhood's ark of refuge— mother's room—echo back only its own restless footsteps? O, how many houses that present only to the careless eye, a blank surface of brick and mortar, are inscribed all over with the handwriting, legible only to those whose baptism has been—tears!

But why count over the tears of the orphans, why tell of their weary days and sleepless nights—of honest Betty's home-spun attempts at consolation—of Mr. Wade's repeated refusals of Mrs. Hereford's invitation for them to spend that part of the day with her in which he was absent at his business? Why tell of the invisible web the cunning Miss Alsop was weaving? Why tell of her speedy success? Why tell of the soft-eyed dove transformed by Hymen to the vulture? Why tell of his astonishment, who prided himself upon his lynx-eyed and infallible penetration of the sex, at being forced to drain to the dregs that bitter cup he had held so unsparingly to the meek lips upon which death had set his seal of silence? Why tell of that pitiful old age, which, having garnered the chaff, and thrown away the wheat of a life-time, finds itself on the grave's brink with no desire for repentance, clutching with palsied hands the treasure of which Death stands ready to rob it!

VISITING AND VISITORS.

"When are you coming to spend the day with us?" asked a lady of my acquaintance of another. "Spend the day with you, my dear!" replied the latter; "I should be tired to death spending the day with you; maybe I'll take tea with you sometime."

I have often pleased myself imagining how the wheels of society would creak greased with such honesty as that! and yet how many, if they but dared to speak their real sentiments, would make a similar response. Now, I respect that old lady; she had made good use of her years; she probably knew what it was to talk at a mark for hours on the stretch, to some one-idea-d statue, who, with crossed hands and starched attitude, seemed remorselessly exacting of her weary tongue—Give—Give! She knew what it was to long for dinner to reprieve her aching jaws, or, at least, afford them a diversion of labor. She knew what it was to be gladder to see one's husband home on such a day, than on any other day in the year; and she knew what it was to have those hopes dashed to earth by that inglorious sneak selfishly retreating behind his newspaper, instead of shouldering the conversation as he ought. She knew what it was to have the hour arrive for her afternoon nap (I won't call it "siesta,") instead of which, with leaden lids, and a great goneness of brain and diaphragm, she must still keep on ringing changes on the alphabet, for the edification of the monosyllabic statue, who—horror of horrors!—had "concluded to stay to tea." She knew what it was in a fit of despair to present a book of engravings to the statue, and to hear that interesting functionary remark as she returned it, that "her eyes were weak." She knew what it was to send in for a merry little chatterbox of a neighbor to relieve guard, and receive for answer, "that she had gone out of town!" She knew what it was to wish that she had forty babies up stairs, with forty pains under their aprons, if need be, that she might have an excuse for leaving the statue for at least one blessed half-hour. She knew what it was to have the inglorious sneak later to tea on that wearisome day than ever before; and on his entrance, blandly and coolly to unfurl a business letter, which, with a Chesterfieldian bow, he hoped the statue would excuse him for retiring to answer; and she knew what it was, five minutes later, to spy the wretch on the back piazza reveling in solitude and a cigar. She knew what it was, when the statue finally—(for every thing comes to an end some time, thank heaven)—took protracted leave—to cry hysterically from sheer weariness, and a recollection of pressing family duties indefinitely postponed, and to think for the forty-eleventh time, what propriety there was in calling her the weaker sex, who had daily to shoulder burdens which the strongest man either couldn't or—wouldn't bear. And so again, I say—sensible old lady— would there were more like her!

And yet we would fain hope that, like ours, this is but one side of her experience. We would hope that she knew what it was to throw her arms about the neck of a friend from whom she had no disguises; whose loving eyes scanned—not the wall for possible cobwebs, nor yet the carpet for darns, nor yet the mirror for fly-specks; but her face, to see what sorrow Time, in his flight, had registered there, which by sympathy she could lighten; what joy, which, by sharing, she could increase. We hope she knew what it was to sit side by side with such a one at the frugal meal—sweeter far than the stalled ox, for the love that seasoned it. We hope she knew what it was to lounge, or sit, or stand, or walk, or read, or sew, or doze even, in that friend's presence, with that perfect love which casteth out fear. We hope she knew what it was to count the hours as they passed, not for their irksomeness, but as a miser tells his hoarded gold; jealous, lest even the smallest fraction should escape. We hope she knew what it was when she unwillingly closed the door upon her retreating form, that shutting it never so securely, kind words, good deeds, loving looks and tones, came flocking in to people the voiceless solitude as with shining troops of white-robed angels.

And we hope she knew what it was to give the cup of cold water to the humble disciple for the Master's sake. We hope that the door of her house and heart were opened as widely for the destitute orphan, in whose veins her own blood flowed—who could repay it only with tearful thanks —as for those who could return feast for feast, and whose tongues were as smooth as their wine. And finally and lastly, lest we ourselves should be making too long a visit—we hope the old lady had no "best chamber," with closed blinds; pillows as ruffled as the chambermaid's temper; forbiddingly polished sheets; smothering canopy; counterpane all too dainty for tumbling; and pincushion, whose lettered words one must not invade, even at the most buttonless extremity! Blessings on the old lady: we trust her carpets were made to be trod on—her chairs to sit down upon—and her windows to open. We hope her house was too small to hold half of her friends, and too hot to hold one of her enemies.

OUR FIRST NURSE.

Now sit down, and I will tell you all about it. Charley and I were engaged. Youth comes but once, you know, and if we waited to be married until we could furnish a house in fashionable style—well, you see, we knew too much for that; we got married, and left other couples to grow gray, if they liked, on the distant prospect of damask curtains, gold salt-cellars, and trains of innumerable servants.

Charley did not know the meaning of a "club-house," and the shopkeepers flashed their diamonds and satins in vain in my face; I never gave them a thought. We had some nice books, and some choice engravings, presented to Charley by an old antiquary who had taken a fancy to him. You might have gone into many a parlor on which thousands had been lavished, and liked ours all the better when you came back. Still, it wanted something—that we both agreed; for no house can be said to be properly furnished without a baby. Santa Claus, good soul, understood that, and Christmas day he brought us one, weighing the usual eight pounds, and as lively as a cricket. Such lungs as it had! Charley said it was intended for a minister.

Well, now it was all right, or would have been, if the baby had not involved a nurse. We had, to be sure, a vague idea that we must have one, and as vague an idea of what a nurse was. We thought her a good kind of creature who understood baby-dom, and never interfered with any little family arrangements.

Not a bit of it!

The very first thing she did was to make preparation to sleep in my room, and send Charley off into a desolate spare chamber. Charley! my Charley! whose shaving operations I had watched with the intensest interest; mixing up little foam seas of "lather" for him, handing him little square bits of paper to wipe his razor upon, and applying nice bits of courtplaster, when he accidentally cut his chin while we were laughing. Charley! whose cravats I had tied to suit my fancy every blessed morning, whose hair I had brushed up in elegant confusion, whose whiskers I had coaxed and trimmed, and—well, any one, unless a bachelor or old maid, who reads this, can see that it was perfectly ridiculous.

Charley looked at me, and I looked at him, and then we both looked at the bran new baby—and there's where she had us. You might have seen it with half an eye, as she folded her hands complacently over her apron-strings, and sat down in my little rocking-chair, opposite the bed. I felt as though I was sold to the Evil One, as she fixed her basilisk eyes on me when Charley left the room. Poor Charley! He did not want to go. He neither smoked, nor drank, nor played billiards; he loved home and—me; so he wandered up stairs and down, sat with his hands in his pockets staring at the parlor fire till he could bear it no longer, and then came up stairs to get comforted. If you'll believe it, that woman came fussing round the bed after him, just as if he were infringing some of her rights and immunities.

What if he did bring me a sly piece of cake in his pocket? Who likes to live on gruel forever? What if he did open the blinds and let a little blessed sunlight in, when she tried to humbug us into the belief that "it would hurt the baby's eyes," because she was too lazy to wipe the dust from the furniture? What if he did steal one of her knitting needles, when she sat there, evening after evening, knitting round, and round, and round that interminable old gray stocking, my eyes following her with a horrid sort of fascination, till my nerves were wound up to the screaming point? What if I did tell him that she always set her rocking-chair on that loose board on the floor, which sent forth that little crucifying squeak, and that she always said "Bless me!" and was always sure to get on to it again the very next time she sat down? What if I did tell him that when she had eaten too much dinner, and wanted to take a sly nap, she would muffle the baby up in so many blankets that it could not cry if it wanted to, and then would draw the curtains closely round my bed, and tell me that "it was high time I took a nap?" I, who neither by stratagem or persuasion, could ever be induced to sleep in the daytime? I, who felt as if my eye-lashes were fastened up to the roots of my hair, and as if legions of little ants were crawling all over me?

What if I did tell him that she got up a skirmish with me every night, because I would not wear a nuisance called a night-cap? What if I did tell him that she insisted upon putting a sticky pitch-plaster upon my neck, for a little ghost of a cough (occasioned by her stirring the ashes in the grate too furiously), and that when I outgeneraled her, and clapped it round the bed-post instead, she muttered, spitefully, that "a handsome neck would not keep me out of my coffin?" What if I did tell him that she tried on my nice little lace collars, when she thought I was asleep at night, and insisted on my drinking detestable porter, that its second-hand influence might "make the baby sleep?" What if I did, was he not my husband? Did I not tell him every thing? laugh with him? cry with him? eat out of his plate? drink out of his cup of tea, because being his, I fancied they tasted better than mine? and didn't he like it, too? Of course he did!

What if I did tell him all this? Poor Charley! he was forlorn, too; his cravats were tied like a fright all the time I was sick, his hair looked like any other man's, the buttons were off his pretty velvet vest, and he had not even the heart to get his boots blacked. Poor Charley!

Well; that nurse had the impudence to tell us one evening "that we acted like two children." "Children!" We! Us! the parents of that eight-pound baby! That was the last drop in our cup. Charley paid her, and I was so glad when she went, that I laughed till I cried.

Then we both drew a long breath and sat down and looked at the new baby—our baby; and Charley asked me about its little sleeping habits, and I told him, with a shake of the head, that I could not speak definitely on that point; and then we discussed, in a whisper, the respective merits of cribs and cradles, and the propriety of teaching it, at an early period, that impressive line of Mrs. Hemans:

"Night is the time for sleep;"

and then Charley got up, and exchanged his musical boots for a noiseless pair of slippers, and changed the position of the shovel, tongs, and poker, and oiled the creaking hinge of the closet door, and laid a chair over the squeaking board in the floor, that he might not tread on it, and with one eye on the baby, gently shaded the lamp; and then he looked at me, and gave a little sort of congratulatory nod, and then he drew off his vest and hung it over a chair, and then—out rattled a perfect tempest of half dollars, quarters, shillings, and sixpences, on the hearth! Of course, the baby woke (frightened out of a year's growth), and screamed until it was black in the face. In vain its poor, inexperienced papa kissed it, scratching its little velvet face with his rough whiskers the while! In vain we both walked the floor with it. The fire went out, the lamp went; and just at daybreak it came to us like a revelation, the sarcastic tone of that hateful old nurse, as she said, "Good-by; I hope you'll get along comfortably with the dear baby!"

And so we did. Do you suppose one night's watching was going to quench our love, either for the baby, or for each other? No—nor a thousand like it! for, as Dr. Watts, or Saxe, hath it, "it was one of the kind that was not born to die."

THE SHADOW OF A GREAT ROCK IN A WEARY LAND.

Man may turn his back upon Revelation, and feed upon the dry husks of infidelity, if he will; but sure I am, that woman can not do without her Saviour. In her happiest estate, she has sorrows that can only be intrusted to an Almighty ear; responsibilities that no human aid can give her strength to meet. But what if earthly love be poisoned at the fountain?—what if her feeble shoulders bend unsupported under the weight of her daily cross?—what if her life-sky be black with gathering gloom?—what if her foes be they of her own household?—what if treachery sit down at her hearth-stone, and calumny await her without, with extended finger? What then—if no Saviour's arms be outstretched to enfold her? What if it be "absurd" (as some tell her) that the God who governs the universe should stoop to interest himself in her petty concerns? What if the Bible to which she flies be "a dead letter?" and "Come unto me all ye who are weary and heavy laden"—only "a metaphor?" What earthly accents can fall upon her ear as sweet as these—"A bruised reed will I not break?" Woman may be "weak;" but blessed be the weakness which leads her to lean on that Almighty arm, which man in his pride rejects; listening rather in his extremity, to the demon whisper—"Curse God and die."

Woman may be "weak;" you may confuse her with your sophistries, deafen her with your arguments, and standing before her in your false strength, exclaim like the unbelievers of old—"Away with him!" and still her yearning soul cries out, with a voice no subtlety of yours can satisfy or stifle—"My Lord and my God!"

TO LITERARY ASPIRANTS.

My heart aches at the letters I am daily receiving from persons who wish to support themselves by their pens; many of these letters, mis-spelt and ungrammatical, show their writers to be totally unfit for the vocation they have chosen; and yet, alas! their necessities are for that reason none the less pressing. Others, unexceptionable in these respects, see no preliminary steps to be taken between avowing this their determination, and at once securing the remuneration accorded to long-practiced writers, who, by patient toil and waiting, have secured a remunerative name. They see a short article in print, by some writer; it reads easy—they doubt not it was written easily; this may or may not be the case; if so— what enabled the writer to produce it in so short a space of time? Long habit of patient, trained thinking, which the beginner has yet to acquire.

You are taken sick; you send for a physician; he comes in, stays ten minutes, prescribes for you a healing medicine, and charges you three or four dollars. You call this "extortionate"—forgetting the medical books he must have waded through, the revolting dissections he must have witnessed and participated in, and the medical lectures he must have digested, to have enabled him to pronounce on your case so summarily and satisfactorily. To return to our subject. These practiced writers have gone through (as you must do), the purgatorial furnace which separates the literary dross from the pure ore. That all who do this should come out fine gold, is impossible; but I maintain, that if there is any thing in a literary aspirant, this process will develop it, spite of discouragement— spite of depression—nay, on that very account.

Now what I would say is this. Let none enter this field of labor, least of all shrinking, destitute women, unless they are prepared for this long, tedious ordeal, and have also the self-sustaining conviction that they have a God-given talent. The reading community is not what it once was. The world is teeming with books—good, bad, and indifferent. Publishers have a wide field from which to cull. There is a great feast to sit down to; and the cloyed and fastidious taste demands dishes daintily and skillfully prepared. How shall an unpracticed aspirant, whose lips perhaps have not been touched with the live coal from the altar, successfully contend with these? How shall the halt and maimed win in such a race?

Every editor's drawer is crammed—every newspaper office besieged— by hundreds doomed to disappointment; not two thirds of the present surfeit of writers, born of the success of a few, obtain even a hearing. Editors have any quantity of MSS. on hand, which they know will answer their purpose; and they have, they say, when I have applied to them for those who have written me to do so, neither time nor inclination to paragraph, punctuate, revise and correct the inevitable mistakes of beginners, even though there may possibly be some grains of wheat for the seeking.

To women, therefore, who are destitute, and rely upon their pen for a support, I would say, again, Do any thing that is honest that your hands find to do, but make not authorship, at least, your sole dependence in the present state of things.

Now, having performed this ungrateful task, and mapped out faithfully the shoals and quicksands, if there are among you those whose mental and physical muscle will stand the strain with this army of competitors— and, above all, who have the "barrel of meal and cruse of oil" to fall back upon—I wish you God speed! and none will be happier than she, who has herself borne the burden and heat of the day, to see you crowned victor.

SUMMER TRAVEL.

Take a journey at this elevation of the thermometer! Not I. Think of the breakfastless start before daybreak—think of a twelve hours' ride on the sunny side of the cars, in the neighborhood of some persistent talker, rattling untranslatable jargon into your aching ears; think of a hurried repast, in some barbarous half-way house; amid a heterogeneous assortment of men, women, and children, beef, pork, and mutton; minus forks, minus spoons, minus castor, minus come-atable waiters, and four shillings and indigestion to pay. Think of a "collision"—disemboweled trunks, and a wooden leg; think of an arrival at a crowded hotel; jammed, jaded, dusty, and dolorous; think of your closetless sentry-box of a room, infested by mosquitoes and Red Rovers; bed too narrow, window too small, candle too short, all the world and his wife a-bed, and the geography of the house an unexplained riddle. Think of your unrefreshing, vapor-bath sleep; think of the next morning, as seated on a dusty trunk, with your hair drooping about your ears, through which the whistle of the cars, and the jiggle-joggle of the brakeman, are still resounding; you try to remember, with your hand on your bewildered forehead, whether your breakfast robe is in the yellow trunk, or the black trunk, and if in either, whether it is at the top, bottom, or in the middle of the same, where your muslins and laces were deposited, what on earth you did with your dressing comb, and where amid your luggage, your toilet slippers may be possibly located. Think of a summons to breakfast at this interesting moment, the sun meanwhile streaming in through the blind chinks, with volcanic power. Think of all that, I say.

Now if I could travel incog. in masculine attire, no dresses to look after, no muslins to rumple, no bonnet to soil, no tresses to keep smooth, with only a hat and things, a neck-tie or two, a change of—of shirts—nothing but a moustache to twist into a horn when the dinner bell rings; just a dip into a wash-basin, a clean dicky, a jump into a pair of—trowsers, and above all, liberty to go where I liked, without being stared at or questioned; a seat in a chair on its hind-legs, on a breezy door-step, a seat on the stairs in a wide hall, "taking notes;" a peep everywhere I chose, by lordly right of my pantaloons; nobody nudging somebody, to inquire why Miss Spinks the authoress wore her hair in curls instead of plaits; or making the astounding discovery that it was hips, not hoops, that made her dress stand out—that now, would be worth talking about: I'll do it.

But stop—I should have to cut my hair short—I should have to shave every morning, or at any rate call for hot water and go through the motions; men would jostle rudely past me, just as if they never had said such pretty things to me in flounces; I should be obliged, just as I had secured a nice seat in the cars, to get up, and give it to some imperious woman, who would not even say "thank you;" I should have to look on with hungry eyes till "the ladies" were all served at table; I should have to pick up their fans, and reticules, and handkerchiefs whenever they chose to drop them; I should have to give up the rocking-chairs, arm-chairs, and sofas for their use, and be called "a brute" at that; I should have to rush out of the cars, with five minutes' grace, at some stopping place, to get a glass of milk, for some "crying baby," with a contracted swallowing apparatus, and be pursued for life by the curses of its owner, because the whistle sounded while his two shilling tumbler was yet in the voracious baby's tight grip. No—no—I'll stay a woman, and what's more, I'll stay at home.

A GENTLE HINT.

In most of the New York shop windows, one reads: "Here we speak French;" "Here we speak Spanish;" "Here we speak German;" "Here we speak Italian." I suggest an improvement—"Here we speak the Truth."

A STORY FOR OLD HUSBANDS WITH YOUNG WIVES.

"I was an old fool! Yes—I was an old fool; that's all there is about it. I ought to have known better; she was not to blame, poor thing; she is but a child yet; and these baubles pleased her ambitious mother's eye. It was not the old man, but his money—his money—I might have known it. May and December—May and December—pshaw! how could I ever have believed, that Mary Terry could love an old fellow like me?" and Mark Ware surveyed himself in the large parlor mirror.

"See!—it reflects a portly old man of sixty, with ruddy face, snow-white hair, and eyes from which the light of youth has long since departed." And yet there is fire in the old man's veins too; see how he strides across the carpet, ejaculating, with fresh emphasis, "Yes, I was an old fool!—an old fool! But I will be kind to her; I'm not the man to tyrannize over a young girl, because her mother took her out of the nursery to make her my wife. I see now it is not in reason for a young girl like her to stay contentedly at home with my frosty head and gouty feet. Poor little Mary! No—I'll not punish her because she can not love me; she shall have what she wants, and go where she likes; her mother is only too proud to trot her out, as the wife of the rich Mark Ware. If that will make them both happy, let them do it; may be"—and Mark Ware paused —"may be, after she has seen what that Dead Sea apple—the world—is made of, she will come back and love the old man a little—may be— who knows? No woman who is believed in, and well treated, ever makes a bad wife; there never was a bad wife yet, but there was a bad husband first; that's gospel—Mark's gospel, anyhow, and Mark Ware is going to act upon it. Mary shall go to the ball to-night, with her mother, and I will stay at home and nurse my patience and my gouty leg. There's no evil in her; she's as pure as a lily, and if she wants to see the world, why—she shall see it; and though I can't go dancing round with her, I never will dim her bright eyes—no—no!"

"That will do, Tiffy; another pin in this lace; now move that rose in my hair a little to the left; so—that will do."

"That will do!" Tame praise, for that small Grecian head, with its crown of braided tresses; for the full, round throat, and snowy, sloping shoulders; for the round, ivory arms, and tapering, rose-tipped fingers; for the lovely bosom, and dainty waist. Well might such beauty dazzle Mark Ware's eyes, till he failed to discern the distance betwixt May and December.

Mark Ware had rightly read Mary. She was guileless and pure, as he had said; and child as she was, there was that in her manner, before which the most libidinous eye would have shrunk abashed.

When the young bride first realized the import of those words she had been made to utter, "till death do us part," she looked forward, with shuddering horror, at the long, monotonous, weary years before her. Her home seemed a prison, and Mark Ware the keeper; its very splendor oppressed her; and she chafed and fretted in her gilded fetters, while her restless heart cried out—anywhere but home! Must she sit there, in her prison-house, day after day, listening only to the repinings of her own troubled heart? Must the bee and the butterfly only be free to revel in the bright sunshine? Had God made her beauty to fade in the stifling atmosphere of darkened parlors, listening to the complaints of querulous old age? Every pulse of her heart rebelled. How could her mother have thus sold her? How could Mark Ware have so unmagnanimously accepted the compulsory sacrifice? Why not have shown her the world and let her choose for herself? O anywhere—anywhere—from such a home!

There was no lack of invitations abroad; for Mary had flashed across the fashionable horizon, like some bright comet; eclipsing all the reigning beauties. No ball, no party, no dinner, was thought a success without her. Night after night found her en route to some gay assemblage. To her own astonishment and her foolish mother's delight, her husband never remonstrated; on the contrary, she often found upon her dressing-table, some choice little ornament, which he had provided for the occasion; and Mary, as she fastened it in her hair, or bosom, would say, bitterly, "He is anxious that I, like the other appendages of his establishment, should reflect credit on his faultless taste."

Mistaken Mary!

Time passed on. Mark Ware was "patient," as he promised himself to be. His evenings were not so lonely now, for his little babe kept him company; the reprieved nurse, only too glad to escape to her pink ribbons and a "chat with John at the back gate." It was a pretty sight—Mark and the babe! Old age and infancy are always a touching sight together. Not a smile or a cloud passed over that little face, that did not wake up all the father in Mark Ware's heart; and he paced the room with it, or rocked it to sleep on his breast, talking to it, as if it could understand the strong, deep love, of which it was the unconscious object.

"I am weary of all this," said Mark's young wife, as she stepped into her carriage, at the close of a brilliant ball. "I am weary of seeing the same faces, and hearing the same stupid nonsense, night after night. I wonder shall I ever be happy? I wonder shall I ever love any thing, or anybody? Mamma is proud of me, because I am beautiful and rich, but she does not love me. Mark is proud of me"—and Mary's pretty lip curled scornfully. "Life is so weary, and I am only eighteen!" and Mary sighed heavily.

On whirled the carriage through the deserted streets; deserted—save by some inveterate pleasure-seeker like herself, from whom pleasure forever flees. Occasionally a lamp twinkled from some upper window, where a half-starved seamstress sat stitching her life away, or a heart-broken mother bent over the dead form of a babe, which her mother's heart could ill spare, although she knew not where to find bread for the remaining babes who wept beside her. Now and then, a woman, lost to all that makes woman lovely, flaunted under the flickering street-lamps, while her mocking laugh rang out on the night air. Mary shuddered, and drew back—there was that in its hollowness which might make even devils tremble. Overhead the sentinel stars kept their tireless watch, and Mary's heart grew soft under their gentle influence, and tears stole from beneath her lashes, and lay like pearls upon her bosom.

"You need not wait to undress me," said Mary to the weary-looking waiting-maid, as she averted her swollen eyes from her gaze—and taking the lamp from her hand, Mary passed up to her chamber. So noiseless was the fall of her light foot upon the carpet, that Mark did not know she had entered. He sat with his back to the door, bending over the cradle of his child, till his snow-white locks rested on its rosy cheeks; talking to it, as was his wont, to beguile his loneliness.

"Mary's forehead—Mary's eyes—Mary's mouth—no more like your old father than a rosebud is like a chestnut-burr. You will love the lonely old man, little one, and perhaps she will, by-and-by; who knows?" and Mark's voice trembled.

"She will—she does"—said Mary, dropping on her knees at the cradle of her child, and burying her face in Mark's hands; "my noble, patient husband!"

"You don't mean that?" said Mark, holding her off at arm's-length, and looking at her through a mist of tears; "you don't mean that you will love an old fellow like me? God bless you, Mary—God forever bless you! I have been very—very lonely,"—and Mark wept for sheer happiness.

The gaping world, the far-sighted world, the charitable world, shook its wise head, when the star of fashion became a fixed star. Some said "her health must be failing;" others, that "her husband had become jealous at last;" while old stagers maliciously insinuated that it were wise to retire on fresh laurels. But none said—what I say—that a true woman's heart may always be won—ay, and kept, too—by any husband who does not consider it beneath him to step off the pedestal of his "dignity" to learn how.

BREAKFAST AT THE PAXES'.

"Morning paper, John?"

"Didn't come this morning, mem; I inquired at the office as I came up with the breakfast, mem; none there, mem."

How provoking! What is breakfast without the morning paper? Coffee and eggs are well enough, but they don't tell a body whether the Pacific has arrived, or Greeley's head is safe on his non-resistant shoulders (I wish that man could fight); or whether breadstuffs have "riz," as every housekeeper knows they ought to; or whether Olmsted's new book is selling as it deserves (were it only for that racy little morceau about his ride with Jenny, the mare); or whether the "Onguent warranted to raise a moustache and whiskers in six weeks" is still on the sprout; or whether Griswold is proven a saint or a sinner; or whether the amiable young man, who advertised the other day for "board in a family where there are no babies," has found his desert-s; or whether the philanthropic firm of M'Mush & Co. are still persisting in that "ruinous sacrifice," for the benefit of a credulous public in general, and themselves in particular; or whether Barnum's head is really under water, or whether he has only made a dive to grab some new mermaid; or whether the Regular Male Line viâ (nobody knows where), is an heir line; or whether there are any lectures to be delivered to-night worth foregoing a cosy fireside, and freezing the tip of one's nose to hear. How am I going to find out all this, I should like to know, without the morning paper? (Long life to the inventor of it!)

Oh! here comes Mr. Pax with one—good soul—he has been out in his slippers, and bought one. Now I shall find out all about every thing, and —who did what. See what a thing it is to have a husband! No, I shan't either: may I be kissed if Pax has not sat down to read that paper himself, instead of giving it to me. Now I like that; I dare say he thinks because he is connected with the Press that he should have the first reading of it. Am not I connected with the Press I'd like to know? I guess you'd have thought so, had you seen me squeezing into the Opera House the other night to hear Everett's lecture.

Perhaps he is going to read it aloud to me—I'll sip my coffee and wait a bit. Good Pax! how I have maligned him; what an impatient wretch I am. I think impatience is a fault of mine. I wonder is it a fault? I wonder if I can help it, if it is? I wonder if people weren't made that way the year I was born? Yes; Pax must be going to read me the paper; that's it. Good Pax—how well he looks in that Turkish breakfast-jacket; he has really a nice profile and pretty hand. I can't say that he has a very saintly under lip, but I have known more saintly looking ones do naughtier things! Yes; I'll sip my coffee—he is undoubtedly going to read the paper to me; no, he isn't either; he means to devour the whole of it solus. I won't stand it—hem—no reply—hem—none so deaf as those who won't hear.

"Pax!"

"Well, dear" (without raising his eyes).

"Pax! what is there interesting in that paper?"

(Pax still reading intently.) "Nothing, my dear, absolutely nothing."

Humph! wonder if it takes a man a whole hour to read "nothing?"

Now, do you suppose I whined about that? cried till my eyes looked as though they were bound with pink tape? Not I. I just sat down and wrote an article about it for the "Weekly Monopolizer," and when it is published, as published it will be, I shall be disinterested enough to hand Pax my paper to read first! Then—when he reads the article, and looking up reproachfully, says: "Mrs. Pax!" it will be my turn not to hear, you know; and when he gets up, and laying his connubial paw on my shoulder, says: "Mrs. Pax, do you know any thing about this article in the Weekly Monopolizer?" I shall reply, with lamb-like innocence: "Nothing, my dear, absolutely nothing!"

Won't that floor him?

GIRLS' BOARDING-SCHOOLS.

Had I twenty daughters, which I regret to say I have not, not one of them should ever enter a "Boarding-school." I beg pardon; I should say "Institute;" schools are exploded; every two-year-older learns his A B C now at an "Institute," though that institute, when hunted down, may consist of a ten-feet-square basement room. But this is a digression.

To every mother who is contemplating sending her daughter to a boarding-school I would say: Let neither your indolence, nor the omnipotent voice of fashion, nor high-sounding circulars, induce you to remove her from under your own personal care and supervision, at a time when the physique of this future wife and mother requires a lynx-eyed watchfulness on your part, which no institute ever has—ever will supply. This is a point which I am astonished that parents seem so utterly to overlook. Every mother knows how fatal wet feet, or insufficient clothing, may be to a young girl at the critical age at which they are generally sent away to school. It is not enough that you place India-rubbers, thick-soled shoes, and flannels in the trunk which bears the little exile company; they will not insure her from disease there. It is not enough that you say to her, "My dear, be careful of your choice of companions," when she has no choice; when her bed-fellows and room-mates—the latter often three or four in number—are what chance and the railroads send; for what teacher, with the best intentions, ever gives this subject the attention which it deserves, or which a mother's anxious heart asks? That the distant home of her daughter's room-mates is located within the charmed limits of fashion; that a carriage with liveried servants (that disgusting libel on republicanism), stands daily before their door; that the dresses of these room-mates are made in the latest style, and their wrists and ears decked with gold and precious stones—is an affirmative answer to these questions to satisfy a true mother?

No—and it is not the blushing country maiden, with her simple wardrobe, and simpler manners, whom that mother has to fear for her child's companion or bed-fellow. It is the over-dressed, vain, vapid, brainless offshoot of upstart aristocracy, who would ridicule the simple gingham in which that country girl's mother studied geography, and which fabric she very properly considers quite good enough for her child, and which is much more appropriate in the school-room than silk or satin. It is this child of the upstart rich mother, whose priceless infancy and childhood have been spent with illiterate servants; with the exception of the hour after dessert, when she was reminded that she had a mother, by being taken in an embroidered robe to be exhibited for a brief space to her guests. It is this girl, whose childhood, as I said, has been passed with servants, peeping into the doubtful books with which doubtful servants often beguile the tedious hours (for there are bad servants as well as bad masters and mistresses)—this girl, lying awake in her little bed, hearing unguarded details of servants' amours, while her mother dances away the hours so pregnant with fate to that listening child. It is such a girl, more to be pitied than blamed, whose existence is to be recognized by her thoughtless mother only, when her "coming out," delayed till the latest possible period, forces her reluctantly to yield to a younger aspirant her own claims to admiration. This girl whose wealth, and the social position arising from it, so dazzles the eyes of proprietors of "Institutes" that they are incapable of perceiving, or unwilling to admit, her great moral and mental delinquencies; it is such a companion that a true mother has to fear for her pure-minded, simple-hearted young daughter, leaving for the first time the guarded threshold and healthful atmosphere of home.

And when after months have passed—and insufficient exercise, [A] imperfect ventilation, and improper companionship, have transformed her rosy, healthy, simple-hearted child, to a pale, languid, spineless, dressy young woman, with a smattering of fashionable accomplishments, and an incurable distaste of simple, home pleasures—will it restore the bloom to her cheek, the spring to her step, the fresh innocence to her heart, to say, "but the school was fashionable and so well recommended?"

[A]Is a formal, listless walk, in a half-mile procession, to answer the purpose of exercise for young, growing girls confined at least ten hours a day over their lessons, and crowded at night into insufficient sleeping-rooms?—from which the highest prices paid for tuition, so far as my observation extends, furnish no immunity.

CLOSET MEDITATIONS,
NOT FOUND IN JAY OR DODDRIDGE.

Shall I ever be unhappy again? Six big closets with shelves and drawers! What a Godsend! You laugh! you are unable to comprehend how such joyful emotions can spring from so trivial a cause.

Trivial! Did you ever board out? Did you ever stand in the midst of your gas-lighted, damask-curtained, velvet-chaired, closetless hotel (yes—hotel) apartments, with a six-cent ink-bottle between your perplexed thumb and finger, taxing your brain, as it was never taxed before, to discover an oasis where to deposit it, when not in use?

Trivial? Did you ever live for a series of years with your head in a trunk? Did you ever see your ghost-like habiliments dangling day after day from pegs in the wall? Did you ever turn away your disgusted eyes, as the remorseless chambermaid whirled clouds of dust over their unprotected fabrics? Did you ever, as you lay in bed of a morning, exhaust your ingenuity in devising some means of relief? Did you ever, exulting in your superior acumen, rush out, and purchase at your own expense, a curtain to cover them? Did you ever jam off all your finger nails trying to drive it up? (for what woman ever yet hit a nail on the head?) Did you ever have that dusty curtain drop down on your nicely-smoothed hair, nine times out of ten when you went to it for a dress? Did you ever set fire to it with a candle, when in an abstracted state of mind?

Trivial? Did you ever implore a white-aproned waiter, with tears in your eyes, and twenty-five cents in your hand, to bring you an empty cigar-box to keep your truant slippers in? Did you ever stifle with closed windows, because if you threw them up, you would throw out your books, which were piled on the window lodge? Were you ever startled in the middle of the night, by the giving way of a solitary nail, on which were hung a bag of buttons, a bag of hooks and eyes, a child's satchel, a child's slate, a basket of oyster crackers, a bag of chess-men, and—your hoops?

Trivial? Did you ever partially carry out the curse which was passed on Eden's tempter, the serpent, as, with a long-handled umbrella, you explored, for some missing shoe, the unknown regions under the bed? Did you ever sit on your best bonnet? Did you ever step into your husband's hat? Did you ever tear a zig-zag rent in your favorite dress, and find, on looking for pieces of the same to mend it, that you had given them away to your washwoman, with other uncounted needfuls, because you had no place to keep them? Did you ever stand in dismay over your furs and woolens in spring, and your muslins, grenadines, and bareges, in autumn?

Trivial? Ah!—you never witnessed the cold-blooded indifference with which hotel-keepers, and landlords generally, shrug their shoulders, as surveying your rooms, and taking a coup d'œil your feminine effects, you pathetically exclaim, with dropped hands and intonation—"No closets!"

A FEMININE VIEW OF NAPOLEON AS A HUSBAND.

It is said that writers of books seldom read many. The "Confidential Letters of Napoleon and Josephine" had not been published when that remark was made. The Napoleon-mad author, Mr. Abbot, says, in his Preface: "We are familiar with him as the warrior, the statesman, the great administrator—but here we behold him as the husband, the father, the brother, moving freely amid all the tender relations of domestic life. His heart is here revealed," etc. I suggest to Mr. Abbot (for whom, apart from this extraordinary hallucination, I have a great respect), the following amendment of the above sentence, viz.: his want of heart is here revealed; but let that pass.

I have devoured the book at a sitting, and it has given me, as do stimulants generally, mental or otherwise, a villainous headache. With the sad fate of the peerless Josephine fresh in my mind, I read with an impatient pshaw! the burning billet-doux, addressed to her by the man who could coolly thrust her aside for his mad ambition. Hear what he once said:

"Death alone can break the union, which love, sentiment, and sympathy have formed. A thousand and a thousand kisses."

Also,

"I hope very soon to be in your arms; I love you most passionately (à la fureur)."

Also,

"I hope in a little time to fold you in my arms, and cover you with kisses burning as the equator."

Also, this consistent lover begs from her whom he afterward deserted,

"Love without bounds, and fidelity without limit."

How very like a man!

Well, I turned over the pages, and read with moistened eyes, for the hundredth time, the wretched state farce enacted at the divorce; and with fresh admiration perused the magnanimous and memorable reply of the queenly Josephine, to the brilliant but cold, intellectual but selfish, imperious yet fascinating Napoleon. Ah! then I would have led away his victim, spite of herself, out of sight, sound, and hearing of this cold, cruel man, who, when it suited his whim, caprice, or convenience; who, when weary of the tame, spiritless Maria Louise, returned secretly to the intoxicating presence of the bewitching Josephine; whom, though repudiating, he yet controlled, down to the lowest menial in her household, down to the color of their jackets and hose; quite safe, in always appending, with gracious condescension, permission "to please herself," to one whose greatest pleasure, he well knew, was to kiss his imperial shoe-tie.

My love and pity for her merge (momentarily) into contempt, when she abjectly begs for the crumbs of his favor, that fall from happier favorites;

for (to quote the touching words of her who would have shared his exile had not death prevented, when the woman for whom she had been cast aside, by a retributive justice, deserted him in his extremity) "he could forget me when he was happy!" Ay, it was when pleasure palled, when friends proved false, when the star of his destiny paled, when heneeded the noble Josephine, that he sought her.

And she? When pealing bells and roaring cannon announced to France that her rival had presented her husband the long-desired heir; she, upon whose quivering heart every stroke of those joyous bells must have smitten like a death-knell; she, the deserted wife, hung festal wreaths over the grave of her hopes, gave jewels to the messenger who brought her the news of his happiness, and ordered a fête in honor of the young heir. Match me that, who can, in the wide annals of man's history? But, oh! when midnight came on, and garlands drooped, and bright eyes closed, and tripping feet were stilled, when the farce was played out, and the iron hand of court etiquette was lifted from off that loving, throbbing, bursting heart, it thus poured itself out to Napoleon:

"She (Maria Louise), can not be more tenderly devoted to you than I; but she has been enabled to contribute more to your happiness, by securing that of France. She has then a right to your first feelings, to all your cares; and I, who was but your companion in times of difficulty, I can not ask more than a place in your affections far removed from that occupied by the Empress Louise. Not till you shall have ceased to watch by her bed, not till you are weary of embracing your son, will you take the pen to converse with your best friend. I will wait."

The answer to the touching letter, from which this is an extract (and every woman with a heart, who reads it, can measure the height and depth of its anguish), was the following verbal, the following delicate message, through Eugene!

"Tell your mother I would have written to her already, had I not been completely absorbed in the pleasure of looking upon my son."

About eleven o'clock that evening she received the much-coveted line from his own hand; in which he seemed to have been able at last to remember somebody beside himself; and for which the all-enduring, all-forgiving Josephine adores as a god, "the man who, when he willed, could be the most delightful of men." Nobody will deny the matchless tact of the lines which dried poor Josephine's tears:

"This infant, in concert with our Eugene, will constitute my happiness, and that of France."

But the man "who could be so delightful when he willed," did not, any more than the rest of his sex, always will it. Motes and butterflies seek the sunbeams, and the friends of poor Josephine's happier days, forsook her for those whom Fortune smiled upon. Malice, always on tiptoe to whisper into the tortured ear, told her of the "happiness" of the inconstant Napoleon; and with the birds, flowers, and fountains of Malmaison mocking her tears, her crushed heart thus sobs itself out to the emperor:

"I limit myself in asking one favor; it is, that you, yourself, will seek means, sometimes to convince me, and those who surround me"—(mark how strong and deathless must be the love that could thus abjectly sue) —"that I have still a place in your memory, and a large share of your esteem and friendship. These means, whatever they may be, will soothe my anguish, without the danger, as it seems to me, of compromising that which is more important than all together, the happiness of your majesty."

Well, what was the answer of "his majesty" to the tortured Josephine, in whose heart, his majesty boasted that "he held the first place, and her children by a former husband next, and that she did right thus to love him!" What was his majesty's answer to her, whom he wished to "cover with kisses burning as the equator," "whom he would wish to imprison in his heart, lest she should escape;" "the beautiful, the good one, all unequaled, all divine," to whom he had "sent thousands of kisses, burning as his heart, pure as her own," whom "he loved à la fureur?" What was his majesty's answer to the weary, weeping, faithful watcher at Malmaison?

"I have received your letter of the 19th of April; it is in a very bad style."

Could any thing be more coolly diabolical? O, foolish Josephine! with all your tact and wisdom, not to have found out that man (with rare exceptions) is unmagnanimous; that to pet and fondle him is to forge your own chains; that the love which is sure is to him worthless; that variety is as necessary to his existence, as a looking-glass and a cigar; and that his vows are made, like women's hearts, to break.

And yet, how surely, even in this world, retribution follows. The dreary rock of St. Helena; the dilapidated, vermin-infested lodgings; the petty, grinding, un-let-up-able tyranny of the lynx-eyed foe; the unalloyed, unassuaged anguish of hydra-headed disease; the merciless separation from the child, who had dug poor Josephine's premature grave; the heaped up, viper, newspaper obloquy which had always free pass to Longwood, when bristling bayonets kept at bay the voices which the ear of its captive ached to hear; the dreary, comfortless death-bed; the last faltering request denied; as if malice still hungered for vengeance when the weary heart it would torture had lost all power to feel. Josephine! Josephine! thou wert indeed avenged!

"FIRST PURE."

I would that I had time to answer the many kind letters I receive from my unknown friends, or power, as they seem to imagine, to reform the abuses to which they call my attention. The subject of licentiousness, upon which I have just received a letter, is one upon which I have thought much and often since my residence in New York. I could not, if I would, ignore it, when at every step its victims rustle past me in the gay livery of shame, or stretch out to me, from beneath tattered garments, the hand, prematurely old, which should, alas! wear the golden pledge of honorable love. But they tell me this is a subject a woman can not understand, and should not write about. Perhaps so; but woman can understand it when, like a blighting mildew, it strips bud, blossom, and verdure, from her household olive-plants; woman can understand it when she weeps in secret over the wrong which she may not whisper even to herself; woman can understand it when the children of the man whom she thought worthy of her maidenly love and honor, sink into early graves, under the inherited taint of his "youthful follies."

And yet they are right; virtuous woman does not understand it; would that she did—would that she sometimes paused to think of her share of blame in this matter; would that she know how much her ready smile, and indiscriminate hand of welcome has to do in perpetuating it; how often it blunts the sting of conscience, and confirms the immoral man in that detestable club-house creed, that woman's virtue depends upon opportunity. Would that mothers would sometimes ask, not—is he a gentleman, or is he accomplished? but, is he moral? is he pure? Pure! Young New York holds its sides in derision at the word. Pure! is he in leading strings? Pure! it is a contemptible reflection on his manhood and free will. Pure! it is a word for old women and priests.

I once expressed my astonishment to a lady, that she should permit the calls of a gentleman whom she knew to be licentious. "That is none of my business, you know, my dear," she replied, "so long as he behaves himself properly in my presence;" and this answer, I am afraid, would be endorsed by too many of my readers. As well might she have said, that it was none of her business that her neighbor's house was in flames, or that they had the yellow fever or the plague. That a man sings well, dresses well, or talks well, is, I am sorry to say, too often sufficient to outweigh his moral delinquency. This is poor encouragement to young men who, not having yet learned to think lightly of the sex to which their mothers and sisters belong, are old-fashioned enough to wish to lead virtuous lives; and some of whom, notwithstanding, have the courage and manhood in these degenerate days to dare to do it.

As to a reform in this matter, I think virtuous women must begin it, by turning the cold shoulder to every man of their acquaintance whom they know to be immoral, and I think a woman of penetration will not be at fault, if she takes pains to sift a man's sentiments in conversation.

Perhaps you will tell me (though I hope it is not so), that this would exclude two thirds of every lady's gentlemen acquaintance. Be it so; better for those ladies, better for their daughters, if they have any, better for the cause of virtue; at least, it would not take long, at that rate, to thin the ranks of vice.

I wonder does man never think, in his better moments, how much nobler it were to protect than to debase woman?—ay, protect her—if need be— even from herself, and ignoring the selfish creed that she has a right to, and is alone responsible for, her own self-disposal, withdraw her, as with a brother's hand, from the precipice over which misery or inclination would plunge her, and prove to the "weaker sex" that he is in the noblest sense the stronger. That, indeed, were God-like.

HOLIDAY THOUGHTS.

Well—New Year's and Christmas are both over: there is a lull equal to that after a Presidential election. What is to be done for an excitement now? Every body is yawning: the men on account of the number of complimentary fibs that they foolishly felt themselves called upon to tell the ladies, on their New Year's calls; and the ladies, because they were obliged to listen as if they did not know them all stereotyped, to be repeated, ad infinitum, at every house on their visiting rounds; the matron, because her handsome carpet is inch-deep in cake crumbs; and her husband, because bills are pouring in from butchers, bakers, grocers, milkmen, tailors, dressmakers, and jewelers, like the locusts of Egypt. Well—we shall not say any thing against New Year's and its jollities, while it frees the poor hack of a clerk, and gives him one day of happiness and rest; while it throws over the indefatigable cook's shoulders the cloak for which she has been vainly toiling and hoping; while it wings the feet of so many bright-eyed children, and lights up the prim parlor of so many hopeless old maids. We shall not say any thing against New Year's, when, after long months of wrong and estrangement, it stretches out the tardy hand of repentance, for which even the Bible bids us to wait, ere we forgive; we shall not say any thing against New Year's, though it reminds us that hands we used to grasp so warmly, are crossed forever over pulseless hearts; though memories sad, but sweet, come thronging thick and fast, of "Happy New Years," from lips upon which Death has set his final seal. And yet not final; thank Him who giveth, and Him who taketh, not final; for even here we trace their noiseless footsteps—even here we see the flitting of their shadowy garments—even here we smile in dreams, at the overshadowing wings of the angels who "have charge to keep us." No, no—not final: our love o'erleaps the dark river, to greet the sister, amid whose orange wreath there crept the cypress vine; to clasp the child, who quickened our heart-throbs ere we saw the lips that called us (alas, for so brief a space), by that blessed name—"Mother." No, no—not final;—else were this fair earth to us a satisfying birth-right; else had the midnight stars no eyes of flame to search the guilty conscience; else had the shimmer of the moonbeam, the ripple of the wave, the crash of the thunder, the flash of the lightning, the ceaseless moan of the vexed sea, no voice to waken the never-dying echo of the immortal in our nature. No—God be praised—not final!

But we had not intended a homily. To return to the observance of New Year's: for our own taste, we should prefer the sugar, which custom so lavishly heaps upon New Year's cake, spread more sparingly upon our slices of "daily bread;" in other words, we should prefer to distribute the compressed courtesies of our friends on this day, equally, through the weeks and months of the year. As to the absurd custom of excluding the daylight, to receive one's visitors by the glare of gas, it is a tacit admission of artificial charms, which one would think even "fashion" would be slow to make. The inordinate display of edibles on such occasions, seems to us as useless as it is disgusting; a cup of coffee, a slice of cake, or a sandwich, being, in our humble estimation, sufficient for any gentleman who is able to distinguish between a private house and a restaurant.

A HEADACHE.

Now I am in for it, with one of my unappeasable headaches. Don't talk to me of doctors; it is incurable as a love-fit; nothing on earth will stop it; you may put that down in your memorandum-book. Now, I suppose every body in the house to-day will put on their creakingest shoes; and every body will go up and down stairs humming all the tunes they ever heard, especially those I most dislike; and I suppose every thing that is cooked in the kitchen will boil and stew over, and the odor will come up to me; and I have such a nose! And I suppose all the little boys in the neighborhood, bless their little restless souls, will play duets on tin-pans and tin-kettles; and I suppose every body who comes into my room to ask me how I do, will squeak that horrid door, and keep squeaking it; and I suppose that unhappy dog confined over in that four-square-feet yard, will howl more deliriously than ever; and Mr. Jones's obnoxious blind will flap and bang till I am as crazy as an omnibus-driver who has a baulky horse, and whose passengers are hopping out behind without paying their fare; and I suppose some poor little child will be running under the window every now and then, screaming "Mother," and whenever I hear that, I think somebody wants me; and I've no doubt there will be "proof" to read to-day, and that that pertinacious and stentorian rag-man will lumber past on his crazy old cart, and insist on having some of my dry goods; and I feel it in my bones that oysters and oranges, and tape, and blacking, and brooms, and mats, and tin-ware, will settle and congregate on this side-walk, and assert their respective claims to my notice, till the sight of an undertaker would be a positive blessing.

Whack! how my head snaps! Don't tell me any living woman ever had such a headache before—because it will fill me with disgust. What o'clock is it? "Twelve." Merciful man! only twelve o'clock! I thought it was five. How am I to get through the day, I would like to know, for this headache won't let up till sundown; it never does. "Read to me." What'll you read? "Tom Moore!" as if I were not sick enough already! Moore! with his nightingales, and bulbuls, and jessamines; and loves and doves, and roses and poesies—till the introduction of an uneducated wildcat, or the tearingest kind of a hyena in his everlasting gardens, would be an untold relief. No—I hate Moore. Beside—he is the fellow who said, "When away from the lips that we love, we'll make love to the lips that are near." No wonder he was baptized more—carnivorous old profligate.

"Will I have a cup of tea?" No; of course I won't. I'm not an old maid. Tea! I'd like a dose of strychnine. There goes my head again—I should think a string of fire-crackers was fastened to each hair. Now the pain is in my left temple; now it is in my eyeballs; now—oh dear—it is everywhere. Sit down beside me, on the bed—don't jar it; now put your cold hand on my forehead—so—good gracious! There's a hand-organ! I knew it—the very one I moved here to get rid of. Playing the same old tune, too, composed of three notes: "tweedle—dum—tweedle—dee!"

Now if that organ-man would pull each of my finger and toe-nails out by the roots, one by one, I wouldn't object, but that everlasting "tweedle—" oh dear!—Or if a cat's tail were to be irretrievably shut into yonder door —or a shirt-sleeve should be suddenly and unexpectedly thrown around an old maid's neck in this room, any thing—every thing but that eternal, die-away "tweedle." What's the use of a city government? What is the use of any thing? What is the use of me?

HAS A MOTHER A RIGHT TO HER CHILDREN?

Most unquestionably, law or no law. Let us begin at the beginning. Let us take into consideration the physical prostration of mind and body endured by mothers antecedent to the birth of their offspring; their extreme nervousness and restlessness, without the ability for locomotion; the great nameless horror which hangs over those who, for the first time, are called upon to endure agonies that no man living would have fortitude to bear more than once, even at their shortest period of duration; and which, to those who have passed through it, is intensified by the vivid recollection (the only verse in the Bible which I call in question being this—"She remembereth no more her pains, for joy that a man-child is born into the world"). Granted that the mother's life is spared through this terrible ordeal, she rises from her sick-bed, after weeks of prostration, with the precious burden in her arms which she carried so long and so patiently beneath her heart. Oh, the continuous, tireless watching necessary to preserve the life and limbs of this fragile little thing! At a time, too, of all times, when the mother most needs relaxation and repose. It is known only to those who have passed through it. Its reward is with Him who seeth in secret.

I speak now only of good mothers; mothers who deserve the high and holy name. Mothers who in their unselfish devotion look not at their capacity to endure, but the duties allotted to them (would that husbands and fathers did not so often leave it to the tombstone to call their attention to the former). Mothers, whose fragile hands keep the domestic treadmill in as unerring motion as if no new care was superadded in the feeble wail of the new-born infant. Mothers whose work is literally neverdone; who sleep with one eye open, intrusting to no careless hireling the precious little life. Mothers who can scarce secure to themselves five minutes of the morning hours free from interruption, to ask God's help that a feeble, tried woman may hold evenly the scales of domestic justice amid the conflicting elements of human needs and human frailties. Now I ask you—shall any human law, for any conceivable reason, wrest the child of such a mother from her frenzied clasp?

Shall any human law give into a man's hand, though that man be the child's own father, the sole right to its direction and disposal? Has not she, who suffered, martyr-like, these crucifying pains—these wearisome days and sleepless nights, earned this her sweet reward?

Shall any virtuous woman, who is in the full possession of her mental faculties, how poor soever she may be, be beggared by robbing her of that which has been, and, thank God! will be the salvation of many a down-trodden wife?

"AND YE SHALL CALL THE SABBATH A DELIGHT."

I like to throw open the windows of my soul on Sabbath morning—air it of the week's fret, and toil, and care—and beckon in the white-winged dove of Peace to sing me a song of heaven. I like to go to church; it is to me like turning from the dusty highway of life into green fields, and, under the friendly shade of some sheltering tree, gazing, through its leafy canopy, into the serene blue depths above. The holy hymn soothes me like a mother's lullaby to her weary child. I care not to read the words of the book which custom places in my hands. I would listen, with closed eyes, while my soul syllables its own secret burden; floating away on that melody to Him who has given us this blessed day of rest; and as the last note dies away, I would cross the sacred threshold, hugging to my heart this holy peace; nor stay to listen to the cold, theoretical, charnel-house sermons to which, Sunday after Sunday—vary the church as I may —I feel myself, unless I do this, a disappointed, disheartened, and wearied listener. No earnestness, no life, no soul; long, dry, windy, wordy skeleton-discourses; tame platitudes, disgusting rant, a school-boy's parrot-lesson, injudicious depreciation of a world which is sweet to live in, and fair to see; injudicious denunciation of innocent, youthful pleasures—proper and healthful for life's young spring-time; an ascetic rendering of that Blessed Book which is, has been, and will be, the soul's life-boat, spite of its listless and blundering clerical expositors—many of whom offer us a Procrustean bed of theology, too short for any healthy creature of God to stretch himself upon. Who can wonder at the rebound? Who can wonder that our young people pass by the church-door, or cross its threshold compulsorily? or that their decorous seniors enter it but to sleep?

A few Sabbaths since I chanced into a church where a hundred and fifty children were assembled for the afternoon service, to be addressed as Sunday-school scholars. The out-door air was a luxury to breathe—it was one of those lovely spring days, which woo every living thing to bask in the warm sunshine. These children, many of them under four, none over fifteen, perspiring in their out-door clothing, were closely packed in those high-backed, uncomfortable seats—their cheeks at fever heat, and every pore in their crucified bodies crying out for ventilation and common sense—neither of which they had for a mortal hour-and-a-half, to speak within bounds. In vain did teachers frown, and nudge, and poke—in vain did the well-meaning but stupidest of possible ministers pound the pulpit cushions, to impress upon their memories, by gesticulation, his long-winded sentences; they were all written—as they deserved to be—in water. Flesh and blood couldn't stand it—least of all that most unperverted, critical, and discerning of audiences—childhood!

That preacher, in my opinion (and I ached to tell him so), did more harm in that hour and a half than he can remedy in a life-time. This may seem a bold assertion. Ithink not. One hundred and fifty little children to carry away with them from that church (not only for that afternoon, but for a long life of Sundays), a disgust of that blessed day, and what should be its sweet and holy services. But what is the use of talking? Every great and good cause is sure to be knocked in the head by some blunderbuss. Why didn't that man tell those children some short, simple story that the youngest child there could understand, appreciate, and be interested in? Why didn't he open wide the church-doors before their attention and interest flagged? Why so enamored of the sound of his own voice, as to keep those steaming, par-boiled little victims in that sacerdotal vapor-bath, after he had said all he could think of to them, to address their teachers, who, if necessary, should have had a meeting by themselves for that infliction? And why—(I ask all of you who have not forgotten how your restless   limbs   ached   when you were   children)—must another minister get up after that, and torture common-sense, and his fainting, frying auditors, by another aimless, inflated, meaningless, and   last-drop-in-the-bucket,   but   (thanks   to   a   kind Providence), final address? And why didn't somebody seize the sexton of that church, who had compelled a hundred and fifty children to breathe the foul air which the morning worshipers had bequeathed, and which he was too lazy to let out the windows—why didn't somebody, I say, seize that sexton, and place him in an exhausted receiver, long enough to give him some faint notion of what he made those par-boiled children suffer in that "protracted meeting?"

"COME ON, MACDUFF."

A correspondent wishes us to "oblige a lady," by publishing a communication containing strictures on Fanny Fern. But, why should we "oblige a lady" whom we do not know, and at the same time disoblige a lady whom all the world knows?—New York Evening Mirror.

"Oblige a lady." She is not the first, or the only lady, who has tried to be "obliged," and obliging, in this way. Dear creatures! how they love me! There was Miss Moses, proper Miss Moses, who had been for a year or more writing for the Scribetown Gazette, when I commenced. How delighted she was at my advent—how pleased she was with my articles —how many things she said about me, personally and literarily, to the editor of the Gazette—what an interest she took in my progress. She never tried to keep my articles out of the paper, (benevolent soul!) "lest they should injure its reputation"—not she; she never, when looking over the exchanges, hid away those in which my articles were copied, and commended—not she, she never, when she found one containing a personal attack on me (written at her own suggestion), marked it with a double row of ink marks, and laid it in a conspicuous place on the editor's table—not she. She liked my articles— liked them so well, that, on several occasions, she appropriated whole sentences and paragraphs; omitting (probably through forgetfulness), to make the necessary quotation marks! Dove-like Miss Moses! I think I see her now looking as though she was going to be translated (which by the way, her works never have been.) Pious Miss Moses, who rang threadbare changes on the ten commandments, and was addicted to meetings and melancholy; she tried hard to extinguish me, but success makes one magnanimous. I forgive her.

And there was Miss Fox, who "never could see any thing to like in Fanny Fern's articles," who knew her to have come from a family, "who always fizzled out"—(on this point this deponent saith nothing)— but who, when she (Miss Fox) had occasion to write a newspaper story, got some kind friend to say in print, "that the story by Rosa, was probably written by Fanny Fern." Sweet Miss Fox!

Then there was Miss Briar, who "wondered if Mr. Bonner, of the New York Ledger, gave Fanny Fern, who had never been out of sight of America, $100 a column for her stupid trash, what he would give her, Miss Briar, who had crossed the big pond, when she touched pen to paper! Fanny Fern, indeed! Humph!"

Lovely creatures! I adore the whole sex. I always prefer hotels, ferry boats, and omnibusses, where they predominate, and abound; how courteous they are to each other, in case of a squeeze! Lord bless 'em! How truly Burns says:

"Auld Nature swears, the lovely dearsHer noblest work she classes,
O:Her 'prentice han' she tried on man,And then she made the lasses,
O.The sweetest hours that e'er I spendAre spent amang the lasses, O."

LOOK ALOFT.

You are "discouraged!" You? with strong limbs, good health, the green
earth beneath your feet, and the broad blue sky above? "Discouraged?"
and why? You are poor, unknown, friendless, obscure, unrecognized, and
alone in this great swarming metropolis; the rich man suffocates you
with the dust of his pretentious chariot wheels.

As you are now, so once was he. Did he waste time whining about it?
No, by the rood! or he would not now be President of the Bank before
which he once sold beer at a penny a glass, to thirsty cabmen and
newsboys. For shame, man! get up and shake yourself, if you are not
afraid such a mass of inanity will fall to pieces. Cock your hat on your
head, torn rim and all; elbow your way through the crowd; if they don't
move for you, make them do it; push past them; you have as much right
in the world as your neighbor. If you wait for him to take you by the
hand, the grass will grow over your grave. Rush past him and get
employment. "You have tried, and failed." So have thousands before
you, who, to-day, are pecuniarily independent. I have the most
unqualified disgust of a man who folds his hands at every obstacle,
instead of leaping over it; or who dare not do any thing under heaven,
unless it be to blaspheme God, wrong his neighbor, or dishonor woman.

I tell you, if you are determined, you can get employment; but you won't
get it by cringing round the doors of rich relations; you won't get it if
you can't dine on a crust, month after month, and year after year, if need
be, with hope for a dessert; you won't get it if you stand with your lazy
hands in your pockets, listening to croakers; you won't do it if you don't
raise your head above every billow of discouragement which dashes over
you, and halloo to Fate, with a stout heart: "Try again, old fellow!" No—
and it is not right you should—you are good for nothing but to go
sniveling through the world, making wry faces at the good fortune of
other people. Bah! I'm disgusted with you.

You despair. Why? "You are a widow." Of how much sorrow is that little word the voice? Oh! I know, poor mourner, how dark earth looks to you. I know that sun and stars mock you with their brightness. I know that you shut out the placid moonbeams, and pray to die. Listen! Are there no bleeding hearts but yours? Your dead sleep peacefully; their tears are all shed; their sighs all heaved; their weary hands folded over quiet hearts; but oh, repiner! the living sorrows that are masked beneath the smiling faces you envy! the corroding bitterness of a dishonored hearth-stone; the mantle all too narrow, all too scant, to hide from prying, malignant eyes, the torturing secret!—bone of your bone, flesh of your flesh, and yet, stranger to you than the savage of the desert—colder to you than the dead for whom you so repiningly grieve. Ah! are there no bleeding hearts save yours? Is the "last vial" emptied on your shrinking head?

But your little children stand looking into your tear-stained face, imploring you for bread—bread that you know not where to procure; your ear aches for the kind words which never come to you. Oh, where is your faith in God? Who says to you in accents sweeter than ever fell from human lips: "A bruised reed will I not break;" "Let your widows trust in me." No kind words? Is it nothing, that those musical little voices call you "mother?" Is the clasp of those soft arms, the touch of those velvet lips, nothing? Is it thus you teach them to put their little hands into that of the Almighty Father, and say, "Give us this day our daily bread?" Oh, get on your knees before those sweet little teachers, who know no danger—no harm, who fear no evil while "mother" is near, and learn of them to watch, and hope, and trust; for sure as the sun shines above your and their heads, so sure is His promise to those who believingly claim it.

"Lonely," are you? Oh, above all loneliness is his, who, having thrown away his faith in God, and bereft of earthly idols, stands like some lightning-reft tree, blossomless, verdureless, scathed, and blasted!

KNICKERBOCKER AND TRI-MOUNTAIN.

The New York woman doteth on rainbow hats and dresses, confectionery, the theater, the opera, and flirtation. She stareth gentlemen in the street out of countenance, in a way that puzzleth a stranger to decide the question of her respectability. The New York woman thinketh it well-bred to criticise in an audible tone the dress and appearance of every chance lady near her, in the street, shop, ferry-boat, car, or omnibus. If doubtful of the material of which her dress is composed, she draweth near, examineth it microscopically, and pronounceth it—"after all—silk." The New York woman never appeareth without a dress-hat and flounces, though the time be nine o'clock in the morning, and her destination the grocer's, to order some superfine tea. She delighteth in embroidered petticoats, which she liberally displayeth to curious bipeds of the opposite sex. She turneth up her nose at a delaine, wipeth up the pavement with a thousand-dollar silk, and believeth point-lace collars and handkerchiefs essential to salvation. She scorneth to ride in an omnibus, and if driven by an impertinent shower therein, sniffeth up her aristocratic nose at the plebeian occupants, pulleth out her costly gold watch to—ascertain the time! and draweth off her gloves to show her diamonds. Arrived at Snob avenue, she shaketh off the dust of her silken flounces against her fellow-travelers, trippeth up her aristocratic steps, and holding up her dress sufficiently high to display to the retreating passengers her silken hose, and dainty boot, resigneth her parasolette to black John, and maketh her triumphant exit.

At the opera, the New York woman taketh the most conspicuous box, spreadeth out her flounces to their fullest circumference, and betrayeth a constant and vulgar consciousness that she is in her go-to-meetin-fixins, by arranging her bracelets and shawl, settling her rings, and fiddling at her coiffure, and the lace kerchief on her neck. She also talketh incessantly during the opera, to show that she is not a novice to be amused by it; and leaveth with much bustle, just before the last act, for the same reason, and also to display her toilette.

On Sunday morning, the New York woman taketh all the jewelry she can collect, and in her flashiest silk and bonnet, taketh her velvet-bound, gilt-clasped prayer-book out for an airing. Arrived at Dives' church, she straightway kneeleth and boweth her head; not, as the uninitiated may suppose, to pray, but privately to arrange her curls; this done, and raising her head, she sayeth, "we beseech thee to hear us, good Lord!" while she taketh a minute inventory of the Hon. Mrs. Peters's Parisian toilette. After church, she taketh a turn or two in Fifth Avenue, to display her elaborate dress, and to wonder "why vulgar people don't confine themselves to the Bowery."

THE BOSTON WOMAN.

The Boston woman draweth down her mouth, rolleth up her eyes, foldeth her hands, and walketh on a crack. She rejoiceth in anatomical and chemical lectures. She prateth of Macaulay and Carlyle; belongeth to many and divers reading-classes, and smileth in a chaste, moonlight kind of way on literary men. She dresseth (to her praise be it spoken) plainly in the street, and considereth india-rubbers, a straw bonnet, and a thick shawl, the fittest costume for damp and cloudy weather. She dresseth her children more for comfort than show, and bringeth them up also to walk on a crack. She maketh the tour of the Common twice or three times a day, without regard to the barometer. She goeth to church twice or three times on Sunday, sandwiched with Bible-classes and Sabbath-schools. She thinketh London, Vienna, or Paris—fools to Boston; and the "Boulevards" and "Tuilleries" not to be mentioned with the Frog Pond and the Common. She is well posted up as to politics—thinketh, "as Pa does," and sticketh to it through thunder and lightning. When asked to take a gentleman's arm, she hooketh the tip of her little finger circumspectly on to his male coat-sleeve. She is as prim as a bolster, as stiff as a ram-rod, as frigid as an icicle, and not even matrimony with a New Yorker could thaw her.

THE NEW YORK MALE.

The New York male exulteth in fast horses, stylish women, long-legged hounds, a coat-of-arms, and liveried servants. Beside, or behind him, may be seen his servant, with folded arms and white gloves, driven out daily by his master, to inhale the gutter breezes of Broadway, to excite the wonder of the curious, and to curl the lips of republicanism. The New York male hath many and divers garments; some of which he weareth bob-tailed; some shanghai, some with velvet collars, some with silk; anon turned up; anon turned down; and some carelessly a-la-flap. The New York male breakfasteth late, owing to pressing engagements which keep him abroad after midnight. About twelve the next morning he lighteth a cigar to assist his blear-eyes to find the way down-town; and with his hands in his pockets, and arms akimbo, he navigateth tortuously around locomotive "hoops;"—indefatigably pursueth a bonnet for several blocks, to get a peep it its owner; nor getteth discouraged at intervening parasols, or impromptu shopping errands; nor thinketh his time or shoe leather wasted. The New York male belongeth to the most ruinous club and military company; is a connoisseur in gold sleeve-buttons, and seal-rings, and diamond studs. He cometh into the world with an eye-glass and black ribbon winked into his left eye, and prideth himself upon having broken all the commandments before he arrived at the dignity of coat-tails.

THE BOSTON MALE.

The Boston male is respectable all over; from the crown of his glossy hat to the soles of his shiny shoes; and huggeth his mantle of self-esteem inseparably about him, that he may avoid contaminating contact with the non-elect of his "set." The Boston male is for the most part good-looking; and a stanch devotee of starch and buckram; he patronizeth jewelry but sparingly, and never discerneth a diamond in the rough. If, as Goethe sayeth, "the unconscious is the alone complete," then is the male Bostonian yet in embryo. He taketh, and readeth all the newspapers and magazines, foreign and domestic; and yet, strange to say, sweareth by the little tea-table "Transcript." When the Boston male traveleth he weareth his best clothes; arrived at his destination he putteth up at the most showy hotel, ordereth the most expensive rooms and edibles, and maketh an unwonted "splurge" generally. He then droppeth the proprieties—pro tem.—being seized with an anatomical desire to dissect the great sores of the city; fancying, like the ostrich, that if his head only be hidden, he is undiscernible.

The Boston male is conservative as a citizen, prosaic as a lover; humdrum as a husband, and hath no sins—to speak of!

MY OLD INK-STAND AND I;
OR, THE FIRST ARTICLE IN THE NEW HOUSE.

Well, old Ink-stand, what do you think of this? Haven't we got well through the woods, hey? A few scratches and bruises we have had, to be sure, but what of that? Didn't you whisper where we should come out, the first morning I dipped my pen in your sable depths, in the sky-parlor of that hyena-like Mrs. Griffin? With what an eagle glance she discovered that my bonnet-ribbon was undeniably guilty of two distinct washings, and, emboldened by my shilling de laine, and the shabby shoes of little Nell, inquired "if I intended taking in slop-work into her apartments?" How distinctly I was made to understand that Nell was not to speak above a whisper, or in any way infringe upon the rights of her uncombed, unwashed, unbaptized, uncomfortable little Griffins. Poor little Nell, who clung to my gown with childhood's instinctive appreciation of the hard face and wiry voice of our jailor. With what venom I overheard her inform Mr. Griffin that "they must look sharp for the rent of their sky-parlor, as its tenant lived on bread and milk, and wore her under-clothes rough-dry, because she could not afford to pay for ironing them!" Do you remember that, old Ink-stand? And do you remember the morning she informed me, as you and I were busily engaged in out first article, that I must "come and scrub the stairs which led up to my room;" and when I ventured humbly to mention, that this was not spoken of in our agreement, do you remember the Siddons-like air with which she thundered in our astonished ears—"Do it, or tramp!" And do you remember how you vowed "if I did tramp," you would stand by me, and help me out of the scrape? and haven't you done it, old Ink-stand? And don't you wish old Griffin, and all the little Griffins, and their likes, both big and little, here and elsewhere, could see this bran-new house that you have helped me into, and the dainty little table upon which I have installed you, untempted by any new papier-mache modern marvel?

Turn my back on you, old Ink-stand! Not I. Throw you aside, for your shabby exterior, as we were thrown aside, when it was like drawing teeth to get a solitary shilling to buy you at a second-hand shop? Perish the thought!

Yes, old Ink-stand, Griffin and all that crew, should see us now. Couldn't we take the wind out of their sails? Couldn't we come into their front door, instead of their "back gate?" Didn't they "always know that there was something in us?" We can forgive them, though, can't we? By the title deed, and insurance policy, of this bran-new pretty house, which their sneers have helped us into, and whose doors shall always be open to those who have cheered us on, we'll do it.

Dropped many a tear into you, have I? Well—who cares? You know, very well, that every rough word aimed at my quivering ears, was an extra dollar in my purse; every rude touch of my little Nell, strength and sinew to my unstrung nerves and flagging muscles. I say, old Ink-stand, look at Nell now! Does any landlady lay rough hands on those plump shoulders? Dare she sing and run, and jump and play to her heart's content? Didn't you yourself buy her that hoop and stick, and those dolls, and that globe of gold-fish? Don't you feed and clothe her, every day of her sunshiny life? Haven't you agreed to do it, long years to come? and won't you teach her, as you have me, to defy false friends, and ill-fortune? And won't you be to my little Nell a talisman, when my eyes grow dim, and hers brighten? Say, old Ink-stand?

THE SOUL—AND THE STOMACH.

There is a good old man. His head is white—his form is bent—his step slow and tremulous. Life has no charms for him, and the opening grave is full of terrors; he wanders up and down—up and down—wringing his withered hands, and says, "I have committed the unpardonable sin; I am lost—lost—lost." They who love him, and their name is Legion, look on dismayed at this good father, good husband, good neighbor, good Christian; and one of them says to me, "Why, if your God be merciful, does he afflict his faithful servant thus? God is not good!"

God is good, though all else fail, and we, like insects, creep and complain; God is good. It is not religion that makes the old man gloomy —it is not that the Word of God shall not stand forever; but He who has bid us care for the soul, bids us also care for the body. "If one member suffer, all the other members suffer with it." If we neglect the laws of health, and abuse our bodies, even in His service, he does not guaranty to the delinquent, a strong mind, an unperverted spiritual vision—clouds and darkness will come between us and the Sun of Righteousness, and though we shall feel after Him, we shall grope like children in the dark. It is an earthly physician which such as that old man needs; a tonic for the body, not a sermon from the pulpit. Let him lean upon your arm; lead him forth to the green fields, where every little bird sings God is good; where waving trees and blossoming flowers pass the whisper round with myriad voices; take away the old man's psalm-book, and let him listen to that anthem, and as the soft breath of spring lifts his white locks from his troubled brow, the film of disease will fall from his eyes, and he, too, shall sing that God is good.

Never lay upon the back of Religion what Dyspepsia should shoulder. The Christian warrior, no more than any other, can afford to neglect or gorge his "rations" when preparing for battle; nor if either faint by the way, in consequence, is it to be laid to the commander.

AWE-FUL THOUGHTS.

"This had, from the very beginning of their acquaintance, induced in her that awe, which is the most delicious feeling a wife can have toward her husband."

"Awe!"—awe of a man whose whiskers you have trimmed, whose hair you have cut, whose cravats you have tied, whose shirts you have "put into the wash," whose boots and shoes you have kicked into the closet, whose dressing-gown you have worn while combing your hair; who has been down cellar with you at eleven o'clock at night, to hunt for a chicken-bone; who has hooked your dresses, unlaced your boots, fastened your bracelets, and tied on your bonnet; who has stood before your looking-glass, with thumb and finger on his proboscis, scraping his chin; whom you have buttered, and sugared, and toasted, and tea-ed; whom have seen asleep with his mouth wide open! Ri—diculous!

A WORD TO PARENTS AND TEACHERS.

Why will New York women be eternally munching cake and confectionery? What is more disgusting than to see a lady devouring at a sitting, ounces of burnt almonds, and sugared wine and brandy-drops, or packing away, in her rosy mouth, uncounted platesful of jelly-cake or maccaroons? "But shopping is hungry business;" that is true, and many a shopper comes hungry distances to perform it; but are cake and confectionery wholesome diet between meals? and is not ice-cream at such a time rank poison? Call for a sandwich or a roll, and you may not be considered suicidal.

Every body knows that young girls are foreordained to go through a regular experience in eating slate-pencils, burnt quills, pickles, and chalk; but this green age passed, one looks for a little common sense. I have often seen New York women, not content with ruining their own constitution in this way (and consequently periling their prospective offspring), buy, before leaving the confectioner's shop, five or six pounds of candy for nursery distribution, and ask Betty, the next day (the sapient mother!), "what can ail those children to fret so?" It were more merciful to purchase a dose of strychnine, and put an immediate end to their misery, than thus murder them by inches. Are the rosy, robust, beautiful English children, candy-fed? Are they suffered to gorge themselves on hot bread, preserves, cake and pastry, ad libitum? Do they have any thing but the plainest puddings, the stalest bread, and the most unmitigated roast and boiled meat, unpoisoned by those dyspepsia-breeding gravies of ours?

It is pitiful, this dwarfing of American children with improper food, want of exercise, and cork-screw clothes. It is inhuman to require of their enfeebled minds and bodies, in ill-ventilated schoolrooms, tasks which the most vigorous child should never have imposed upon his tender years. As if a child's physique were not of the first importance!—as if all the learning in the world could be put to any practical use by an enfeebled body! As if a parent had a right, year after year, thus to murder the innocents.

Think of one of those candy-and-cake-fed young girls, bending over her tasks in school, from nine o'clock till three, with perhaps ten or fifteen minutes intermission (spent in the close air of the school-room) and two days out of a week at three, after another ten minutes' intermission, and another cake-and-candy feed, commencing drawing, or music lessons, to last till five; her mother, meanwhile, rocking away as comfortably, in her chair at home, as if her daughter's spine were not crooking irretrievably. I will not speak of the utter impossibility that this young girl should have a steady hand for drawing, under such circumstances, because any fool can understand that to be impossible.

I ask what right have you to require of your child, your growing, restless child, what it would be impossible for you to do yourself? You know very well that you could not keep your mind on the stretch for so many hours to any profit; or your body in one position for such a length of time, without excessive pain and untold weariness. Then add to this the tasks which must be conned on the return home for the next day's lesson, and one marvels no longer at the sickly, sallow, narrow-chested, leaden-eyed young girls we are in the habit of meeting.

What would I have? I would have teachers less selfishly consult their own convenience, in insisting upon squeezing into the forenoon what should be divided between forenoon and afternoon, as in the good old-fashioned way of keeping school, with time to eat a wholesome dinner between. A teacher's established constitution may possibly stand this modern nonsense (though I am told not long); but that children should be thus victimized, without at least a remonstrance on the part of their natural guardians, I can only ascribe to the criminal indifference of parents to the welfare of their offspring.

LADY DOCTORS.

And so the female doctors are prospering and getting practice. I am sure I am heartily glad of it, for several reasons; one of which is, that it is an honest and honorable deliverance from the everlasting, non-remunerating, consumptive-provoking, monotonous needle. Another is, that it is a more excellent way of support, than by the mercenary and un-retraceable road, through the church-door to the altar, into which so many non-reliant women are driven. Having said this I feel at liberty to remark that we all have our little fancies, and one of mine is, that a hat is a pleasanter object of contemplation in a sick-room than a bonnet. I think, too, that my wrist reposes more comfortably in a big hand than a little one, and if my mouth is to be inspected, I prefer submitting it to a beard than to a flounce. Still, this may be a narrow prejudice—I dare say it is—but like most of my prejudices, I am afraid no amount of fire will burn it out of me.

A female doctor! Great Esculapius! Before swallowing her pills (of which she would be the first), I should want to make sure that I had never come between her and a lover, or a new bonnet, or been the innocent recipient of a gracious smile from her husband. If I desired her undivided attention to my case, I should first remove the looking-glass, and if a consultation seemed advisable, I should wish to arm myself with a gridiron, or a darning-needle, or some other appropriate weapon, before expressing such a wish. If my female doctor recommended a blister on my head, I should strongly doubt its necessity if my hair happened to be handsome, also the expediency of a scar-defacing plaster for my neck, if it happened to be plump and white. Still, these may be little prejudices; very like they are; but this I will say, before the breath is taken out of me by any female doctor, that while I am in my senses I will never exchange my gentlemanly, soft-voiced, soft-stepping, experienced, intelligent, handsome doctor, for all the female M. D.'s who ever carved up dead bodies or live characters—or tore each other's caps.

THE CHERUB IN THE OMNIBUS.

They stepped in together—the man and his wife—honest, healthy country-folk. She—rosy and plump; he—stalwart, broad-chested, and strong-limbed, as God intended man and woman to be. I might not have noticed them particularly, but they had a baby; and such a baby! None of your flabby city abortions; but a flesh-and-blood baby—a baby to make one's mouth water—ay, and eyes, too! Such a baby as might have been born in the Garden of Eden, had the serpent never crept in; born of parents fed on strawberries and pomegranates—pure in soul, pure in body, and healthy and vigorous as purity alone can be.

Such a baby! such eyes—such a skin—such bewildering lips—such a heaven-born smile; my eyes overflowed as I looked at it. I was not worthy to hold that baby, but my heart yearned for it, and I held out my hands invitingly.

See! the little trusting thing leaps from its father's arms and sits smiling on my knee. Ah! little baby, turn away those soft blue eyes from mine; is it not enough that my soul is on its knees to you? Is it not enough, that for every bitter word wrung from my tortured soul by wrong and suffering, I could cry: "God be merciful to me a sinner?"

And yet, little baby, I was once like thee. Like thee, I stretched out the trusting hand to those who——ah, little baby—I am not like thee now; yet stay with me, and perhaps I shall be. Jesus "took a little child and set him in the midst." Take hold of my hand, and lead me to heaven.

Going? then God be with thee, as surely as he has been with me, in thy pure presence. I shall see thee again, little baby, if I heed thy teachings; thou hast done thy silent mission.

FANNY FORD.

CHAPTER I.

It was a mad freak of dame Nature to fashion Mary Ford after so dainty a model, and then open her blue eyes in a tumble-down house in Peck-lane. But Mary cares little for that. Fortune has given her wheel a whirl since then, and Jacob Ford is now on the top. Mary sees the young and the old, the grave and the gay, the wise and the ignorant, smile on her sweet face; as she passes, men murmur "beautiful," and women pick flaws in her face and figure. She can not sleep for serenades, and her little room is perfumed, from May to January, with the rarest of hot-house flowers. Lovers, too, come wooing by the score. And yet, Mary is no coquette; no more than the sweet flower, which nods, and sways, and sends forth its perfume for very joy that it blossoms in the bright sunshine, all unconscious how it tempts the passer-by to pluck it for his own wearing. A queenly girl was the tailor's daughter, with her Juno-like figure, her small, well-shaped head, poised so daintily on the fair white throat; with her large blue eyes, by turns brilliant as the lightning's flash, then soft as a moonbeam; with her pretty mouth, and the dimple which lay perdu in the corner, with the flossy waves of her dark brown hair; with her soft, white hands, and twinkling little feet; with her winsome smile, and floating grace of motion.

Percy Lee was conquered. Percy—who had withstood blue eyes and black, gray eyes and hazel. Percy—for whom many a fair girl had smiled and pouted in vain. Percy the bookworm. Percy—handsome as Apollo, cold as Mont Blanc. Percy Lee was fettered at last, and right merrily did mischievous Cupid forge, one by one, his chains for the stoic. No poor fish ever so writhed and twisted on the hook, till the little word was whispered which made him in lover's parlance, "the happiest of men."

Of course, distanced competitors wondered what Mary Ford could see to admire in that book-worm of a Percy. Of course, managing mammas, with marriageable daughters, were shocked that Miss Ford should have angled for him so transparently; and the young ladies themselves marveled that the aristocratic Percy should fancy a tailor's daughter; of course the lovers, in the seventh heaven of their felicity, could afford to let them think and say what they pleased.

The torpid sexagenarian, or frigid egotist, may sneer; but how beautiful is this measureless first love, before distrust has chilled, or selfishness blighted, or the scorching sun of worldliness evaporated the heart's dew; when we trust with childhood's sweet faith, because we love; when care and sorrow are undiscernible shapes in the distance; when at every footstep we ring the chime of joy from out the flowers. What can earth offer after this sparkling draught has been quaffed? How stale its after spiritless effervescences!

Percy's love for Mary was all the more pure and intense, that he had hitherto kept his heart free from youthful entanglements. Fastidious and refined to a degree, perhaps this with him was as much a matter of necessity as of choice. In Mary both his heart and taste were satisfied; true, he sometimes wondered how so delicate and dainty a flower should have blossomed from out so rude a soil; for her father's money could neither obliterate nor gild over the traces of his innate vulgarity; in fact, his love for his daughter was his only redeeming trait—the only common ground upon which the father and lover could meet. The petty accumulation of fortune by the penny, had narrowed and hardened a heart originally good and unselfish; the love of gold for its own sake had swallowed up every other thought and feeling. Like many persons of humble origin, whose intellects have not expanded with their coffers, Jacob Ford overrated the accident of birth and position, and hence was well pleased with Mary's projected alliance with Percy.

"Well, to be sure, Lucy, beauty is a great thing for a girl," he one day said to his wife. "I did not dream of this when Mary used to climb up on the counter of my little dark shop in Peck-lane, and sit playing with the goose and shears."

"Nor I," replied Lucy, as she looked around their handsome apartment, with a satisfied smile; "nor I, Jacob, when, after paying me one Saturday night for my week's work, you said, 'Lucy, you can be mistress of this shop if you like.' I was so proud and happy: for, indeed, it was lonesome enough, Jacob, stitching in that gloomy old garret I often used to think how dreadful it would be to be sick and die there alone, as poor Hetty Carr did. It was a pity, Jacob, you did not pay her more, and she so weakly, too. Often she would sit up all night, sewing, with that dreadful cough racking her."

"Tut—tut—wife," said Jacob; "she was not much of a seamstress; you always had a soft heart, Lucy, and were easily imposed upon by a whining story."

"It was too true, Jacob; and she had been dead a whole day before any one found it out; then, as she had no friends, she was buried at the expense of the city, and the coffin they brought was too short for her, and they crowded her poor thin limbs into it, and carried her away in the poor's hearse. Sometimes, Jacob, I get very gloomy when I think of this, and look upon our own beautiful darling; and, sometimes, Jacob—you won't be angry with me?" asked the good woman, coaxingly, as she laid her hand upon his arm—"sometimes I've thought our money would never do us any good."

"Pshaw!" exclaimed Jacob, impatiently shaking off his wife's hand; "pshaw, Lucy, you are like all other women, weak and superstitious. A man must look out for number one. Small profits a body would make to conduct business on your principles. Grab all you can, keep all you get, is every body's motto; why should I set up to be wiser than my neighbors?"

Lucy Ford sighed. A wife is very apt to be convinced by her husband's reasoning, if she loves him; and perhaps Lucy might have been, had she not herself known what it was to sit stitching day after day in her garret, till her young brain reeled, and her heart grew faint and sick, or lain in her little bed, too weary even to sleep, listening to the dull rain as it pattered on the skylight, and wishing she were dead.

A pressure of soft lips upon her forehead, and a merry laugh, musical as the ringing of silver bells, roused Lucy from her reverie.

"Good-by—mother dear," said Mary; "I could not go to ride with Percy without a kiss from you. Come to the window—look! Are not those pretty horses of Percy's? They skim the ground like birds! And see what a pretty carriage! Now acknowledge that my lover's taste is perfect."

"Yes—when he chose you," said Jacob, gazing admiringly on Mary's bright face and graceful form. "You would grace a court, Mary, if you are old Jacob Ford's daughter."

Mary threw her arms around the old man's neck, and kissed his bronze cheek. To her the name of father was another name for love; nurtured in this kindly atmosphere, she could as little comprehend how a child could cease to worship a parent, as she could comprehend how a parent, when his child asked for bread, should mock his misery with a stone. Unspoiled by the world's flatteries, she had not learned to undervalue her doting father's love, that it was expressed in ungrammatical phrase; she had not yet learned to blush at any old-fashioned breach of etiquette (on his part), in the presence of her fastidious young friends; and by her marked deference to her parents in their presence, she in a measure exacted the same from them. It was one of the loveliest traits in Mary's character, and one for which Percy, who appreciated her refinement, loved and respected her the more.

"Have your fortune told, lady?" asked a withered old woman, of Mary, as she tripped down the steps to join Percy.

"Of course," said the laughing girl: "suppose you tell me whom I am to marry," with a gay glance at Percy; and she ungloved her small white hand, while the dame's withered fingers traced its delicate lines.

"Retribution is written here," said the old woman, solemnly; "your sun will set early, fair girl."

"Come away, Mary," said Percy, with a frown, shaking his whip at the woman, "the old thing is becrazed."

"Time will show," muttered the beldame, pocketing the coin with which Mary had crossed her hand; "time will show; brighter eyes than yours, fair lady, have wept themselves dim."

"What can she mean?" said Mary, drawing involuntarily close to the side of her lover. "I almost wish we had not seen her."

The spirits of youth are elastic. The April cloud soon passed from Mary's brow, and before the fleet horses had skimmed a mile, her laugh rang out as merrily as ever.

The lovers had both a trained eye for natural beauty, and the lovely road through which they passed, with its brown houses half hidden in foliage —the lazy grazing cattle—the scent of new-mown hay and breath of flowers—the rude song of the plowman and the delicate twitter of the bird—the far-off hills, with their tall trees distinctly defined against the clear blue sky—the silver stream and velvet meadows—the wind's wild anthem, now swelling as if in full chorus, then soft and sweet as the murmur of a sleeping babe, all filled their hearts with a quiet joy.

"Life is very sweet," said Mary, turning her lustrous eyes upon her lover. "People say that happiness and prosperity harden the heart; when I am most blest I feel most devotional. In vain might the infidel tell me 'there is no God,' with such a scene as this before me, or fetter my grateful heart-pulses as they adored the Giver."

"You dear little saint," said Percy, with a light laugh, "how well you preach. Well—my mother was neck-deep in religion; the prayers and hymns she taught me, stay by me now, whether I will or no. I often catch myself saying 'Now I lay me,' when I go to bed, from the mere force of habit; but your rosy lips were never made to mumble pater nosters, Mary: leave that to crafty priests, and disappointed nuns. Religion, my pet, is another name for humbug, all the world over; your would-be-saint always cheats in proportion to the length of his face and his prayers. Bah! don't let us talk of it."

"Don't—dear Percy," said Mary. "I like you less well when you talk so; religion is the only sure basis of character. Every superstructure not built on this foundation—"

"Must topple over, I suppose," said Percy. "Don't you believe it, my angel. I am a living example to the contrary; but Cupid knows I would subscribe to any article of faith emanating from your rosy lips;" and Percy drew rein at the door of his father-in-law's mansion, and leaping out, assisted Mary to alight.

"Such a lovely drive as we have had, dear mother," said Mary, throwing her hat upon the table. "Percy has just gone off with a client on business; he will be back presently. Dear Percy! he's just the best fellow in the world—a little lax on religious points, but he loves me well enough to be influenced there. Now I will sit down at this window while I sew, and then I shall see Percy when he comes up the street."

Nimbly her fingers moved; her merry song keeping time the while. Now a blush flitting over her cheek, then a smile dimpling it. She was thinking of their beautiful home that was to be, and how like a fairy dream her life would pass, with that deep, rich voice lingering ever in her ear; cares, if they came, lightened by each other's presence, or turned to joys by mutual sympathy. And then, she was so proud of him; A woman's love is so deepened by that thought.

God pity her, who, with a great soul, indissolubly bound, must walk ever backward with a mantle (alas! all too transparent), to cover her husband's mental nakedness!

CHAPTER II.

"A gentleman, sir, to see you," said a servant to Jacob Ford, as he ushered in his old friend, Mr. Trask.

"Ah, Trask, how are you? Glad to see you," said Jacob, with one of his vice-like shakes of the hand. "Come for a rubber at whist? That's right. I was thinking to-day, how long it was since you and I had a quiet hour together. How's trade, Trask? You ought to be making money. Why, what's the matter, man?" clapping him on the shoulder; "never saw you this way before; hang me if you don't look as solemn as old Parson Glebe. Why don't you speak? Why do you stare at me so?"

"Jacob," replied Mr. Trask, and there he stopped.

"Well—that's my name; Jacob Ford: as good a name as you'll find on 'change. I never have done any thing to make me ashamed of it."

"I wish every body could say as much," said Trask, gravely.

"What are you driving at?" asked Jacob Ford; "don't talk riddles to me— they get me out of temper. If you have any thing to tell, out with it. I've seen fifty years' wear and tear; I'm not frightened by trifles."

"But this is no trifle, Ford. I can't do it," said the soft-hearted Mr. Trask. "Jacob, my old friend—I—can't do it," and he sat down and covered his face with his hands.

"Come—come," said Jacob; "take heart, man. If you have got into a scrape, Jacob Ford is not the man to desert an old friend; if a few hundreds or more will set it all right, you shall have it."

"For God's sake, stop," said Trask; "the shadow has fallen on your threshold, not on mine."

"Mine?" replied Jacob, with a bewildered look. "Mine? defalcations? banks broke? hey? Jacob Ford a beggar, after fifty years' toil?"

"Worse—worse," said Trask, making a violent effort to speak. "Percy Lee is arrested for embezzlement, and I have proofs of his guilt. There—now I've said it."

"Man! do you know this?" said Jacob, in a hoarse whisper, putting his white lips close to his friend's ear, as if he feared the very walls would tell the secret.

"Before God, 'tis true," said Trask, solemnly.

"Then God's curse light on the villain," said Jacob Ford. "My Mary—my bright, beautiful Mary! Oh! who will tell her? Listen, Trask, that's her voice—singing. Oh, God—oh God, this is too dreadful"—and the old man bowed his head upon his breast, and wept like a child.

"What does all this mean?" asked Lucy Ford, opening the door. "Jacob—husband—Trask—what is it?" and she looked from one to the other, in bewildered wonder.

"Tell her, Trask," whispered Jacob.

"Don't weep so, dear Jacob," said Lucy; "if money has gone, we can both go to work again; we both know how. Mary will soon have a home of her own."

Jacob sprang to his feet, and seizing Lucy by the arm, hissed in her ear, "Woman, don't you name him. May God's curse blight him. May he die alone. May his bones bleach in the winds of heaven, and his soul be forever damned. Lucy—Percy Lee is a—a—swindler! There—now go break her heart, if you can. Lucy?—Trask?"—and Jacob, overcome with the violence of his feelings, wept again like a child; while poor Lucy, good Lucy, hid her face on her husband's breast, repressing her own anguish that she might not add to his.

"Who's going to tell her, I say?" said Jacob. "May my tongue wither before I do it. My darling—my loving, beautiful darling—who will tell her?"

"I," said the mother, with ashen lips, as she raised herself slowly from her husband's breast, and moved toward the door.

Clutching at the balustrade for support, Lucy dragged herself slowly up stairs. Ah! well might she reel to and fro as she heard Mary's voice:

"Bring flowers, bring flowers for the bride to wear,They were born to blush in her shining hair;She is leaving the home of her childhood's mirth,She hath bid farewell to her father's hearth,Her place is now by another's side;Bring flowers for the locks of the fair young bride."

A trembling hand was laid upon Mary's shoulder. She shook back her long bright hair, and looked smilingly up into her mother's face.

"Mary," said Lucy, solemnly, "you will never marry Percy Lee."

"Dead? Percy dead? Oh—no—no," gasped the poor girl. "My Percy!—no—no!"

"Worse—worse," said Lucy, throwing her protecting arms around her child. "Mary, Percy Lee is a swindler; he is unworthy of you; you must forget him."

"Never," said Mary—"never! Who dare say that? Where is he?—take me to him;" and she sunk fainting to the floor.

"I have killed her," said the weeping mother, as she chafed her cold temples, and kissed her colorless lips. "I have killed her," she murmured, bending over her, as Mary passed from one convulsive fit to another.

"Will she die, Jacob?" asked Lucy, looking mournfully up into her husband's pallid face. "Will she die, Jacob?"

"Better so," groaned the old man. "God's curse on him who has done this. She was my all. What's my gold good for, if it can not bring back the light to her eye, the peace to her heart? My gold that I have toiled for, and piled up in shining heaps: what is it good for?"

"The curse was on it, Jacob," groaned Lucy. "Oh, Jacob, I told you so. God forgive us; it was cankered gold."

"Why did the villain blast my home?" asked Jacob, apparently unconscious of what Lucy had said; "kill my one ewe lamb; all Jacob had to love—all that made him human? Lucy, I never prayed, but perhaps He would hear me for her;" and he knelt by his child. "Oh God, make my soul miserable forever, if thou wilt, but spare her—take the misery out of her heart."

"If it be Thy will," responded Lucy.

"Don't say that, Lucy," said Jacob. "I must have it so;—what has she done, poor lamb?"

CHAPTER III.

Percy Lee a defaulter—a swindler! The news flew like wildfire.

"No great catch, after all," said a rival beauty, tossing her ringlets.

"I expected something of that sort," said a modern Solomon.

"Hope he'll be imprisoned for life," said a charitable tailor, whom Jacob Ford had eclipsed, "this will bring Jacob's pride down a trifle, I'm thinking."

"How lucky you did not succeed in catching him," said a mother, confidentially, to her daughter.

"I?" exclaimed the young lady. "I? Is it possible you can be so stupid, mamma, as to suppose I would waste a thought on Percy Lee! I assure you he offered himself to Mary Ford in a fit of pique at my rejection. Don't imagine you are in all my secrets," said the dutiful young lady, tossing her head. "Well—her disappearance from society is certain— thank goodness—not that she interferes with me; but her pretended simplicity is so disgusting! What the men in our set could see to admire in her, passes me; but chacun à son gout."

"Of course, Lee will get clear," said a rough dray-man to his comrade. "These big fish always flounder out of the net; it is only the minnows who get caught. Satan! it makes me swear to think of it. I will be sure to stand at the court-house door when he is brought for trial, and insult him if I can. I hope the aristocratic hound will swing for it."

"Come, now, Jo," said his friend, taking out his penknife, and sitting down on a stump to whittle. "You are always a railing at the aristocracy, as you call 'em. I never knew a man who talks as you do, who was not an aristocrat at heart, worshiping the very wealth and station he sneered at. Don't be a fool, John. We are far happier, or might be, with our teams, plenty of jobs, and good health, than these aristocrats, as you call them, who half the time are tossing on their pillows, because this ship hasn't arrived in port, or that land speculation has burst up, or stocks depreciated, or some such cursed canker at the root of all their gourds. Now there's poor Jacob Ford; of what use are all his riches, now his daughter's heart is broke? And Percy Lee, too—will his fine education and book learning get him out of the clutches of the law? Have a little charity, Jo. It hurts a man worse to fall from such a height into a prison, than it would you or me, from a dray-cart. Gad—I pity him; his worst enemy couldn't pile up the agony any higher."

"Pity him!" said Jo, mockingly—"a swindling rascal like that—to break a pretty girl's heart!"

"Jo," said his friend, shutting up his penknife, and looking him steadily in the eye, "have you always said no to the tempting devil in your heart? Did you never charge a stranger more than the law allows for a job? Did no poor girl ever curse the hour she saw the light, for your sake?"

"Well, Mr. Parson, what if all that were true?" asked Jo, with an abortive attempt at a laugh. "I can't see what it has to do with what we are talking about; hang it."

"Just this," answered his friend. "He who is without sin, only, is to cast the first stone."

"O, get out," said Jo, cracking his whip over his horse's head, and taking refuge, like many other cornered disputants, in flight.

And Percy Lee! From the hour in which he passed from the heaven of Mary's smile, up to the present moment, in which he paced like a caged lion up and down his narrow bounds, what untold agonies were his! Why had he wrecked happiness, love, honor, all in one fatal moment? Why had he prostituted his God-given talents so madly to sin? Let those answer who have in like manner sinned, and who have expiated that sin, by a life-long brand upon the brow and a life-long misery in the heart. "Let him who thinketh he standeth, take heed lest he fall."

CHAPTER IV.

"I can't remember," said Mary, two months after Percy's arrest, "I can't remember," raising herself, and laying her emaciated hand upon her brow. "Have I been sick, mamma?"

"Yes, Mary," replied her mother, repressing her tears of joy at the sound of her child's voice.

"Where's Percy, mamma?"

But before Lucy could answer, she again relapsed into stupor. Another hour passed—there was reason in her glance. "Mamma? Percy—take me to him"—said Mary, with a burst of tears, as she strove vainly to rise from her couch.

"By-and-by, darling," said her mother, coaxingly, laying her gently back upon the pillow, as she would an infant, "by-and-by, Mary, when you are stronger."

"No—now" she replied, a spasm of pain contracting her features. "Is he —is he—there? How long have I lain here?"

"Two months, Mary."

"Two months," exclaimed poor Mary, in terror, "two months. O, mamma, if you ever loved me, if you want me to live—take me to him. Two months! He will think!—O, dear, mamma, take me to Percy!"

"Yes—yes, you shall go," said Jacob, "only don't cry. I would shed my heart's blood to save you one tear. You shall go, Mary, even to that curs —"

"Well—well, I won't say it," said the old man, kissing her forehead; "but mind, it is only for your sake—here—Lucy, quick, she is fainting."

Another week passed by, poor Mary making superhuman efforts to sit up, to gain strength to accomplish her heart's wish. Jacob would look at her wasted figure, till the curse rose to his lip, and then rush suddenly from her presence.

"I did not think I could do this, even for her," muttered Jacob, on the morning of their visit to the prison. "I don't know what has come over me, Lucy—sometimes I wonder if I am Jacob. I don't care for any thing, so she don't grieve."

The carriage came—in silence the sad trio moved toward the prison.

"Can't do it," whispered Jacob to Lucy, as they stopped before the door; "I thought I could go in with her; but I can't do it, not even for Mary. The old feeling has come back. I can't look on that man's face without crushing him as I would a viper;" and the old man left them in the turnkey's office, returned to the carriage, twitched down the blinds, and threw himself back upon the seat.

Ah! how much the poor heart may bear! Mary sat in the prison office—still—motionless!—but a bright spot burned upon her cheek, and her tone was fearful in its calmness, and Lucy asked her again "if she were strong enough to go through with it." How distinctly the turnkey's clock ticked! What a quantity of false keys and other implements which had been taken from refractory prisoners, were on exhibition in the glass case! How the clerk stared at them as they registered their names in the book! What a mockery for that little bird to sing in his cage, over Mary's head! How crushed and broken-hearted the poor woman looked in the black bonnet, on the bench, waiting to see her prodigal son! How sad his young wife beside her, with the unconscious baby sleeping on her breast! The room grew smaller—the air grew stifled.

"You can go now, ma'am," said the turnkey, rattling his keys and addressing Lucy.

"In a moment, please," said Lucy, with a quivering lip, as Mary fell from her chair:—"Some water quick, please, sir"—and she untied the strings of Mary's hat.

"Now," said Mary, after a pause. And again the bright spot burned upon her cheek—and as with faltering step, she followed the turnkey, the young wife's tears fell on her baby's face, while she murmured, "God help her, and it's my own heart that has the misery, too."

CHAPTER IV.

The huge key grated in the lock. In the further corner of the cell, crouched Percy—his chin in his palms, his eyes bloodshot, and his face livid as death.

As Mary tottered through the door, Percy raised his head, and, with a stifled groan, fell at her feet. Pressing his lips to the hem of her robe, he waved her off with one hand, as if his touch were contamination. Mary's arms were thrown about his neck, and the words, "I love you," fell upon his doomed ear, like the far-off music of heaven. When Percy would have spoken, Mary laid her hand upon his mouth—not even to her, should he humiliate himself by confession. And so, in tears and silence, the allotted hour passed—He only, who made the heart, with its power to enjoy or suffer, knew with what agonizing intensity.

"Well, I've seen a great many pitiful sights in my day," said the old jailor, as the carriage rolled away with Mary; "but never any thing that made my eyes water like the sight of that poor young cretur. Sometimes I think there ain't no justice up above there, when I see the innocent punished that way with the guilty. I hope these things will all be made square in the other world; I can't say they are clear to my mind here. I get good pay here, but I'd rather scull a raft than stay here to have my feelin's hurt all the time this way. If I didn't go in so strong for justice, I should be tempted, when I think of that young woman, to forget to lock that fellow's cell some night. 'Five years' hard labor!' 'Tis tough, for a gentleman born—well, supposing he got out? if he is a limb of the devil, as some folks say, he will break her heart over again some day or other. It would be a shorter agony to let her weep herself dead at once. God help her."

CHAPTER V.

The Bluff Hill penitentiary was called "a model prison." A "modern Howard" was said to have planned it, and passed his oracular judgment, ratified by the authorities of the State in which it was located, upon its cells, prison-yards, work-shops, chapel, eating-rooms, and ingenious instruments of torture.

That the furnaces failed to keep the prisoners from freezing in winter, or that there was no proper ventilation in summer, was, therefore, nobody's meddling business. Better that they should suffer, year in and year out, than that a flaw should be publicly picked in any scheme set afoot by the "modern Howard." The officers elected to preside over Bluff Hill prison, were as stony as its walls, and showed curious visitors round the work-shops, amid its rows of pallid faces, pointing out here a disgraced clergyman, there a ruined lawyer, yonder a wrecked merchant, with as much nonchalance as a brutal keeper would stir up the caged beasts in a menagerie, for the amusement of the crowd; with as little thought that these fallen beings were men and brothers, as if the Omniscient eye noted no dark stain of sin, hidden from human sight, on their souls.

They gave you leave to stop as long as you pleased, and watch the muscles of your victim's face, work with emotion under your gaze. You could take your own time to speculate upon the scowl of defiance, or the set teeth of hate, as you flaunted leisurely past their prison uniform, in your silk and broadcloth; or you could stand under the fair blue sky, in the prison-yard, when the roll beat for dinner, and see them in file, by twos—guarded—march with locked step and folded arms, to their eating-room. The beardless boy branded in your remembering eye for life, wherever you might hereafter meet him, for this his first crime, how hard soever against fearful odds, he might struggle upward to virtue and heaven. You might follow the sad procession to thair meals, where the fat, comfortably-fed chaplain craved a blessing over food, from which the very dog at his door would have turned hungry away; or you could go into the prison hospital, and view the accommodation (?) for the sick— the cots so narrow that a man could not turn in them; or you could investigate "The Douche," which the keeper would tell you, with a bland smile, "conquered even old prison birds;" or you could peep into the cells (philanthropically furnished by this "modern Howard" with a Bible), so dark that at the brightest noonday no prisoner could read a syllable; or you could see the row of coffins standing on an end in the hall, kept on hand "for sudden emergencies;" or any other horrors of the place, for which your morbid curiosity was appetized.

Or, if you had a human heart beating within your breast, if you could remember ever kneeling to ask forgiveness of your God, you could turn away soul-sick from such unfeeling exhibitions, and refuse to insult their misery—fallen as they were—by your curious gaze. You could remember in your own experience, moments of fearful temptation, when the hot blood poured like molten lead through your veins. You could place in the balance, as God does—as man does not—neglected childhood—undisciplined youth. You could remember, that at a kindly word, whispered in those felon cars, the hardest rock might melt; and you could wish that if prisons must be, they who pass under their iron portals might pass unrecognizable in after life by the world's stony eyes—you could wish that when freedom's air again fanned their pallid temples, no cursed scornful finger might lash to fury the hydra-headed monster Sin, in their scarred hearts.

Heaven speed the day when the legislative heart, pitiful as God's, shall temper this sword of justice with more mercy.

"Which is he?" asked an over-dressed, chubby, vulgar-looking fellow, to the keeper of Bluff Hill prison.

"That tall fellow yonder," replied the keeper, "with the straight nose, and high forehead—that's he—see? reefing off flax yonder."

"Don't say," said the man, with his bloated eyes gloating over Percy. "How old is he?"

"Nineteen only," said the keeper.

"Humph!" said the man, loud enough for Percy to hear—"Pre—co—cious; wasn't intended for that sort of work, I fancy, by the look of his hands; they are as small and white as a woman's. Ask him some question, can't ye? I wish I was keeper here; I'd like to break his spirit," said Mr. Scraggs, as Percy answered the keeper's question without raising his eyes. "Bah! how these fuzzy bits of lint and flax fly about the room; my throat and nose are full. I should think this would kill a fellow off before long."

"It does," said the keeper, coolly.

"And what's that horrible smell? Faugh—it makes me sick."

"That? Oh, that's the oil used in the machinery."

"Why the fury don't you ventilate, then?" asked Mr. Scraggs, thinking more of his own lungs than the prisoners', adding, with a laugh, as he recollected himself, "I don't suppose the Governor of your State is particular on that p'int;" then, with another stare at Percy, he said, "they say he seduced old Ford's daughter before he stole the money."

The words had hardly left his lips, when, with a bound like a panther, Percy instantly felled him to the earth, the blood spouting from his own mouth and nostrils with the violence of his passion.

Scraggs lay for some hours insensible, though not dangerously wounded, and Percy was led off in irons, to reflect on this new misery in solitary confinement.

CHAPTER VI.

"I stepped in to inquire after poor Mary, this morning," said a neighbor of Lucy Ford. "Poor dear! she's to be pitied!"

They who have suffered from the world's malice, know that the most simple words may be made to convey an insult, by the tone in which they are uttered. Lucy Ford was naturally unsuspicious, but there was something in Miss Snip's tone which grated harshly on her ear.

"I regret to say Mary is no better," Lucy replied, with her usual gentle manner. "If I could persuade her to take more nourishment, I should be glad; but she sits rocking to and fro, seemingly unconscious of every thing."

"I should like to see the poor dear," said Miss Snip.

Lucy hesitated; then blushing, as if she felt ashamed of her doubts, she led the way to Mary's room. Every thing about it bore marks of the taste of the occupant. There lay her silent guitar; there a half finished drawing; here a book with the pearl folder still between the leaves, where she and Percy had left it. The beautiful tea-rose he had given her, drooped its buds in the window, for want of care, and the canary's cage was muffled, lest its song should quicken painful memories. And there sat Mary, as her mother had said, rocking herself to and fro, with her hands crossed listlessly on her lap, her blue-veined temples growing each day more startlingly transparent.

"Quite heart-rending, I declare," said Miss Snip, "and as if the poor dear hadn't enough to bear, just think of the malice of people. I said it was a shame and that of course nobody would believe it of Miss Mary, and I never spoke of it, except to lawyer Beadle's wife, and one or two of our set; but a rumor is a rumor, and when it is once set rolling, it has got to go to the bottom of the hill; but nobody, I'm sure, that ever knew Miss Mary, would believe she would be seduced by Percy Lee!"

"Lord-a-mercy! you don't suppose she heard me?" exclaimed Miss Snip, as Mary fell forward upon the floor.

"Cursed viper!" shouted Jacob Ford, emerging from the ante-room, and unceremoniously ejecting Miss Snip through the door. "Cursed viper!"

"That's what I call pretty treatment, now," muttered Miss Snip, as she stopped in the hall, to settle her false curls; "very pretty treatment—for a disinterested act of neighborly kindness. Philanthropy never is rewarded with any thing but cuffs in this world, but I shan't allow it to discourage me. I know that I have my mission here below, whether I have the praise of men or not. All great reformers are abused—that's one consolation. I'll step over to Mrs. Bunce's now, and see if it is true that her husband takes a drop too much. They do say so, but I don't believe a word of it."

"Lucy," said Jacob—and the poor old man's limbs shook beneath him —"this must be the last arrow in the quiver. Nothing can come after this. Let her be, Lucy,"—and he withdrew his wife's hands, as she bathed Mary's temples—"let her be: 'tain't no use to rouse her up to her misery —to kill her by inches this way. I am ready to lie down side of her. Lucy —I couldn't muster heart to tell you, till a worse blow came, that we are beggars. 'Tain't no matter now."

"God be merciful!" said Lucy, overwhelmed with this swift accumulation of trouble.

"Yes, you may well say that. Just enough left to keep us from starving. My heart has been with her, you see," said Jacob, looking at Mary, "and my head hasn't been clear about things, as it used to be, and so it has come to this. I wouldn't mind it, if she only—" and Jacob dropped his head hopelessly upon his breast. Then raising it again, and wiping his eyes, as he looked at Mary, he said: "She never will look more like an angel than she does now. I thought she'd live to close these old eyes, and that my grand-children would play about my knee, but you see how it has gone, Lucy."

The red flag of the auctioneer, so often the signal of distress, floated before Jacob Ford's door. Strange feet roved over the old house; strange eyes profaned the household gods. Careless fingers tested the quality of Mary's harp and guitar; and voices which in sunnier days had echoed through those halls in blandest tones, now fell upon the ear, poisonous with cold malice. When once the pursuit is started, and the game scented, every hound joins in the cry; each fierce paw must have its clutch at the quivering heart, each greedy tongue lap up the ebbing life-blood. Never was beauty's crown worn more winningly, more unobtrusively, less triumphantly, than by Mary Ford; but to those whom nature had less favored, it was the sin never to be forgiven; and so fair lips hoped the stories were not true about her, while they reiterated them at every street corner; and bosom friends, when inquired of as to their truth, rolled up their eyes, sighed like a pair of bellows, and with a deprecating wave of the hand, replied, in melancholy tones, "don't ask me," thus throwing the responsibility upon the listener to construe it into little or much; pantomimic looks and gestures not yet having been pronounced indictable by the statute book; others simply nodded their heads, in a mysterious manner, as if they had it at their charitable option to send the whole family to perdition, with a monosyllable.

CHAPTER VII.

Jacob Ford's new home was a little cottage, just on the outskirts of the city; for Lucy said, "maybe the flowers, and the little birds, and the green grass might tempt Mary out of doors, where the wind might fan her pale cheek." It was beautiful to see Lucy stifling her own sorrow, while she moved about, performing uncomplainingly the household drudgery. Mary would sit at the window, twisting her curls idly over her fingers, or leaning out, as if watching for Percy. Sometimes she would sit on the low door-step, when the stars came out, with her head in Jacob's lap, while his wrinkled fingers strayed soothingly over her temples. She seldom or never spoke; did mechanically what she was bid, except that she drew shuddering back, when they would have led her across the threshold. Once she wept when Jacob brought her a violet, which he found under the cottage window. Jacob said, "dear heart! why should a little blossom make the poor thing cry?" Lucy's womanly heart better solved the riddle: it was Percy's favorite flower.

Their rustic neighbors leaned over each other's fences, and wondered "who on airth them Fords was," and why "the old man didn't take no interest in fixin' his lot. The trees wanted grafting, the grass wanted mowing, the gooseberries were all over mildew, the strawberries, choked with weeds; and it did really 'pear to them as though the old fellow must be 'ither a consarned fool, or an idiot, to let things run out that way. And the poor sick girl, she looked like a water-lily—so white, so bowed down; why didn't they put her into a shay, and drive her out, to bring a little color into her waxen cheeks?"

The thrifty housewives said, "it was clear to them that the old lady hadn't her wits, narry more than the old man, for she left her clothes'-line out all night, when every body knew that dew and rain would rot it; but what could you expect from shiftless city folks?"

For all this the country people were kind-hearted. New neighbors did not grow on every bush. Topics were scarce in Milltown, and every new one was hunted down like a stray plum in a boarding-school pudding. Yes, you might have gone further, and found worse people than the Milltown-ites. The little sun-burnt children learned to loiter on their way to school, "to pick a nosegay for the pretty pale lady." Widow Ellis, under the hill, picked her biggest strawberries, and put them in a tempting little basket, covered with green leaves, for her curly-pated Tommy to carry to "poor Miss Mary." Miss Trodchom baked an extra loaf of 'lection-cake, "in hopes the Fords' daughter might nibble a bit, poor thing." And farmer Jolly dropped his whip on purpose, over Jacob's fence, to get a chance to tell the old man "that he had a mare as was as easy as a cradle, and a prettyish side-saddle that the sick girl might have, and welcome, if she took a notion." And Mr. Parish, the minister, came, but he could not make much of Jacob, who told him "that if it was religion to be willing to see one's own flesh and blood suffer, he did not want it."

Poor old Jacob! Every earthly reed had broken beneath him, his unsteady steps were tottering toward the grave, and yet he threw aside the only sure Staff. He did not know, poor old man, so gradually had his heart hardened by contact with the world, "that it is easier for a camel to go through a needle's eye than for a rich man to enter the kingdom of God." Through no rift in the dark cloud which shadowed him, could he see bright Mercy's sunbeam. One by one the lights had gone out in his sky, and still he groped about, blind to the rays of Bethlehem's star. Poor old Jacob!

It was Sabbath morning. Jacob stood at his cottage door, gazing out. Each tiny blade of grass bent quivering under its glistening dew-drop. The little ground-birds on the gravel walk were picking up their early breakfast; the robins were singing overhead. The little swallows flew twittering round the cottage eaves. The leaves were rustling with their mysterious music. The silver mist wreathed playfully over the hill-sides, whose summits lay bathed in sunshine. Every thing seemed full of joyous life. Where was the Master hand which regulated all that harmony? The birds sang—the leaves danced—the brooks sparkled—the bee hummed—why did He make man only to suffer? It was all a riddle to poor Jacob. He took his staff, and sauntered away under the drooping lindens. The Sabbath bell was calling the simple villagers to church. Across the meadows, down the grassy lane—the rosy maiden, the bent old man, and the lisping little child. Jacob looked after them as they went. Jacob never had been to church—not since he was a little child. Sunday he always posted his books, squared up his accounts, wrote business letters and the like of that; shortening the day at both ends by getting up later and going to bed earlier. Sunday to him was no different from any other day in the week—except that he transferred his business from his counting-room to his parlor; and yet—here he was, leaning on his staff, before the village church, almost wishing to go in with its humble people. He looked about as if he expected somebody to be astonished that Jacob Ford should be standing so near a church door; but nobody seemed to notice it, or look at all surprised. By-and-by he crept on a little further, and seated himself on a stone bench in the porch, with his chin upon his staff. The butterfly and the bee passed in and out; even the little birds flew in at the church door, and out at the open window; and still old Jacob sat there—he could scarcely have told why. Now he hears the choir sing,

"Jesus, I my cross have taken,All to leave, and follow Thee;Naked—poor—despised—forsaken—Thou from hence my all shalt be.

"Though the world despise and leave me,They have left my Saviour too;Human hearts and hopes deceive me,Thou art not like them, untrue."

As the song died away, old Jacob's tears flowed down his cheeks; the words soothed his troubled spirit like a mother's lullaby.

"Come unto me all ye that labor and are heavy laden, and I will give you rest."

Who promised that?

How did the minister know how "heavy laden" was Jacob's spirit?

How did he know that for sixty years he had been drawing water from broken cisterns? Chasing shadows even to the grave's brink?

How did he know that on that balmy Sabbath morning, his heart was aching for something to lean on that would not pass away?

"Come unto me."

Old Jacob took his staff, and tottered out into the little church-yard He did not know he was praying, when his soul cried out, "Lord help me;" but still his lips kept murmuring it, as he passed down the grassy road, and under the drooping lindens, for each time he said it, his heart seemed to grow lighter; each time it seemed easier for old Jacob to "come." And so he entered his low doorway, and as he stooped to kiss his daughter's cheek, the bitterness seemed to have gone from out his heart, and he felt that he could forgive even Percy, for His sake of whom he had just so recently craved forgiveness.

"What is it?" asked Lucy, awed by the strange expression of Jacob's face, and laying her hand tenderly upon his arm; "what is it, Jacob?"

"Peace!" whispered the old man, reverently; "God's peace—here Lucy;" and he laid his hand on his heart.

Lucy took old Jacob's staff and set it in the corner. Good, kind Lucy! She did not think when she did so, that he would need it no more. She did not know when the sun went down that night, that death's dark shadow fell across her cottage threshold. She did not know, poor Lucy, when she slumbered away the night hours so peacefully by his side, that, leaning on a surer Staff, old Jacob had passed triumphantly through the dark valley; and when at length the little twittering sparrows woke her with their morning song, and she looked into the old man's cold, still face, the pale lips, though they moved not, seemed to whisper, "Peace, Lucy—God's peace."

CHAPTER VIII.

"Is it possible you care for that girl yet, Tom? A rejected lover, too? Where's your spirit, man? Pshaw—there's many a fairer face than Mary Ford's; besides, she is more than half crazy. Are you mad, Tom? You wouldn't catch me sighing for a girl who had cried her eyes out for the villainy of my rival."

"Curse him!" said Tom Shaw, striking his boots with a light cane he held in his hand; "he is safe enough, at any rate, for some time to come; good for a couple more years, I hope, for striking that fellow in prison. When he comes out, if he ever does, he will find his little bird in my nest. Half-witted or whole-witted, it matters little to me. I am rich enough to please my fancy, and the girl's face haunts me."

"Pooh!" said Jack; "you are just like a spoiled child—one toy after another, the last one always the best. I know you—you'll throw this aside in a twelvemonth; but marriage, let me tell you, my fine fellow, is a serious joke."

"Not to me," said Tom, "for the very good reason that I consider it dissolved when the parties weary—or at any rate, I shall act on that supposition, which amounts to the same thing, you know."

"Not in law," said Jack.

"Nonsense," replied Tom; "I am no fool; trust me for steering my bark clear of breakers. At any rate, I'll marry that girl, if perdition comes after it—were it only to spite Percy. How he will gnash his teeth when he hears of it, hey? The old man is dead, and the old woman is left almost penniless. I'll easily coax her into it. In fact, I mean to drive out there this very afternoon. Mary Ford shall be Mrs. Tom Shaw, d'ye hear?"

"Good day, Pike! Haven't got a pitchfork you can lend a neighbor, have ye? Ours is broke clean in two; I'm dreadful hard put to it for horseflesh, or I would drive to the village and buy a new one. You see that pesky boy of mine has lamed our mare; it does seem to me, Pike, that boys allers will be boys—the more I scold at him, the more it don't do no good."

"And the more it won't," said the good-natured farmer Rice. "Scolding never does any good no how—the boy is good enough by natur'—good as you was, I dare say, when you was his age. I wouldn't give a cent for a boy that hain't no friskiness about him, no sperrit like; but you see you don't know how to manage him. You are allers scolding, just as you say. It's 'John, go weed those parsnips; ten to one, you careless dog, you'll pull up the parsnips instead of the weeds;'—or, 'John, go carry that corn to mill; ten to one, you'll lose it out of the wagon going.' I tell you, Pike, it is enough to discourage any lad, such a constant growling and pecking; now I want my boys to love me when they grow up. I don't want them glad to see the old man's back turned. I don't want them happier any where than at their own home. That's the way drunkards and profligates are made—that's the way the village tavern thrives. I tell you, Pike, if you lace up natur too tight, she'll bust out somewhere. Better draw it mild."

"O, don't talk to me, neighbor," said Rice, impatiently. "Them's modern notions; thrash children, I say. When I was a lad, if I did my duty, it was well; if I didn't, I knew what to expect. It is well enough for your children to love you; of course they oughter, when you've brought them into the world; but I say they've got to mind, any how; 'obey your parents;' that's it; plain as preaching."

"Yes," said farmer Rice, "I believe in that; but there's another verse in the same book, that runs this way—'Parents provoke not your children to anger, lest they be discouraged.'"

"Well—well," said Mr. Pike, uneasily, "I hate argufying, as I do bad cider. Your neighbor, Mr. Ford, dropped off sudden like, didn't he? What's the matter of him?"

"Some say one thing—some another; but I think, neighbor, it was just here. That ere old man has been in harness these sixty years—it was a sort of second natur to him to be active. Well, he was taken right out of the whirl and hubbub of the city, where people can't hardly stop long enough to bury one another, and sot right down in this quiet place, where there's nothing a-going but frogs and crickets, with nothing to do but to brood over his troubles. Well, you see such a somerset at his time o' life wan't the thing; of course it upsot him. He'd lean over this fence, and lean over that, and put on his hat, and take it off, and walk a bit, and sit down a bit, and act just like an old rat in a trap, trying to gnaw his way out. It was just as if you should pull up that old oak-tree, that has grown in that spot till its roots strike out half a mile round, and set it out in some foreign sile; it wouldn't thrive—of course not."

"No," said Mr. Pike, "I see, I see—it would be just so with me, if I was set down where he came from—that etarnal rumbling and whiz buzz would drive me clean distracted. The last time I staid in the city over night, I thought every minute the last day had come, there was such a tearin' round. But what's become of the old woman and her sick darter?"

"She took it hard—she did—but the girl is sort of image-like—don't feel nothing, I reckon. Pretty, too—it's a nation pity. They've got enough left to keep them alive, milk and fresh air, like the rest on us. I don't want no better fare. There's some talk, so my old woman says, about a fellow who drives out here, who is going to marry the girl;—nothing but woman's gabble, I guess; you know if they didn't talk they wouldn't say nothing."

"Fact," said Mr. Pike, profoundly, "I often think on't; but come, I can't stay prating here all day—where's the pitchfork you was going to lend me?"

"There it is," said Mr. Rice; "and now remember what I told you about that boy of yourn; there's more good in that Zekiel, than you think for;—remember now, a little oil makes machinery work easy, Pike."

"Yes, oil of birch," said farmer Pike, chuckling at his own wit, and cracking his horse-whip at a happy little vagrant robin, as he went through the gate and down the road.

CHAPTER IX.

Summer had danced by—the chill wind whistled through the trees—the nuts were dropping in showers, and the leaves rusted beneath the traveler's foot; the golden-rod and barberry clusters alone remained to deck the hedges, and the striped snake crawled out on the rock to sun himself only at midday. Widow Ford's cottage looked lonely and desolate, stripped of its leafy screen; but the squirrels might be seen leaping from tree to tree as merrily as if old Jacob still sat watching them in the door-way. Lucy moved about, sweeping, dusting, replenishing the fire—but the silver hair glistened on her temples, and her step was slow and weary. Now and then she would lean against the mantel, and look at Mary—and then wander restlessly into the little bedroom—then, back again to the mantel.

"You still think it best to consummate this marriage?" said the clergyman to Lucy, in a low voice.

"Only that I would not leave her alone," said Lucy, tremulously. "I shall soon be in the church-yard by the side of Jacob. Mr. Shaw knows all—he loves her, and wishes to make her his wife. I believe he will be kind to her. As for Mary, poor thing, you see how it is," and she glanced at her daughter, who sat with locked fingers—her long lashes sweeping her colorless cheek. One might have taken her for some beautiful statue, with those faultless marble features, and that motionless attitude.

Mr. Parish sighed, as he looked at Mary; but he had little time to discuss matters, if that were his intention, for the sound of approaching carriage-wheels announced Mr. Shaw.

"At twelve, then, to-morrow," said he, as he took up his hat, "if you are of the same mind, I will perform the ceremony as you desire."

Mr. Parish walked home in a very thoughtful mood. Through his acquaintances in the city, he had learned the history of the family. He knew the length and breadth of the shadow which had fallen across their hearth-stone. He saw that it was true, as Lucy had said, that her own strength was fast failing; still it seemed to him sacrilege to bestow Mary's hand in marriage, when her heart was so benumbed and dead. He would have offered her a shelter in his own house, had he been master of it; but, unfortunately, he had married a lady who lost no opportunity to remind him that her dowry of twenty thousand dollars was payment in full for the total abnegation of his free will. This was not the first occasion on which the clanking of this gentleman's golden fetters had sounded unmusically in his reverend ears; in truth, he would much have preferred his liberty, even at the expense of eking out a small salary by farming, as did the neighboring country clergy. Mrs. Parish lost no opportunity to remind her husband that he was sold, by such pleasant remarks as the following: That it was time her house was re-painted, or her barn re-roofed, or her carry-all re-cushioned. When she felt unusually hymeneal, she would say, "Mr. Parish, you can use my horses to-day, if you will drive carefully." That she invariably and sweetly deferred to her husband's opinion in company, was no proof of the absence of a private conjugal understanding, that he was to consider himself merely her echo.

Little did his brother clergymen who exchanged with him in their thread-bare suits of black, dream of the price at which his pleasant parsonage surroundings were purchased. Little did they dream, when they innocently brought along their wives and babies on such occasions, the suffering it entailed on "brother Parish."

No, poor simple souls, they went home charmed with the hospitality of their host and hostess, charmed with their conjugal happiness, and marveling as they returned to their own houses, what made their rooms seem so much smaller, and their fare so much more frugal than before. Had they been clairvoyantly endowed, they might have seen brother Parish, after he had smilingly bowed them down the nicely rolled gravel walk to their wagons, return meekly to the parlor, to be reminded for the hundredth time, by Mrs. Parish, of that twenty thousand dollar obligation. Well might personal feelings come in, to strengthen his ministerial scruples, lest he should join carelessly in wedlock, hands which death only could unclasp.

"He oughter be ashamed of hisself marrying that poor crazed thing, even if the old lady is willing," said farmer Jones' wife, as Tom Shaw's smiling face peered out of the carriage window, on his wedding day. "It hardens the heart awful to live in the city; riches can't make that poor cretur happy; a pebble stun and a twenty dollar piece, are all one to her. Now my daughter Louizy is no beauty; she is clumsy and freckled, and brown as a butternut; but she is too fair in my eyes, to be sold that way. I wish I knew what crazed that Mary Ford. Ah—here comes parson Parish; maybe I'll get it out of him."

"Good day, sir—met the bridal carriage, I suppose, on the road—queer wedding that, of Miss Mary's. Is it true, that Squire Ford's house took fire, and Miss Mary lost her wits by the fright?"

"I never heard of it," replied the parson—taking the Maltese cat in his lap, and manipulating her slate-colored back.

Mrs. Jones might have added, "Nor I either," but nothing daunted, she tried another question.

"Scarlet fever p'rhaps, parson? that allers leaves suthing behind it, most commonly. My George would have been left blind, likely, if he hadn't been left deaf. They say it was scarlet fever that done it."

"Do they?" asked the parson.

"Confound it," thought Mrs. Jones; "I'm sure the man knows, for he was very thick there at the cottage. I'll see if my gooseberry wine won't loosen his tongue a little;" and she handed the minister a glass.

"Sometimes I've wondered, parson, what made old Ford walk round so like an unquiet sperrit. He didn't do nothing he hadn't oughter, did he? It wasn't that that crazed Miss Mary, I s'pose? That old man got up and sat down fifty times a minute."

"So I have heard," answered the impenetrable parson, sipping his wine.

"She wasn't crossed in love nor nothing, was she?" asked the persevering querist; "that sometime plays witchwork with a woman."

"Oh, that reminds me," said the parson. "I hear Zekiel Jones is engaged to your Louisa."

"My Louizy!" screamed Mrs. Jones, walking straight into the trap; "My Louizy engaged to Zekiel Jones! a fellow who don't know a hoe-handle from a hay-cutter. I guess there'll be a tornady in this house afore that marriage comes off. I do wish people would mind their own business, and not meddle with what don't consarn 'em. Now who told you that, parson?"

"Well, I really don't remember," replied the minister; "but you know it matters little, so there's no truth in it," and dexterously escaping through the dust he had raised, he bowed himself down the garden walk; while Mrs. Jones stood with her arms a-kimbo, in the doorway, ejaculating: "Zekiel Jones and my Louizy—a fellow who goes to sleep in the middle of the day in haying time, and a gal who can churn forty pounds of butter a day! Gunpowder and milk! I guess so."

CHAPTER X.

"How shall we manage to kill time to-day, Jack?" asked Tom Shaw; "race-course—billiards—club—pistol gallery?"

"Kill time! You—a bridegroom of six months! Well, you can't say you weren't warned. You remember I told you you would soon weary of your new toy. A six-months' bridegroom!" and Tom laughed merrily.

"Long enough to make love to a statue, were it ever so faultless," replied Tom, with a yawn. "I'm bored to death, Jack, and I don't care who knows it. My mother-in-law, who, to do her justice, is clever enough, strolls over the house like a walking tomb-stone. My wife is as lifeless as if half the women in town were not dying for me. It's cursed monotonous; hang me if I'm not sick of it."

"Does your wife never speak to you?" asked Jack.

"Never," said Tom; "there she sits in her chair, playing with her fingers, or else at the window, looking this way, and that, as if she were expecting somebody; when she does so, it seems to worry the old lady, who looks nervously at me, and tries to coax her away—the Lord only knows why; and two or three times I have seen her coax away a faded flower that Mary has a fancy for holding between her fingers. It's all Greek to me. Confound it, I feel as if I were in a nest of lunatics. It makes me as nervous as the devil. Come, let's be off. What has become of Susy, the little ballet-girl? Did she take my marriage to heart?"

"Not she, the delicious little monkey; she tossed her pretty head, and said with an arch smile: 'Mark what I say: he'll be back to me in six months.'"

"Pretty prophet!" replied Tom.

The two young men locked arms and sauntered down the crowded street, whiffing their cigars; now attracted by some brilliant shop-window, now bandying jests with those miserable women, who, but for just such as they, might have lifted their womanly brows to the starry sky—pure as when first kissed by a mother's loving lips. Pale seamstresses glided by, unguarded, save by Him who noticeth the sparrow's fall. Young men of their own age, weary of the slowly accumulating gains of honest toil, looked enviously upon their delicately kidded hands, fine apparel, and care-for-naught air. Passing, at length, the long line of carriages in front of the opera house, they disappeared under the lighted vestibule, and took possession of one of the boxes.

Fair young girls were there, unveiling to the libidinous eye, at Fashion's bidding, charms of which they should have been chary to the moon. Faded belles throwing out bait at which nobody even nibbled. Married men groaned, looked at their watches, and leaning back in their seats, computed the rise and fall of stocks; married women gazed anxiously around to see if their laces, diamonds, or cashmeres were eclipsed by their neighbors'. Every body was bored to death, stifled by the heat, blinded, by the gas, and scientifically inappreciative of the music, but every body willing to endure ten times as much, rather than not be "in the fashion." The moon, to be sure, silvered the pretty fountain in the park, close by, and the cool, sweet evening breeze played through the blossoming trees; but the "working people" were stretched upon its benches; the poor man's child laid his soft cheek to the cool grass; the ragged little urchin, escaping from the stifled air of the noisome lane, threw up his brimless hat in the gravel walk. The parks were plebeian, opera boxes were beyond the reach of "the vulgar."

But look! Now the audience show signs of animation. All is astir. See, the ballet! A fleecy cloud sails in, enveloping "Susy." Susy, the favorite pro tem.—Susy, with her jetty locks, creamy skin, and dimpled shoulders. Susy, with her pretty ankles and rounded waist. Susy, with her jeweled arms and rose-banded hair. Susy, with her rounded bosom and twinkling feet. Young men and old men level their glasses in breathless admiration, as Susy languishingly twirls, and tip-toes, and pirouettes. Young girls, who have long since ceased blushing at such exhibitions, wish, for the nonce, that they were Susy, as bouquets and diamond rings are thrown upon the stage. Tom Shaw's eyes sparkle, and relieving his enthusiasm by some expressive expletives, he leaves Jack for a behind-the-scene tête-à-tête with the danseuse.

CHAPTER XI.

"Day dawned—within a curtained room,Filled to faintness with perfume,A lady lay at point of doom.Morn broke—an infant saw the light,But for the lady, fair and bright,She slumbered in undreaming night."

Life and death had passed each other on the threshold! Lucy Ford's tears were the baptism of Mary's motherless babe. The poor weary heart, whose pulse had beat so unevenly above it, had ceased its flutterings. It was nothing new to see Mary lie with marble face, folded hands, and softly-fringed, closed eyes. But, sometimes, the thin hand had been kindly outstretched toward Lucy; sometimes, the glossy head had raised itself, and leaned tenderly on the maternal bosom; sometimes, the blue eye had lingered lovingly on her wrinkled face. Small comfort, God knows—and yet it was much to poor Lucy. She looked at the little gasping, helpless thing before her—a tenant already for her rifled heart— a new claimant for her love and care. Oh, how could she else but welcome it? With soft folds she wrapped its fragile limbs, with motherly care she soothed it on her sunken breast, and with a prayer to God, as she pressed her lips to Mary's brow, she promised Death to be faithful to the trust of Life.

Days and nights—weeks, months and years came and went, blanching the prisoner's lip and cheek, but failing to subdue a love which yet had not saved him from incurring a doom so terrible. Had Mary forgotten him? for, since that dreadful, happy day, when he clasped her in his cell, he had heard nothing save the damning sneer of the villain Scraggs. Perhaps she was dead—and his bloodless lip quivered at the thought. Nay—worse—perhaps they might have married her, in her despair, to another. Percy tossed on his narrow cot in agony.

He even welcomed the day-light, which recalled him to his task. Oh, those long, long nights, when locked in his cell, remorse kept him silent company! or worse, the dreary, idle Sunday, when taken out once to chapel, then remanded back to his dark cell, he lay thinking of the pleasant Sabbaths he had passed with Mary, in the little parlor, on the sofa by her side. He could see her now, in the pretty blue dress she wore to please him; the ring he had given her, sparkling on her white hand— her glossy hair, worn the very way he liked to see it, the book opened at the passage he liked best, the little flower pressed between its leaves, because he gave it. Then the little arbor in the garden—where they used to sit the pleasant Sabbath evenings—the song Mary sang him there—with her head upon his breast. Oh, happiness—oh, misery!

Percy knew it was summer, for as he passed through the prison-yard he saw that the green blades of grass were struggling up between the flag-stones, and now and then, he heard the chirp of a passing bird. The sky, too, was softly blue, and the breeze had been where clover and daisies had bloomed, and rifled their sweetness.

Percy looked down on his shrunken limbs, clad in his felon garb—then on his toil-worn hands. He passed them slowly over his shaven crown. Merciful Heaven! he—Percy Lee—Mary's lover! Fool—thrice-accursed fool; life—liberty—happiness—love—all laid at the feet of the tempting fiend—for this! No tears relieved the fierce fire, which seemed consuming his heart and brain. How long could he bear this? Was his cell to be his grave? Once, seized with a sudden illness, he had been taken to the prison hospital, where the doctor tried pleasant little experiments on the subjects who came under his notice. Around him were poor wretches, groaning under every phase of bodily and mental discomfort. Now roused out of some Heaven-sent slumber, when it suited the doctor to show them to visitors; or to descant upon the commencement and probable duration of their disease, coupled with accounts of patients who had died in those beds, and whom he could have cured under different circumstances.

It was here that Percy shed the only tears which had moistened his eyes since his incarceration. A party of visitors were passing through the wards, listening to the doctor's egotistical details, and peeping into the different cots. A sweet little girl had strayed away from the rest of her party, and was making her tour of childish observation alone. Her eye fell upon Percy. She stood for a moment, gazing at him with the intensest pity written on her sweet face. Then gliding up to his side, she drooped her bright curls over his pillow, and placing a flower between his fingers, she whispered, "I'll pray to God to make you well and let you go home."

"Mary! come here," said a shrill female voice, recalling the child; "don't you know that is a horrid bad man! he might kill you."

"No, he is not," said the little creature, confidently, with a piteous glance of her soft, blue eyes at Percy; "no, he is not."

"What makes you think so?" asked one of the party.

"I don't know," replied the child; "something tells me so—here;" and she laid her hand on her breast.

"Won't you please let him go home?" asked she of the doctor.

"Home."

As the sweet pleader passed out, the room seemed to grow suddenly dark, and Percy turned his face to his pillow, and wept aloud.

Heavenly childhood! that the world should ever chill thy Christ-like heart. That scorn should uproot pity. That suspicion should stifle love. That selfishness should dry up thy tears, and avarice lock thine open palm, with its vice-like grasp! Oh, weep not ye who straighten childhood for the grave; over whose household idols the green grass waves; heaven's bright rain showers and spring flowers bloom. Let the bird soar, while his song is sweetest, before one stain soil his plumage, or with maimed wing he flutter helplessly. Let him soar. The cloud which hides him from thy straining eye, doth it not hide him from the archer?

CHAPTER XII.

"The top o' the mornin' to yez, Bridget," said Pat, poking his head into the kitchen. "Is the ould lady up yet? Sorry a plight masther was in the night—dhrunk as a baste—and he cares no more for his own flesh and blood than I do for a Protestant—bad 'cess to 'em."

"Thrue for you, Patrick, and may I niver confess again to the praste, if his light o' love is not misthress here before long; he is as bould-faced about it as if poor Misthress Mary wasn't fresh under the sod. God rest her sowl."

Bridget's prediction was not long being verified. Upholsterers were soon in attendance, re-modeling and re-furnishing poor Mary's apartments, of which the pretty danseuse shortly took unblushing and triumphant possession. It was understood in the house, that her will was to be law; and implicit obedience to the same the surest passport to head-quarters. Poor Lucy, willing to bear any thing rather than separation from the child —chased from one room to another—finally took refuge with her charge in the attic, whither poor Mary's portrait had long since been banished. For the little Fanny's sake, she patiently endured every humiliation; she heeded not the careless insolence of the new régime of servants. She bore every caprice of the tyrannical little danseuse. Patiently her feeble limbs tottered up stairs and down, performing the offices of nurse and servant to her grandchild; patiently she soothed it when ill, or amused it when fretful; uncomplainingly she bore from her son-in-law his maudling curses, when they passed each other on the stairs, or in the hall. Every thing—any thing, but separation from Mary's child, which nestled every day closer to her heart; and whose soft eyes and glossy curls reminded her every day more forcibly of her lost daughter. Every day she prayed to God to spare the withered trunk till the vine which clambered round it should gather strength to brave the winds and storms. Fanny slept securely on her breast, while the bacchanalian song resounded through the house, and obscene jests, and curses loud and deep, made night hideous. And when the moonbeams penetrated the little window, and, falling upon Mary's portrait, revealed her in all her beauty, before the shadow had fallen on her fair brow, or dimmed her lustrous eyes, or robbed that dimpled mouth of its sunny smile, poor Lucy would nestle closer to little Fanny, and pray God that so bitter a cup might pass from her.

Dear little Fanny! with her plump little arms thrown carelessly over her curly head, her pearly teeth just gleaming through her parted lips, as if some kind angel even then were promising her exemption from such a doom.

Time crept on, blanching Lucy's cheek to deadly paleness, tinting Fanny's with a lovelier rose; thinning Lucy's silver hair, piling the golden clusters round Fanny's ivory brow; bending Lucy's shrunken limbs, rounding Fanny's into symmetry and grace.

True, the child never left the attic; but what place, how circumscribed soever, will not Love beautify and brighten? True, "mamma's" pictured semblance responded not to the little upturned face and lisping lips, but who shall say that age and infancy were the only tenants of that lonely room?

Fanny knew that she had a "papa" somewhere in the house, but "papa" was always "sick," or "busy," so grandmamma said; that must be the reason why he never came up to see his little girl. Sometimes Fanny amused herself by climbing up to the little window, overlooking the square where a silvery fountain tossed its sparkling diamonds to the sun, who turned them all sorts of pretty colors, and sent them quivering back again. Little Fanny liked that! Then she saw little children playing round the fountain, sailing their tiny boats on its bosom, and clapping their hands gleefully when they rode safely into port. Great shaggy Newfoundland dogs, too, jumped into the water, and swam, with their black noses just above the surface, and ever and anon sprang out upon the mossy bank, shaking their shaggy coats upon the more dainty ones of mamma's little pets, quite regardless of lace, silk, or ribbon. It was a pretty sight, and little Fanny wanted to go to the fountain too; but grandmamma was so feeble, and she had so much running to do up and down stairs, that she had no strength left to walk; and then grandmamma had to make all Fanny's little dresses, and keep them tidy and nice; and by the time the sun moved off of mamma's picture in the afternoon, she was quite ready to go to bed with little Fanny.

Poor old grandmamma! Fanny handed her her spectacles, and a cricket to put her poor tired feet upon, and picked up the spools of cotton when they rolled upon the floor, and learned too to thread her needles quite nicely, for grandmamma's eyes were getting dim; and sometimes Fanny would try to make the bed, but her hand was so tiny that she could not even cover one of the small roses of its patch-work quilt. Dear little thing! He who blessed little children, recorded of her, "She hath done what she could."

One day Fanny heard a great noise—a great bumping and tumbling, as if some heavy body were falling down the stairs. Then she heard a deep groan—and then such a shriek! If she lived to be as old as grandma, that shriek would never go out of her ears; then there was a great running to and fro, Patrick and Bridget wrung their hands, and said ochone! ochone! and then grandmamma's face grew very white, as she took Fanny by the hand and hurried down stairs; and when they got into the lower entry, there lay a gentleman very still on the floor. A beautiful lady was kneeling on the floor beside him, chafing his temples—but it was of no use; feeling of his pulse—but it was quite still. Then the beautiful lady shrieked again—oh, so dreadfully! and then she fell beside him like one dead.

Fanny's grandma whispered to her, that the gentleman "was her papa," and that he had fallen down stairs and broken his neck—grandma did not say that he was drunk when he did it. Fanny crept up to him, for she had wanted so much to see her papa—so she put her little rosy face close to his, and said, "Wake up, please, papa, and see me." But he did not open his eyes at all; then she put her hand on his face, and then she seemed frightened—her little lip quivered, and she clung to her grandmother's dress—then some men came and carried papa up stairs, and the maid-servants laid the beautiful lady on the sofa, in the parlor; and she and grandma went back up into the attic—and all that day, grandma did not seem to see mamma's picture at all; and when Fanny came up to her, she wept and said, "God help you—my poor lamb."

CHAPTER XIII.

The bell sounded at Bluff Hill Prison, to call the prisoners to their tasks. They passed out from their cells and crossed, two by two, the prison-yard to their workshops. Percy and a stout negro were the last couple in the file. Just as they were about passing in, the African, who had received the punishment of the douche the day previous, for dilatoriness at his task, sprang upon the officer in waiting, and seized him by the throat. Percy, whose pugilistic science was a match for the African's muscle, grappled with and secured him in an instant, receiving, as he did so, a severe bite from the fellow's teeth, in his left shoulder. The negro was handcuffed, and Percy carried to the hospital, to have his wound dressed. The officer, in the flush of his gratitude, assured him, as he left, that the case should be laid before the governor, and would undoubtedly result in his pardon.

Percy's eye brightened, as he bowed his head in reply, but in truth he took no credit for the deed; it was only following an irresistible impulse to save the life of a fellow-creature.

Liberty! it would be sweet! But, pshaw! why dream of it? Men were proverbially ungrateful. Ten to one, the officer would never think of his promise again; or if he did, the governor would lay it on the table, to be indefinitely postponed, or forgotten, or rejected, with a thousand other troublesome applications. No—suns would rise and set just as they had done, and time for him would be marked only by the prison-bell, with its clanging summons to labor. He should see, every day, as he had done, the poor lame prisoner sunning himself in his favorite corner in the yard —he should see the prisoners' mattresses, hung on the rails to air—he should see the gleam of the blacksmith's forge, and hear the stroke of the stonecutter's hammer; the shuttle would fly, and the wheel turn round. He should sit down to his wooden plate, his square bit of salt meat, and his one potato, and drink water out of his rusty tin cup. He should gasp out the starry nights in his stifling cell; he should hear the rustling of silken robes, as ladies went the prison rounds, and his heart would beat quick as he thought of Mary; he should burn forever with the fire of remorse and shame—yet never consume; the taper would flicker and flicker—yet never go out.

So Percy sat carelessly down on the hospital bench, to have his wound dressed; and listened to the asthmatic breathing of the sick man at his side, and saw the hospital cook stirring in a cauldron some diluted broth, and watched the doctor, as he compounded a plaster, and leisurely smoked a cigar; and looked at a green branch which the wind ever and anon swept across the grated window, showering its snowy blossoms, as if in mockery, on the prison floor.

O, no—liberty was not for him—and why should it be? Had he not forfeited it by his own rash act?—was not his punishment just?—had he not lost the confidence of his fellow men?—crushed the noblest and purest heart that ever God warmed into life and love? It was all too true, and there had been moments when he meekly accepted his punishment, when he toiled in his prison uniform, not as if under the eye of a taskmaster, but willingly, almost cheerfully, as if by expiatory penance he could atone to himself for the wrong he had done that guileless heart. O, did it still beat? and for him? for the thousandth time he questioned. Could Mary look on him? smile on him? love him still? O, what mockery were liberty else! What mattered it how brightly the sun shone, if it shone not on their love purified and intensified by sorrow? What matter how green the earth, if they walked not through it side by side? What mattered it how fresh the breeze—how blue the sky—how soft the moonbeams—how sweet the flowers—how bright the stars—if day and night found not their twin hearts beating like one? Better his cell should be his tomb.

CHAPTER XIV.

"I like to live here," said little Fanny, running up to Lucy, with her sun-bonnet hanging at the back of her neck; her cheeks glowing, and her apron full of acorns, pebbles, pine leaves, grasses and flowers; "see here, I tied them up with a blade of grass for you, and here's a white clover; a great bumble bee wanted it, he buzzed and buzzed, but I ran off with it; won't you go with me, grandmother, and help me find a four-leaved clover? Don't sew any more on those old vests. Who taught you to make vests?" asked the little chatterbox.

"O, I learned many—many—years ago," replied Lucy, with a sigh, as she thought of Jacob; "and now you see, dear, what a good thing it is to learn something useful when one is young. If I did not know how to make these vests, I could not pay for this room we live in, you know; here, thread my needle, darling, either the eye is too small, or my eye is too dim; I can't see as well as I used."

"I wish I could do something useful," said Fanny, as she handed back the needle. "I can only brush up the hearth, and fill the tea-kettle, and pick up your spools, and thread your needle, and—what else, grandma?"

"Make this lonely old heart glad, my darling," said Lucy, pressing her lips to Fanny's forehead.

"Why didn't my papa ever come kiss me?" asked Fanny. "Was I too naughty for my papa to love?"

"No—no, my darling," said Lucy, turning away her head to restrain her tears, "you are the best little girl that—but run away, Fanny," said she, fearing to trust herself to speak. "Go find grandma a pretty four-leaved clover."

The child sprang up and bounded toward the door. Standing poised on one foot on the threshold, with her little neck bending forward, she exclaimed eagerly, "Oh, grandma, I dare not; there's a man climbing over the stile into the meadow, with a pack on his back; won't he hurt me?"

"No," said Lucy, peering over her spectacles at the man, and then resuming her seat, "it is only a peddler, Fanny; shops are scarce in the country, so they go round with tapes, needles, and things, to sell the farmers' wives. I am glad he has come, for I want some more sewing-silk to make these button-holes."

"Good day, ma'am," said the peddler, unlading his pack. "Would you like to buy any thing to-day? Combs—collars—needles—pins—tapes—ribbons—laces? buy any thing to-day, ma'am?"

"May I look?" whispered Fanny to Lucy, attracted by the bright show in the box.

"There's a ribbon for your hair," said the peddler, touching her curls caressingly; "and here is a string of beads for your neck. You will let me give them to you, won't you? because I have no little girl to love;" and his voice trembled slightly.

"May I love him, grandma?" whispered Fanny, for there was something in the peddler's voice that brought tears into her eyes. "May I give him some milk to drink, and a piece of bread?" and hardly waiting for an answer, she flew to the cupboard, and returned with her simple lunch.

"Thank you," said the peddler, in a low voice, without raising his eyes.

The sewing-silk was purchased, and the box rearranged, and strapped up, but still the peddler lingered. Lucy, thinking he might be weary, invited him to stop and rest awhile.

"I will sit here on the door-step awhile, if you please, with the little girl," said the peddler. "Are you fond of flowers?" said he to Fanny, again touching her shining curls.

"Oh, yes," she replied; "only I don't like to go alone to get them—the cows stare at me so with their great big eyes, and the little toads hop over my feet, and I am afraid they will bite; they won't bite, will they?" asked Fanny, looking confidingly up in his face.

"I should not think any thing could harm you," replied the peddler, drawing his fingers across his eyes.

"What are you crying for?" asked Fanny, "'cause you haven't any little girl to love you?"

"The dust, dear, in the road, quite blinded me to-day," replied the peddler.

"I will bring you some water for them, in my little cup," said Fanny. "Grandma bathes her eyes when they ache, sewing on those tiresome vests."

"No—no"—said the peddler, catching her by the hand as she sprang up —"don't go away—sit down—here—close by me—I will make a wreath of flowers for your hair; your eyes are as blue as this violet."

"They are mamma's eyes," said Fanny. "Grandma calls them 'mamma's eyes.' We have a pretty picture of mamma—see—that's it," and she bounded across the room and drew aside a calico curtain which screened it. "There, isn't it pretty?—why don't you look?"

The peddler slowly turned his head, and replied, in a husky voice, "Yes, dear."

"Mamma is dead," said Fanny, re-seating herself by his side. "What makes you shiver? are you cold?—he is sick, grandma," said Fanny, running up to Lucy.

"A touch of my old enemy, the ague, ma'am," said the peddler, respectfully—and Lucy returned to her needle.

"Yes, my mamma is dead," said Fanny. "Are you sorry my mamma is dead? Sometimes I talk to her—grandma likes to have me; but mamma's picture never speaks back. Don't you wish my mamma would speak back?" said Fanny, looking up earnestly in his face.

The peddler nodded—bending lower over the wreath he was twining.

"My papa is dead, too," said Fanny—"are you sorry my papa is dead? Nobody loves me but grandma and God."

"And I"—said the peddler, touching her curls again with his fingers.

"Why do you keep touching my hair?" asked the little chatterbox.

"Because it is so like—oh, well—I am sure I don't know," said the peddler, placing the wreath over her bright face, and touching his lips to her forehead. "Good-by, dear, don't forget me. I will make you a prettier wreath sometime, shall I?"

"O yes," said Fanny; "let me tell grandma. Grandma is so deaf she can't hear us;" and the child ran back into the room to tell the news.

"I like peddlers," said little Fanny, as she watched her new friend saunter slowly down the road. "He gave me this pretty wreath and this ribbon; I am sorry he didn't like mamma's picture; he hardly looked at it at all."

"The peddler never heard of your mamma, my darling; you must not expect strangers to feel as you and grandma do about it."

"Yes," replied Fanny, in a disappointed tone;—"but it is a pity, because I like him. There he goes; now he has climbed the fence, and is crossing the meadow. Good by, Mr. Peddler."

Yes—across the meadow, down the little grassy lane, over the stile—far into the dim—dim woods, where no human eye could penetrate, prostrate upon the earth, shedding such tears as manhood seldom sheds, lay the peddler. Still in his ears lingered that bird-like voice, still in his veins thrilled the touch of that tiny hand, and those silken curls, in whose every glossy wave shone out Mary's self. Mary—yet not Mary; Mary's child—yet not his child!—And Lucy, too;—O, the sorrow written in every furrow of that kindly face, and—O God—by whom?

The stars glimmered through the trees, the night-winds gently rocked the little merry birds to sleep—midnight came on with its solemn spirit-whispers—followed the gray dawn with its misty tears, and still—there lay the peddler, stricken, smitten, on Nature's kindly breast; for there, too (but all unconscious of his misery—deaf to his penitence), lay pillowed the dear head which had erst drooped so lovingly upon his breast.

CHAPTER XV.

"Very well done; button-holes strong and even, lining smooth; stitching, like rows of seed pearl. This is no apprentice work," said Mr. John Pray, as he held Lucy's vests up to the light for a more minute inspection. "That's a vest, now, as is a vest; won't disgrace John Pray's shop; it would gladden even the eyes of my old boss, Jacob Ford; and mighty particular he was, too, and mighty small wages the old man paid, as I have occasion to know. Well, I made a vow then, and thank God I have had grace to keep it, that if ever John Pray became a master workman, he would do as he would be done by. So, I don't ask what wages other tailors give; that don't matter to me. I don't want to die with any body's groans in my ears. So, when a piece of work is finished and handed in, I say, 'Now, John Pray, what should you think was a fair price for you to receive, if you had done that 'ere job?' That's it; no dodging behind that question. 'Specially when a man has been through the operative mill himself. So, there's your pay, Zekiel, weighed out in that ere pair of Bible scales; and you may tell the old lady, as you call her, that if she had served a regular apprenticeship at the trade, she couldn't have done better. What did you say her name was? However, that's no consequence —as long as she does the work well. Here's some more vests for her."

"Well, I really don't know," said Zekiel, "I never heern tell her name. She's a bran new neighbor, and as I was coming into town every day with my cart, she axed me, civil like, if I'd bring these vests to you. So, I brung 'em. I don't mind doing a good turn for a fellow creetur, now and then, specially when it 'taint no bother," added Zekiel, with a grin.

"What did you spoil it for by saying that?" said John Pray. "I was just going to clap you on the back for a clever fellow."

"You might go further, and clap a worse fellow on the back," answered Zekiel. "But I never boasts, I don't. 'Tain't no use. If the ministers tell the truth, we've all got to be weighed in the big scales up above, where there ain't no false weights—bad deeds agin good deeds. Farmer Reed, I'm thinking, will be astonished when the balance on his account is struck. But, good day; my parsnips and cabbages ought to be in the market, instead of wilting at your door—even though you city folks don't know the taste of a fresh vegetable. Good day."

CHAPTER XVI.

Rain—rain—rain; patter, patter. No sunshine to help Lucy's purblind eyes in stitching the dark vests; no sunshine to kiss open the buttercups for Fanny. The birds took short and hasty flights from tree to tree; the farmers slouched their hats over their faces, and whipped up their teams; the little school children hurried back and forth with their satchels, without stopping to look for chipmunks or for ground-birds' nests; the bells on the baker's cart lost their usual merry tinkle, and the old fishman's horn, as he went his Friday round, gave forth a discordant, spiritless whine.

Little Fanny had righted her grandmother's work-basket, read "Jack and his Bean-Stalk," made houses on the slate, put the black kitten to sleep in the old barrel, blown soap bubbles, till she was tired, in the tin bowl, and had finally crept up on the little cot bed and fallen asleep.

Lucy sat back in her chair, and began counting over the money Zekiel had brought her. It would relieve their present necessities. Fanny should have some new clothes out of it, when farmer Smith's rent was paid. But the future? Lucy's eyes were growing dimmer every day, and her limbs more feeble. She might drop off suddenly, and then who would befriend poor little Fanny? What lessons of sorrow had that loving little heart to learn? By what thorny path would she thread life's toilsome journey?

Dear little Fanny! She could no more live without love than flowers without sunshine. That she should ever weep tears, that no kindly hand should wipe away; that she should hunger or thirst—shiver with winter's cold—faint under summer heat; that a harsh voice should ever drive the blood from her lip or cheek—that her round limbs should bend with premature toil—that sin should tempt her helplessness—that sorrow should invite despair—that wrong should ever seem right to Mary's child! Poor Lucy bowed her head and wept.

The peddler looked in through the little casement window. He saw the falling tears, he saw Lucy's sorrowful gaze at the rosy little dreamer. He needed no explanation of the tableau. He knocked at the door; Lucy's tones were tremulous, as she bade him come in.

"I thought you might be wanting some more silk," said he, respectfully, with his eyes fixed upon little Fanny.

"Sit down—sit down," said Lucy; for the tones of his voice were kindly, and her heart in its loneliness craved sympathy. "It is dull weather we have, sir; one don't mind it when all is right here," and she laid her hand on her heart.

"True," said the peddler, in a low voice, still gazing at Fanny.

"The child sleeps," said Lucy. "It was of her I was thinking when you came in; it would be very bitter to die and leave her alone, sir;" and Lucy's tears flowed again.

"Have you no relatives—no friends, to whom you could intrust her?" asked the peddler, with his eyes bent on the ground.

"None, God help us," replied Lucy.

"Sir," and Lucy drew her chair nearer to the peddler, "a great sorrow may sometimes be in the heart, when smiles are on the face."

The peddler nodded, without trusting himself to speak.

"This poor heart has borne up until now, with what strength it might; but now"—and she glanced at little Fanny—"O, sir—if I could but take her with me."

"God will care for her," said the peddler, stooping to remove his hat, that Lucy might not see his emotion.

"Sometimes I feel that," replied Lucy; "and then again—O, sir, trouble makes the heart so fearful. My poor daughter—she was our idol, sir—the sunbeam in our home; so good—so beautiful—so light-hearted, till the trouble came. It was like a lightning bolt, sir—it scathed and withered in one moment what was before so fresh and fair; it blighted all our hopes, it blackened our hearth-stone, it killed my husband—poor Jacob. Pardon me, sir, I talk as if you had known our history. It was Mary's lover, sir; he was taken up for swindling, at our very door;—and yet I loved the lad —for the ground she walked on he loved—for Mary's sake."

"She forgave him?" asked the peddler, in a voice scarcely audible.

"She?—poor dear—she? All the world could not have made her believe ill of him. She? Why, sir, she would sit at the window for hours, watching the way he used to come. It crazed her, poor thing; and then she would come and go just as she was bid. Her father saw her fade, day by day, and cursed him;—he forgot business—every thing went wrong—one way and another our money went, and then Jacob died."

"He forgave him—your daughter's lover, before he died?" asked the peddler, tremulously.

"You have a kind heart, sir," said Lucy. "Yes, Jacob's heart softened at the last;—he said we all needed God's mercy. His last words were 'Peace.'"

"God be thanked," murmured the peddler; then adding, quickly, "it must have made you so much happier; you say you loved the lad."

"Yes," said Lucy, "even now. We all err, sir. He was only nineteen—young to marry; but Mary's heart was bound up in him. He didn't mean it, sir—I don't know how it was. God help us all.

"Well, we buried Jacob; then we had none to look to—Mary and I. We were poor. I was feeble. Then Mary's lover came—the rich Mr. Shaw. You are ill, sir?"

"No—no," replied the peddler; "go on—your story interests me."

"Well, he wanted to marry Mary, although he saw how it was. It was all one to her, you know, sir. She was crazed like—though so sweet and gentle. I did it for the best, sir," said Lucy, mournfully. "I thought when I died Mary would have a home."

"Go on," said the peddler. "He treated her kindly?" he asked, with a dark frown.

"For a little," answered Lucy. "He wearied after a while. I might have known it—I was to blame, sir—her heart was broken. When the babe opened its eyes, she closed her's, and I alone mourned for her."

"O, God!" groaned the peddler.

"It moves you, sir," said Lucy; "perhaps you, too, have known trouble."

The peddler bowed his head without replying.

"Then, sir, he brought a gay young thing into the house—his mistress—not his wife. He never looked upon his child; he cursed me and it. I gave it our name; I called it Fanny Ford; and we crept away, the babe and I, up in the attic;—then all was confusion—extravagance—ruin;—then he died, sir—and since—you see us here—you know now, sir, why I, leaning over the grave's brink, yet shrink back and cling to life for her sake," and she looked at Fanny.

"Would you trust her with me?" asked the peddler, with his eyes bent upon the ground. "I am all alone in the world—I have none to love—none who love me—I am poor, but while I have a crust, she shall never want."

"It is a great charge," replied Lucy. "If you should weary, sir?"

"Then may God forget me," said the peddler, earnestly, kneeling at Lucy's feet.

Lucy bent on him a gaze searching as truth, but she read nothing in that upturned face to give the lie to those solemn words. Pointing to Fanny, she said,

"Before God—and as you hope for peace at the last?"

The peddler bowed his head upon Lucy's withered hand, and faltered out, "I promise."

CHAPTER XVII.

"Good morning, Zekiel," said John Pray. "Glad to see you—you must tell the old lady to go ahead and finish this pile of vests in a twinkling; business is brisk now. Why, what's this?" said he. "These vests unfinished? How's that? Don't the pay suit? What's the trouble now?"

"Don't," said Zekiel—"don't—stop a bit—I'm as tough as any man—but there's some things I can't stand;" and he dashed a tear away.

"What's the matter now?" asked John. "Is the old lady dissatisfied with her pay?"

"Don't—I say," said Zekiel;—"hold up—don't harrow a man that way—she's dead—I tell you stone dead. She never'll make no more vests for nobody. I never shall forget what I saw there this morning, never.

"You see she was old and infirm, and wan't fit to work for any body any how; but she had a little gran'child, fresh as a rose-bud, and she did it for her, you see. Well, this morning I harnessed the old gray horse—the black one is lame since Sunday—and reined up at her door, as usual, to get the bundle. I knocked, and nobody came; then I knocked again, then little rose-bud came tip-toeing to the door, with her finger on her pretty lip, so—and whispered, 'grandma is asleep; she has not woke up this great while.' So I said—'You'd better speak to her and say, here's Zekiel, come for the bundle, cause you know she is partiklar like about sending it.' So the little rose-bud went up to the bed-side, and said —'Grandma, here is Zekiel, come for the vests.' The old lady didn't say nothing, and rose-bud asked me to speak to her. I went up, and—John Pray—the old lady was stone dead, and how was I going to tell that to little rose-bud?"

"You don't mean to tell me that the child was all alone with the corpse—nobody to see to the poor thing?" asked John.

"But I do, though," said Zekiel; "it was enough to break a body's heart, and she so innocent like. I never was so put to it in my life, to know what to do. There she had gone and tidied up the kitchen, hung the tea-kettle on the fire as well as she knew how, and sat waiting for her gran'mother to 'wake up,' as she called it. How could I tell her she was dead? Blast me if I could, to this minute."

"But you didn't come away and leave her so?" asked John.

"No," replied Zekiel, "for a peddler came in, and little rose-bud ran up, glad-like, to see him; then I beckoned him one side, and told him just how it was, and he turned as white as a turnip, and great big tears rolled down his face, as he took little rose-bud up in his arms and kissed her. Then he told me he was a kind of a relation like, and poor, but that he would take the child and do the best he could by her; and I knew he must be clever, for children are powerful 'cute, and never take to cranky folks, any how—and so I left them, and came blubbering into town. I vow it was enough to make the very stones cry, to see little rose-bud take on so, after the old lady."

There was no litigious will to be read, no costly effects to quarrel about, in Lucy Ford's poor cottage, and yet Golconda's mines were all too poor to buy the priceless treasures to which the peddler fell heir—Mary's picture and Mary's child!

With such talismans, what should he fear? what could he not accomplish? He no longer walked with his head bowed upon his breast. The pure love of that sinless little one restored his long-lost self-respect. Life was dear to him. His eye regained its luster; his step its firmness. Even his humble calling, now more than ever necessary, became to him dignified and attractive. Fanny should have an education worthy of Mary's child. For the present, till he had amassed a little capital, he must find her a home in some quiet farmer's family, where he could oversee her, in his occasional visits.

Dear little Fanny! with her smiles and tears, she had already twined herself round every fiber of his heart. "Cousin John," as the peddler taught her to call him, "was to take care of her always, and she was to love him dearly—dearly—better than any body, but mamma and grandma."

CHAPTER XVIII.

Ah! there is Mrs. Quip's head, poked out of the north chamber window. A sure sign that it is five o'clock to the minute. Now she scuds across the yard, making a prodigious flutter with her flying calico long-short, among the hens and chickens, who take refuge in an upturned old barrel. Snatching some sticks from the wood-pile, she scuds back again to the kitchen, twitches a match from the mantel, lights the fire, hangs on the tea-kettle, jerks out the table, rattles on the cups and saucers, plates, knives, forks, etc., and throws open every blind, door, and window. This done, she flies up stairs, pokes Susan in the ribs, drags Mary out on the floor, throws a mug of water in "that lazy John's face," and intimates that "breakfast will be on the table in less than fifteen minutes."

John rubs the water out of his eyes, muttering a few unmentionable words. Susan and Mary make a transient visit to the looking-glass, and descend the stair's just as the coffee smokes upon the table. Mrs. Quip frightens the chickens into the barrel again with her calico long-short and the great bell that she ring at the barn-door to "call the men folks to breakfast," and takes her accustomed seat at the table.

"Brown bread or white? baked beans or salt meat? doughnuts, cheese, or apple-pie? which'll you have?" said Mrs. Quip to little Fanny.

"Ma'am?" said Fanny, with a bewildered look.

"Oh, dear; Susan Quip, for gracious' sake find out what that peddler's child wants; hurry, all of you. Baking to be done to-day; yesterday's ironing to finish; them new handkerchers to hem; John's trowsers to mend; buttery shelves to scour; brown bread sponge to set; yeast to make; pickles to scald; head-cheese to fix: hurry, all of you. Susan Quip, there's the cat in the buttery, smack, and—scissors—right into that buttermilk, arter a mouse. Scat—scat; Susan Quip, that's your doings—leaving the buttery door open. John Quip, do you drownd that cat to-day. Don't talk to me of kittens; kittens is as plenty as peddlers' children. Hand me that coffee, Susan Quip. Lord-a-mercy, there's the fishman: run, John—two mackerel, not more than sixpence a-piece; pinch 'em in the stomach, to see if they are fresh. If they are flabby, don't take 'em; if they ain't, do. Yes, every thing to do, to-day, and a little more beside. Soft soap to——Heavens and earth, John Quip, that mackerel man hasn't given you the right change by two cents. Here, stop him! John Quip—Susan—get out of the way, all of you; I'll go myself," and the calico long-short started in full pursuit of the mackerel defaulter.

Poor little Fanny! no Green Mountain boy, set down in the rush of the city, ever felt half so crazy. Mrs. Quip, with her snap-dragon, touch-me-not-manners, high-pitched voice, and heavy tramp, was such a contrast to her dear grandmother, with her soft tones, noiseless step, and gentle ways. Fanny was afraid to move for fear she should cross Mrs. Quip's track. She did not know whether she were hungry or thirsty. She marveled at the railroad velocity with which the food disappeared, and pitied Mrs. Quip so much for having such a quantity of things to do all in a minute!

The next day after Fanny's arrival at Butternut farm, was Sunday. Mrs. Quip was up betimes, as usual, but her activity took a devotional turn. She was out to the barn fifty times a minute, to see "if the horse and waggin was getting harnessed for meetin',"—not but Mr. Quip was still above ground, but as far as he had any voice in family matters, he might as well have been under. Mrs. Quip was up in Susan's room (or, as she pronounced it, Sewsan), to see if she was learning her catechise; she was padlock-ing John Quip's Sunday temptation, in the shape of the "Thrilling Adventures of Jack Bowsprit;" she was giving the sitting-room as Sabbatical and funereal an aspect as possible, by setting the chairs straight up against the walls, shutting all the blinds, and putting into the cupboard every thing that squinted secular-wise.

Fanny, oppressed by the gloom within doors, crept out into the warm sunshine, and seating herself under a tree in the yard, was looking at a few clover blossoms which she had plucked beside her. She was thinking of the pleasant Sundays she had passed with her dear grandmother, and how she used to sit on the door-step of the cottage, and tell her how God taught the little birds to build their cradle nests, and find their way through the air; and how He provided even for the little ants, who so patiently, grain by grain, built their houses in the gravel walk; and how He kept the grass green with the dew and showers, and ripened the fruit, and opened the blossoms with the warm sunshine, and how He was always watching over us, caring for our wants, listening to our cries, pitying us for our sorrows, and making His sun to shine even on those who forget to thank Him for it. But see—Fanny has dropped her clover blossoms, for Mrs. Quip has seized her by the arm, and says,

"You wicked child, you! To think of picking a flower Sunday! What do you expect will become of you when you die? What do you think the neighbors will think? Sinful child! There"—slamming her down on a cricket in the sitting-room—"sit down, and see if you can learn what the chief end of man is, afore meeting time. Flowers of a Sunday! or flowers any day, for the matter of that, I never could see the sense of 'em. Even the Bible says, 'they toil not, neither do they spin.' Gracious goodness— Sewsan Quip, Mrs. Snow's kerriage has just started for meetin'. Get your things, all of you. Sewsan, see to that peddler's child; mind that she don't take no flowers to the Lord's temple; John Quip, you shan't wear them gloves; they cost twenty-five cents at the finding-store; and if you think that I bought 'em for you to drive in, you are mistaken; now put 'em in your pocket till you get into the meetin'-us porch; that will save 'em a sight; them leather reins will wear 'em all threadbare in less than no time.

Mercy on us, the string is off my bunnet. Sewsan, that's your doing. Run and bring me a pin off the third shelf in the buttery, under the yellow quart bowl. I picked it up and put it there this morning. Make haste, now. John Quip, stop cracking your whip that way on the holy Sabbath day. What do you suppose your dead grandpa would think, if he should hear it?"

The wagon was brought, and its living freight stowed carefully away in the remote corners. The oil-cloth covering was buttoned carefully down on all sides, as it had been during the winter; Mrs. Quip said it was hot, but maybe it would crack the oil-cloth to roll it up for the breeze to play through. Susan, Mary, and Fanny, therefore, took a vapor bath, on the back seat. Mrs. Quip, seated at John's side, excluded, with her big black bonnet, any stray breeze which might have found entrance that way, to the refreshing of the gasping passengers. Dobbin moved on; he had been up that hot, dusty hill, many a Sunday before, and understood perfectly well how to keep his strength in reserve for the usual accession to his load on the village green, in the shape of the Falstaffian Aunt Hepsibah, Miss Butts, the milliner, and Deacon Tufts, who were duly piled in on the gasping occupants behind. Mrs. Quip being also on the alert to fill up any stray chinks in the "waggin" with "them children who stopped to rest in the road, when they oughter go straight to meetin'."

The unlading of Mrs. Quip's wagon at the meeting-house door, was an exhibition much "reckoned on" by the graceless young men of the village, who always collected on the steps for the purpose, and with mock gallantry assisted Mrs. Quip in clambering over the wheels, suppressing their mirth at her stereotyped exhortation, as she glanced at Dobbin, "to see that they didn't start the critter."

It was a work of time to draw out the unctuous Aunt Hepsibah; Deacon Tufts, more wiry and agile, "helped hisself," as Mrs. Quip remarked. The crowning delight was the evacuation of the wagon, by Miss Butts—who, with a mincing glance at the men, circumspectly extended one finger of her right hand—gingerly exposed the tip of the toe of her slipper, and with sundry little shrieks and exclamations, prolonged indefinitely the delicious agony of her descent, as the young gentlemen by turns profanely touched her virgin elbows. Thirty-nine years of single blessedness had fully prepared her to appreciate these little masculine attentions, of which she always made an exact memorandum in her note-book (affixing the date) on reaching her seat in church. The unappropriated Miss Butts wore rose-buds in her bonnet, as emblematical of love's young spring-time, and dressed in shepherdess style; nature, perhaps, suggesting the idea, by placing the crook in her back.

Poor little Fanny was as much out of her element at Butternut farm as a humming-bird in a cotton-mill. She could not "heel a stocking," although Mrs. Quip "knew how as soon as she was born." She could neither chain-stitch, cross-stitch, button-hole-stitch, nor cat-stitch, though she often got a stitch in her side trying to "get out of Mrs. Quip's way." She did not know "whether her grandmother was orthodox or Unitarian;" whether Cousin John "belonged to the church," or not; in fact, as Mrs. Quip remarked, the child seemed to her "not to have the slightest idea what she was created for."

"Cousin John" came at last! with an empty pack, a full purse, and a fuller heart. Fanny flew into his outspread arms, and nestled into his bosom, with a fullness of joy which the friendless only can feel. Out of sound of Mrs. Quip's trip-hammer tongue, out of sight of Mrs. Quip's omniscient eyes, Fanny whispered in "Cousin John's" ear, crying, laughing, and kissing the while, all her little troubles. Cousin John did not smile, for he knew too well how keenly the little trusting heart, which beat against his own, could suffer or enjoy; so he wiped her tears away, and told her that she should say good-by to Butternut farm, and accompany him on his next trip, as far as Canton, where he would leave her with a nice old lady, who had a red and green parrot, and who taught a school for the village children.

It was a pretty sight—Cousin John and Fanny; she, skipping on before him to pluck a flower, then returning to glide her little hand in his, and walk contentedly by his side; or, standing on some stile, waiting to be lifted over, with her bonnet blown back, and her bright little face beaming with smiles; Cousin John sometimes answering her questions at random, as the tones of her voice, or the expression of her face, recalled her lost mother; sometimes looking proudly upon the bud, as he thought how sweet and fair would be the blossom, but more often gazing at her tearfully, as Lucy's last solemn words rang in his ears.

Percy was a riddle to himself. In the child's pure presence, every spot upon his soul's mirror he would have wiped away. Lips which had never framed a prayer for themselves, now murmured one for her. Feet which had strayed into forbidden paths, would fain have found for her tiny feet the straight and narrow path of life.

Insensibly "a little child was leading him"—nearer to Thee, O God, nearer to Thee.

Little Fanny's joy on this pedestrian tour was irrepressible; but the journey was not all performed on foot: many a good-natured farmer gave them a lift of a mile or two, and many a kind-hearted farmer's wife offered Fanny a cake, or a drink of milk, for the sake of her own sun-burnt children, yet blessed in a mother's love. Then there were friendly trees to shade them from the scorching noon-day sun, where the peddler could unstrap his pack, and Fanny throw off her bonnet and go to sleep in his lap. Sparkling brooks there were, to lave their faces, or quench their thirst, and flowers whose beauty might have tempted on tardier feet than Fanny's. Their only trouble was "Cousin John's pack;" and Fanny's slender stock of arithmetic was exhausted in trying to compute how many pieces of tape, how many papers of needles, how many skeins of thread, must be sold before he could buy a horse and wagon to help him to carry his load. The peddler, too, had his air-castles to build, to which the afore-mentioned tape, needles, and thread were but the stepping-stones. Fanny once placed where she could be contented, and kindly treated, and Cousin John must leave her, to woo Dame Fortune, for her sake, more speedily.

Fanny shed a few tears when she heard this, poor child! and wondered if there were many Mrs. Quips in the world; but the motherly face of Mrs. Chubbs, with her three chins, the queer gabble of the red and green parrot, and more than all, the society of playfellows of her own age, were no small mitigations of the parting with Cousin John.

Mrs. Chubbs would most decidedly have been turned out of office by any modern school committee. When a little creature who should have been in the nursery, was sent to her charge, "to be out of the way," Mrs. Chubbs oftener allowed it to stretch its little limbs on the grass-plat, front of the door, than she set it poring over a spelling-book. She never thumped geography or arithmetic into her pupils with a ferule. A humming-top string, or a kite-tail fragment protruding from a childish pocket, excited in her no indignation. A bit of gingerbread, or an apple, munched by a little urchin who had made an early or an indifferent breakfast, did not appear to her old-fashioned vision an offense worthy of the knout or the guillotine. In fact, Mrs. Chubb's heart was as capacious as her pockets, and their unfathomable depths were a constant marvel to her pupils.

As to the parrot, he constituted himself "a committee" of one, and called out occasionally, "Mind your lessons, I say," to Fanny's great diversion. And Fanny did "mind" them; for she loved good Mrs. Chubb, and then she had a little private plan of her own for astounding Cousin John, one of these days, with her profound erudition.

And so time passed—the little homesick lump in her throat had quite disappeared; she sang—she skipped—she laughed—a merrier little grig never danced out a slipper.

Will my indulgent reader skip over ten years with me?—he might take a more dangerous leap—and enter yonder substantial-looking building, in which young ladies are "finished." Passing by the long dining-hall, with its bare tavern-y looking table, and rows of bamboo chairs, let us ascend yonder marble stairs (for the school-house, let me tell you, was once an aristocratic old mansion), and turn down that long passage to the right. Now let us stop before No. 29. Remove your hat, if you please, because I am about to usher you into the presence of two very pretty girls, and though I do not approve of eaves-dropping, suppose we just step behind that friendly screen, and listen to what they are saying.

CHAPTER XIX.

"Fanny, what pains you are taking with your hair to-day!" said Kate. "Is this Cousin John who has written you such interminable letters from 'El-Dorado,' to turn out, after all, your lover? I hope not, for I fancy him some venerable Mentor, with a solemn face, and oracular voice, jealous as Bluebeard of any young man who looks at you. How old is this paragon?—handsome or ugly? I am dying to know."

"Thirty-six," replied Fanny; "and as I remember him, with dark, curling hair, a broad, expansive brow, eyes one would never weary looking into, a voice singularly rich and sweet, and a form perfect but for a trifling stoop in the shoulders. That is my Cousin John," said Fanny, drawing the comb through her ringlets.

"Stoop in the shoulders! I thought as much," mockingly laughed the merry Kate. "If he had 'a stoop in the shoulders' ten years ago, how do you suppose your Adonis looks now?"

"It matters very little to me," replied Fanny, with a little annoyance in her tone; "it matters very little to me, were he as ugly as Caliban."

"How am I to construe that?" asked Kate, crossing her two forefingers ("it matters very little to you"). "Does it mean that love is out of the question between you two, or that you would have him if Lucifer stood in your path?"

"Construe it as it best suits you," replied Fanny, with the most provoking nonchalance.

"But 'a stoop in the shoulders,'" persisted the tormenting Kate. "I don't care to have a man's face handsome, provided it is intelligent, but I do insist upon a fine form, correct morals, and a good disposition."

Fanny laughed—"I suppose you think to wind your husband round your little finger, like a skein of silk."

"With Cupid's help," replied Kate, with mock humility.

"Of course you will be quite perfect;—never, for instance, appear before your husband in curl papers, or slip-shod?" asked Fanny; "never make him eat bad pies or puddings?"

"That depends," answered Kate, "if he is tractable—not; if not—why not?"

"You will wink at his cigars?"

"He might do worse."

"You will patronize his moustache?"

"If he will my snuff-box," said Kate, laughing. "Heigho—I feel just like a cat in want of a mouse to torment. I wish I knew a victim worthy to exercise my talents upon."

"Talons, you mean," retorted Fanny—"I pity him."

"He would get used to it," said Kate; "the mouse—the husband, you know—I should let him run a little way, and then clap my claws on him. I've seen it tried; it works like a charm."

"Kate, why do you always choose to wear a mask?" asked Fanny; "why do you take so much pains to make a censorious world believe you the very opposite of what you are?"

"Because paste passes as current as diamond; because I value the world's opinion not one straw; because if you own a heart, it is best to hide it, unless you want it trampled on. But I don't ask you to subscribe to all this, Fanny, with that incomparable Cousin John in your thoughts; there he is—there's the door-bell—Venus! how you blush! but 'a stoop in the shoulders.' How can you, Fanny? Thirty-six years old, too—Lord bless us!"

CHAPTER XX.

Was this "little Fanny?" this tall, graceful creature of seventeen, the little thing who bade him good-by at Mrs. Chubb's door, ten years since, with her pinafore stuffed in the corner of her eye? "Little Fanny," with that queenly presence? Cousin John almost felt as if he ought to ask leave to touch her hand; ah—she is the same little Fanny after all—frank, guileless, and free-hearted. She flies into his arms, puts up her rosy lips for a kiss, and says "Dear Cousin John."

"God bless you," was all he could find voice to say, for in truth, she was Mary's own self.

Yes—Fanny was very lovely, with those rippling waves of silken hair, and the light and shadow, flitting like summer clouds over her speaking face. Cousin John held her off at arm's length. Yes, she was very lovely. "How much she had changed!"

"And you, too," said Fanny, seating herself beside him. "You look so much better; the stoop in your shoulders is quite gone; you are bronzed a little, but all the better for that."

"Thank you," said Cousin John, "more especially as I could not help it, not even to please 'little Fanny.'"

"Ah—but I am no longer little Fanny," she said, blushing slightly. "I have crammed a great many books into my head since I saw you, and done considerable thinking beside."

"And what has your thinking all amounted to?" asked Cousin John, half playfully, half seriously.

"Just to this—that you are the very best cousin in the world, and that I never can repay you for all you have been to the poor, little friendless orphan," said Fanny, with brimming eyes.

"God bless you," said Cousin John. "I am more than repaid in these last ten minutes."

Hours flew like seconds, while Percy narrated his adventures by sea and land, and listened to Fanny's account of herself; the old duenna, meanwhile, walking uneasily up and down the hall, occasionally making an errand into the sitting-room, and muttering to herself as she went out, that she had heard before of boarding-school "cousins," and that he was altogether too handsome a man to be allowed such a long tête-à-tête with Miss Fanny; and so she reported at head-quarters, but the Principal being just then unfortunately engaged in examining a new French teacher, who had applied for employment, could not give the affair the attention Miss Miffit insisted upon.

Mr. Thurston Grey, too, was on the anxious seat; for the mischievous Kate had informed him "that Fanny was holding a protracted meeting in the best parlor, with the handsomest man she ever saw."

Nothing like a rival to precipitate matters! The declaration which had so long been trembling on Mr. Grey's lips, found its way into a billet-doux, and was forwarded to Fanny that very night, and presented by Kate in the presence of Cousin John, "to test," as she said, "the quality of his cousin-ship."

Cousin John was not jealous of "little Fanny!" how absurd! Little Fanny! whom he had carried in his arms, who had slept on his breast. In fact he laughed quite merrily at the idea, louder than was at all necessary to convince himself of the nonsense of the thing, when he read Mr. Grey's proposal; (for Fanny had no secrets from "Cousin John.") True he wound up his watch twice that morning, and put on odd stockings, and found it quite impossible to decide which of his cravats he should wear that day, and looked in the glass very attentively for some time, and forgot to smoke, but he wasn't jealous of little Fanny. Of course he wasn't!

CHAPTER XXI.

"A gin-sling, waiter! Strong, hot, and quick; none of your temperance mixtures for me; and waiter, here, a beef-steak smothered in onions; and waiter, some crackers and cheese, and be deuced quick about it, too. I'm not a man to be trifled with, as somebody besides you will find out, I fancy," said Mr. Scraggs, hitching his heels to the mantel, as the waiter closed the door.

Mr. Scraggs was a plethoric, pursy, barrel-looking individual, with a peony complexion, pink, piggy eyes, and a nose sky-wardly inclined. His neck-cloth was flashy and greasy; his scarlet vest festooned with a mock chain; his shirt bosom fastened with green studs, and his nether limbs encased in a pair of snake-skin pantaloons. As the waiter closed the door to execute his order, he delivered himself of the following soliloquy, between the whiffs of his cigar:

"Ha-ha! pardoned out, was he? turned peddler, did he? fathered the little gal, and sold tape to pay her board, hey? put her to boarding-school, and went to New Orleans to seek his fortin'? got shipwrecked and robbed, and the Lord knows what, and then started for Californy for better luck, did he? Stuck to gold-digging like a mole—made his fortin', and then came back to marry the little gal, hey? That'll be as I say. She's a pretty gal—may I be shot, if she ain't; a deuced pretty gal—but she don't come between me and my revenge. Not 'xactly! That blow you struck in the prison, my fine fellow, is not forgotten quite yet. John Scraggs has a way of putting them little things on file. Hang me if it don't burn on my cheek yet. Your fine broadcloth suit don't look much like your red and blue prison uniform, Mr. Percy Lee. Your crop of curly black hair is rather more becoming than your shaven crown; wonder what your pretty love would say if she knew all that? if she knew she was going to marry the man who killed her own mother? and, pretty as she is, by the eternal, she shall know it. But, patience—John Scraggs; a little more billing and cooing first; a little more sugar before the drop of gall brims over the cup. Furnish the fine house you have taken, Mr. Percy Lee, pile up the satin and damask, and picters, and statters, and them things—

chuckle over the happiness you are not a going to have—for by the
eternal, the gal may go the way the mother did, but my hand shall
crush you; and yet, I ain't got nothing agin the gal, neither: she's as
pretty a piece of flesh and blood as I've seen this many a day. A delicate
mate for a jail-bird, ha—ha."

"Waiter! waiter another gin-sling; hotter and stronger than the last; 'gad
—fire itself wouldn't be too strong for me to swallow to-day. Percy
Lee's wedding-day, is it? We shall see!

"He will curl his fine hair, don his broad-cloth suit, satin vest and white
gloves; look at his watch, and be in a devil of a hurry, won't he? ha—ha.
He will get into a carriage with his dainty bride, and love her all the
better for her blushing and quivering; he will look into her pretty face till
he would sell his very soul for her; he will lead her by the tips of her
little white gloved fingers into church; then they'll kneel before the
parson, and he will promise all sorts of infernal lies. Then the minister
will say, 'if any one present knows any reason why these two shouldn't
be joined in the holy state of matrimony, let him speak, or forever after
hold his peace.'

"Then is your time, John Scraggs—leap to his side like ten thousand
devils; hiss in the gal's ear that her lover is a jail-bird—that he's her
mother's murderer—laugh when she shrinks from his side in horror, and
falls like one stone dead; for by the eternal, John Scraggs is the man to
do all that—and yet I ain't got nothing agin the gal either.

"But, stay a bit; that will be dispatching the rascal too quick. I'll make
slower work of it. I'll prolong his misery. I'll watch him writhe and twist
like a lion in a net. I'll let the marriage go on—I'll not interrupt it; and
then I'll make it the hottest hell! The draught shall be ever within reach
of his parched lips, and yet, he shall never taste it; for his little wife shall
curse him. She shall be ever before him, in her tempting, dainty beauty,
and yet a great gulf shall separate them. That's it—slow torture; patience
—I won't dispatch him all at once. I'll lop off first a hand, then a foot,
pluck out an eye, touch up a quivering nerve, maim him—mangle him—
let him die a thousand deaths in one. Good! I'll teach the aristocrat to fell
me to the earth like a hound. A jail-bird—ha, ha; salt pork and mush,
instead of trout cooked in claret; water in a rusty tin cup, instead of old
Madeira, and Hock, and Sherry, and Champagne. Mush and salt pork—

ha, ha. Too cursed good, though, for the dainty dog. I wish I'd been warden of the Bluff Hill prison. I'd have lapped up his aristocratic blood, drop by drop."

CHAPTER XXII.

"Mine forever," whispered Percy, as he drew Fanny's hand within his arm, on their wedding morning, and led her to the carriage.

Not a word was spoken on the way; even the rattling Kate vailed her merry eyes under their soft lashes, and her woman's heart, true to itself, sent up a prayer for the orphan's happy future. And Percy; he was to be all to Fanny—father, brother, husband; there were none to divide with him the treasure he so jealously coveted.

Happy Percy! The lightning bolt, indeed, had fallen; riving the stately tree, dissevering its branches, but again it is covered with verdure and blossoms, for lo—the cloud has rolled away, the rainbow arches the blue sky, and hopes, like flowers, sweeter and fresher for nature's tears, are springing thick in his pathway.

All this and more, passed through Percy's mind as he watched the shadows come and go on Fanny's changeful cheek.

"Get out of the way," thundered the coachman, to a man who, with slouched hat, and Lucifer-ish frown, stood before the carriage. "Get out of the way, I say;" and he cracked his whip over his shoulders. "Staring into the carriage window that way, at a young 'oman as is going to be married. Get out of the way!"

"Go to ——," muttered the man. "Get out of the way! ha—that's good—it will be a long time before I get out of the way, I can promise you. But, drive on—drive on—I'll overtake you—and ride over you all, too, rough-shod, hang me, if I don't. 'The horns of the altar,' as the ministers call it, will prove the horn of a dilemma to you, Mr. Percy Lee, or there was no strength in the horn I swallowed this morning."

The words were said which never may be unsaid; the twain were one—joy to share together—sorrow to bear together—smooth or rough the path, life's journey to travel together. A few words from holy lips—a short transit of the dial's fingers—a blush—perchance a tear—a low response—and heaven or hell, even in this world, was to be their portion.

The bridal party turn from the altar. Through the stained windows—under the grand arches—past the fluted pillars, the dim light slants lovingly upon the soft ripples of the young bride's hair—upon the fleecy folds of her gossamer vail—upon the sheen of her bridal robe; the little satin shoe peeps in and out from under the lustrous folds, whose every rustle is music to Percy's ear.

Hark! Fanny's lip loses its rose—as she clings, tremblingly, to Percy's arm. A scuffle—curses—shouting—the report of a pistol—then a heavy fall—then a low groan!

"Is he quite dead? Does his pulse beat?"

"Not a flutter," said the policeman, laying the man's head back upon the church steps.

"How did it happen?"

"Well, you see, he was intoxicated like, and 'sisted upon coming in here, to see the wedding, though I told him it was a private 'un. Then he muttered something about jail-birds and the like 'o that—intending to insinivate something ag'in me, I s'pose. Well, I took him by the shoulder to carry him to the station-house, and in the scuffle, a loaded pistol he had about him went off; and that's the end of him. His name is in his hat, there. 'John Scraggs.' A ruffianly-looking dog he is, too; the world is none the worse, I fancy, for his being out of it."

As at the birth, so at the bridal, Life and Death passed each other on the threshold; new-born love to its full fruition; the still corpse to its long home.

There are homes in which Love folds his wings contented forever to stay. Such a home had Fanny and Percy.

"The love born of sorrow, like sorrow is true."

MORAL MOLASSES;
OR, TOO SWEET BY HALF.

The most thorough emetic I know of, is in the shape of "Guide to Young Wives," and kindred books; as if one rule could, by any possibility, apply to all persons; as if every man living did not require different management (bless me, I did not intend to use that torpedo word, but it is out now); as if, when things go wrong, a wife had only to fly up stairs, read a chapter in the "Young Wife's Guide," supposed to be suited to her complaint, and then go down stairs and apply the worthless plaster to the matrimonial sore. Pshaw! as well might a doctor send a peck of pills into a hospital, to be distributed by the hands of the nurse, to any and every male patient brought there, without regard to complaints or constitutional tendencies. I have no patience with such matrimonial nostrums.

"Always meet your husband with a smile." That is one of them. Suppose we put the boot on the other foot, and require the men to come grinning home? no matter how many of their notes may have been protested; no matter how, like Beelzebub, their business partner may have tormented them; no matter how badly elections go—when they do it, may I be there to see! Nor should they. Passing over the everlasting monotony of that everlasting "Guide Book" smile, let us consider, brethren (sisters not admitted), what matrimony was intended for. As I look at it, as much to share each other's sorrows, as to share each other's joys; neither of the twain to shoulder wholly the one or the other. Those of you, brethren, who agree with me in this lucid view of the subject, please to signify it by rising.

'Tis a vote.

Well then, do people in moments of perplexity generally grin? Is it not asking too much of female, and a confounded sight too much of male nature, to do it when a man's store burns down, and there is no insurance? or when a misguided and infatuated baby stuffs beans up its nose, while its mamma is putting new cuffs on her husband's coat, hearing Katy say her lesson, and telling the cook about dinner? And when this sorely afflicted couple meet, would it not be best to make a clean breast of their troubles, sympathize together over them, have a nice matrimonial cry on each other's shoulders, and wind up with a first-class kiss?

'Tis a vote.

Well then—to the mischief with your grinning over a volcano;—erupt, and have done with it! so shall you love each other more for your very sorrows; so shall you avoid hypocrisy and kindred bedevilments, and pull evenly in the matrimonial harness. I speak as unto wise men.

Lastly, brethren, what I particularly admire, is the indirect compliment to your sex, which this absurd rule I have quoted implies; the devotion, magnanimity, fortitude, and courage, it gives you fair-weather sailors credit for! But what is the use of talking about it? These guide books are mainly written by sentimental old maids; who, had they ever been within kissing distance of a beard, would not so abominably have wasted pen, ink, and paper; or, by some old bachelor, tip-toeing on the outskirts of the promised land, without a single clear idea of its resources and requirements, or courage enough to settle there if he had.

A WORD TO SHOP-KEEPERS.

In one respect—nay, in more, if so please you—I am unfeminine. I detest shopping. I feel any thing but affection for Eve every time I am forced to do it. But we must be clean and whole, even in this dirt-begrimed, lawless city; where ash-barrels and ash-boxes, with spikes of protruding nails for the unwary, stand on every sidewalk, waiting the bidding of balmy zephyrs to sift their dusky contents on our luckless clothes. All the better for shop-keepers; indeed, I am not at all sure, that they and the street-cleaning gentry do not, as doctors and druggists are said to do, play into each other's hands!

Apart from my natural and never-to-be-uprooted dislike to the little feminine recreation of shopping, is the pain I experience whenever I am forced to take part in it, at the snubbing system practiced by too many shop-keepers toward those whose necessities demand a frugal outlay. Any frivolous female fool, be she showily dressed, may turn a whole storefull of goods topsy-turvy at her capricious will, although she may end in taking nothing away but her own idiotic presence; while a poor, industrious woman, with the hardly-earned dollar in her calico pocket, may not presume to deliberate, or to differ from the clerk as to its most frugal investment. My blood often boils as I stand side by side with such a one. I, by virtue of better apparel, receiving respectful treatment; she— crimsoning with shame, like some guilty thing, at the rude reply.

Now, gentlemen, imagine yourselves in this woman's place. I have no need to do so, because I have stood there. Imagine her, with her fatherless, hungry children by her side, plying the needle late into the night, for the pitiful sum of seventy-five cents a week, as I once did. Imagine her, with this discouraging price of her eye-sight and strength, creeping forth with her little child by the hand, peeping cautiously through the glass windows of stores, to decide unobtrusively upon fabrics and labeled prices, or vainly trying to read human feeling enough in their owners' faces to insure her from contemptuous insult at the smallness and cheapness of her contemplated purchase. At length, with many misgivings, she glides in amid rustling silks and laces, that drape hearts which God made womanly and tender like her own, but which Fashion and Mammon have crushed to ashes in their vice-like clasp; hearts which never knew a sorrow greater than a misfitting dress, or a badly-matched ribbon, and whose owners' lips curl as the new-comer holds thoughtfully between her thin fingers the despised fabric, carelessly tossed at her by the impatient clerk.

Oh, how can you speak harshly to such a one? how can you drive the blood from her lip, and bring the tear to her eye? how can you look sneeringly at the little sum she places in your hand, so hardly, virtuously, bravely earned? She has seen you!—see her, as she turns away, clasping so tightly that little hand in hers, that the pained child would tearfully ask the reason, were it not prematurely sorrow-trained.

Oh, you have never (reversing the order of nature) leaned with a breaking heart, upon a little child, for the comfort and sympathy that you found nowhere else in the wide world beside. You never wound your arms about her in the silent night, drenching brow, cheek and lip with your tears, as you prayed God, in your wild despair, dearly as you loved her, to take her to himself; for, living, she, too, must drink of the cup that might not pass away from your sorrow-steeped lips.

It is because I have felt all this that I venture to bespeak your more courteous treatment for these unfortunates who can only weep for themselves.

A MUCH-NEEDED KIND OF MINISTER'S WIFE;
OR, A HAIR-BREADTH ESCAPE FOR SOME PARISH.

I once had a narrow escape from being a minster's wife. No wonder you laugh. Imagine a vestry-meeting called to decide upon the width of my bonnet-strings, or the proper altitude of the bow on that bonnet's side. Imagine my being called to an account for asking Mrs. A. to tea, without including the rest of the alphabet. Imagine my parishioners expecting me to attend a meeting of the Dorcas Society in the morning, the Tract Society in the afternoon, and the Foreign Mission Society in the evening, five days in the week—and make parish calls on the sixth— besides keeping the buttons on my husband's shirts, and taking care of my "nine children, and one at the breast." Imagine a self-constituted committee of female Paul Prys running their arms up to the elbows in my pickle-jar—rummaging my cupboards—cross-questioning my maid-of-all-work, and catechizing my grocer as to the price I paid for tea. Imagine my ministerial progeny prohibited chess and checkers by the united voice of the parish. Christopher!

Still, the world lost a great deal by my non-acceptance of that "call." What would I have done? I would not, on Saturday afternoon (that holiday which should never, on any pretext, be wrested from our over-schooled, over-taught, children), have put the finishing touch to the crook in their poor little spines, by drumming them all into a Juvenile Sewing Society, to stitch pinafores for the Kankaroo heathen. What would I have done? I would have ate, drunk, slept, and laughed, like any other decent man's wife. I would have educated my children as do other men's wives, to suit myself, which would have been to turn them out to grass till they were seven years old, before which time no child, in my opinion, should ever see the inside of a school-room; and after that, given them study in homœopathic, and exercise in allopathic quantities. I would have taken the liberty, as do other men's wives, when family duties demanded it, to send word to morning callers that I "was engaged." I should have taken a walk on Sunday, if my health required it, without asking leave of the deacons of my parish. I would have gone into my husband's study, every Saturday night, and crossed out every line in his forthcoming sermon, after "sixthly." I would have encouraged a glorious beard on my husband's sacerdotal chin, not under the cowardly plea of a preventive to a possible bronchitis, but because a minister's wife has as much right to a good-looking husband as a lay-woman. I would have invited all the children in my parish to drink tea with me once a week, to play hunt the slipper, and make molasses candy; and I would have made them each a rag-baby to look at, while their well-meaning, but infatuated Sunday-school teachers, were bothering their brains with the doctrine of election. That's what I would have done.

PARENT AND CHILD;
OR, WHICH SHALL RULE.

"Give me two cents, I say, or I'll kick you!"

I turned to look at the threatener. It was a little fellow about as tall as my sun-shade, stamping defiance at a fine, matronly-looking woman, who must have been his mother, so like were her large black eyes to the gleaming orbs of the boy. "Give me two cents, I say, or I'll kick you," he repeated, tugging fiercely at her silk dress to find the pocket, while every feature in his handsome face was distorted with passion. Surely she will not do it, said I to myself, anxiously awaiting the issue, as I apparently examined some ribbons in a shop-window; surely she will not be so mad, so foolish, so untrue to herself, so untrue to her child, so belie the beautiful picture of healthy maternity, so God-impressed in that finely-developed form and animated face. Oh, if I might speak to her, and beg her not to do it, thought I, as she put her hand in her pocket, and the fierce look died away on the boy's face, and was succeeded by one of triumph; if I might tell her that she is fostering the noisome weeds that will surely choke the flowers—sowing the wind to reap the whirlwind.

"But the boy is so passionate; it is less trouble to grant his request than to deny him." Granting this were so; who gave you a right to weigh your own ease in the balance with your child's soul? Who gave you a right to educate him for a convict's cell, or the gallows? But, thoughtless, weakly indulgent, cruel-kind mother, it is not easier, as you selfishly, short-sightedly reason, to grant his request than to deny it; not easier for him—not easier for you. The appetite for rule grows by what it feeds on. Is he less domineering now than he was yesterday? Will he be less so to-morrow than he is to-day? Certainly not.

"But I have not time to contest every inch of ground with him." Take time then—make time; neglect every thing else, but neglect not that. With every child comes this turning point: Which shall be the victor—my mother or I? and it must be met. She is no true mother who dodges or evades it. True—there will be a fierce struggle at first; but be firm as a rock; recede not one inch; there may be two, three, or even more, but the battle once won, as won it shall be if you are a faithful mother, it is won for this world—ay, perhaps for another.

"But I am not at liberty to control him thus; when parents do not pull together in the harness, the reins of government will slacken; when I would restrain and correct him, his father interferes; children are quick-witted, and my boy sees his advantage. What can I do, unsustained and single-handed?" True—true—God help the child then. Better for him had he never been born; better for you both, for so surely as the beard grows upon that little chin, so surely shall he bring your gray hairs with sorrow to the grave; and so surely shall he curse you for your very indulgence, before he is placed in the dishonored one your parental hands are digging for him.

These things need not be—ought not to be. Oh! if parents had but a firm hand to govern, and yet a ready ear for childish sympathy; if they would agree—whatever they might say in private—never to differ in presence of their children, as to their government; if the dissension-breeding "Joseph's coat" were banished from every hearthstone; if there were less weak indulgence and less asceticism; if the bow were neither entirely relaxed, nor strained so tightly that it broke; if there were less out-door dissipation, and more home-pleasures; if parents would not forget that they were once children, nor, on the other hand, forget that their children will be one day parents; if there were less form of godliness, and more godliness (for children are Argus-eyed; it is not what you preach, but what you practice), we should then have no beardless skeptics, no dissolute sons, no runaway marriages, no icy barriers between those rocked in the same cradle—nursed at the same breast.

THE LAST BACHELOR HOURS OF TOM PAX.

To-morrow, at eleven, then, I am to be married! I feel like a mouse conscious of coming cheese. Is it usual for bachelors to feel this way, or am I a peculiar institution? I trust the parson, being himself a married man, will be discreet enough to make a short prayer after the ceremony. Good gracious, my watch has stopped! no it hasn't, either; I should like to put the hands forward a little. What to do with myself till the time comes, that's the question. It is useless to go over to Mary's—she is knee-deep in dressmaker's traps. I never could see, when one dress is sufficient to be married in, the need women have to multiply them to such an indefinite extent. Think of postponing a man's happiness in such circumstances, that one more flounce may be added to a dress! Phew! how stifled this room is! I'll throw up the window; there now—there goes a pane of glass; who cares? I think I will shave; no I won't—I should be sure to cut my chin—how my hand trembles. I wonder what Mary is thinking about? bless her little soul. Well, for the life of me I don't know what to do with myself. Suppose I write down

TOM PAX'S LAST BACHELOR WILL AND TESTAMENT.

In the name of Cupid, Amen.—I, Tom Pax, being of sound mind, and in immediate prospect of matrimony (praised be Providence for the same), and being desirous of settling my worldly affairs while I have the strength and capacity to do so, I do, with my own hand, write, make, and publish this, my last Will and Testament:

And in the first place, and principally, I commit my heart to the keeping of my adorable Mary, and my body to the parson, to be delivered over at the discretion of my groomsmen, to the aforesaid Mary; and as to such worldly goods as a kind Providence hath seen fit to intrust me with, I dispose of the same in the following manner (I also empower my executors to sell and dispose of my real estate, consisting of empty demijohns, old hats, and cigar boxes, and invest the proceeds in stocks or otherwise, to manage as they may think best; all of which is left to their discretion):

I give and bequeath to Tom Harris, my accomplice in single blessedness, my porcelain punch-bowl, white cotton night-cap, and large leathern chair, in whose arms I first renounced bachelordom and all its evil works.

I give and bequeath to the flames the yellow-covered novels and plays formerly used to alleviate my bachelor pangs, and whose attractions fade away before the scorching sun of my prospective happiness, like a snow wreath between a pair of brass andirons.

I give and bequeath to Bridget Donahue, the chambermaid of this lodging-house (to be applied to stuffing a pin-cushion), the locks of female hair, black, chestnut, brown, and tow-color, to be found in my great coat breast pocket.

I give and bequeath to my washwoman, Sally Mudge, my buttonless shirts, stringless dickeys, gossamer-ventilator stockings, and unmended gloves.

I give and bequeath to Denis M'Fudge, my bootblack, my half box of unsmoked Havanas, which are a nuisance in my hymeneal nostrils.

I give and bequeath to my benighted and unconverted bachelor friend, Sam Scott, my miserable and sinful piejudices against the blessed institution of matrimony, and may Cupid, of his infinite loving-kindness, take pity on his petrified heart.

In witness whereof, I, Tom Pax, the Testator, hereunto set my hand and seal, as my last Will and Testament, done this twelfth day of January, in the year of our Lord one thousand eight hundred and fifty-six.

TOM PAX. [L.S.]

Witness,FANNY FERN.

TOM PAX'S CONJUGAL SOLILOQUY.

Mrs. Pax is an authoress. I knew it when I married her. I liked the idea. I had not tried it then. I had not a clear idea what it was to have one's wife belong to the public. I thought marriage was marriage, brains not excepted. I was mistaken. Mrs. Pax is very kind: I don't wish to say that she is not. Very obliging: I would not have you think the contrary; but when I put my arm round Mrs. Pax's waist, and say, "Mary, I love you," she smiles in an absent, moonlight-kind of a way, and says, "Yes, to-day is Wednesday, is it not? I must write an article for 'The Weekly Monopolizer' to-day." That dampens my ardor; but presently I say again, being naturally affectionate, "Mary, I love you;" she replies (still abstractedly), "Thank you, how do you think it will do to call my next article for 'The Weekly Monopolizer,' 'The Stray Waif?'"

Mrs. Pax sews on all my shirt-buttons with the greatest good humor: I would not have you think she does not; but with her thoughts still on "The Weekly Monopolizer," she sews them on the flaps, instead of the wristbands. This is inconvenient; still Mrs. Pax is kindness itself; I make no complaint.

I am very fond of walking. After dinner I say to Mrs. Pax, "Mary, let us take a walk." She says, "Yes, certainly, I must go down town to read the proof of my article for 'The Monopolizer.'" So, I go down town with Mrs. Pax. After tea I say, "Mary, let us go to the theater to-night;" she says, "I would be very happy to go, but the atmosphere is so bad there, the gas always escapes, and my head must be clear to-morrow, you know, for I have to write the last chapter of my forthcoming work, 'Prairie Life.'" So I stay at home with Mrs. Pax, and as I sit down by her on the sofa, and as nobody comes in, I think that this, after all, is better, (though I must say my wife looks well at the Opera, and I like to take her there). I put my arm around Mrs. Pax. It is a habit I have. In comes the servant; and brings a handful of letters for her by mail, directed to "Julia Jesamine!" (that's my wife's nom-de-plume). I remove my arm from her waist, because she says "they are probably business letters which require immediate notice." She sits down at the table, and breaks the seals. Four of them are from fellows who want "her autograph." Mrs. Pax's autograph! The fifth is from a gentleman who, delighted with her last book, which he says "mirrored his own soul" (how do you suppose Mrs. Pax found out how to "mirror his soul?") requests "permission to correspond with the charming authoress." "Charming!" my wife! "his soul!" Mrs. Pax! The sixth is from a gentleman who desires "the loan of five hundred dollars, as he has been unfortunate in business, and has heard that her works have been very remunerative." Five hundred dollars for John Smith, from my wife! The seventh letter is from a man at the West, offering her her own price to deliver a lecture before the Pigtown Young Men's Institute. I like that!

Mrs. Pax opens her writing desk; it is one I gave her; takes some delicate buff note-paper; I gave her that, too; dips her gold pen (my gift) into the inkstand, and writes—writes till eleven o'clock. Eleven! and I, her husband, Tom Pax, sit there and wait for her.

The next morning when I awake, I say, "Mary dear?" She says, "Hush! don't speak, I've just got a capital subject to write about for 'The Weekly Monopolizer.'" Not that I am complaining of Mrs. Pax, not at all; not that I don't like my wife to be an authoress: I do. To be sure I can't say that I knew exactly what it involved. I did not know, for instance, that the Press in speaking of her by her nom-de-plume would call her "Our Julia," but I would not have you think I object to her being literary. On the contrary, I am not sure that I do not rather like it; but I ask the Editor of "The Weekly Monopolizer," as a man—as a Christian—as a husband—if he thinks it right—if it is doing as he would be done by—to monopolize my wife's thoughts as early as five o'clock in the morning? I merely ask for information. I trust I have no resentful feelings toward the animal.

TEA AND DARNING NEEDLES "FOR TWO!"

Not long since, John Bull, in the columns of an English newspaper, growled out his intense disgust at the "trash in the shape of American lady books," which constantly afflicted him from the other side of the Atlantic.

Here is a book called "Letters from the United States, Canada, and Cuba," by the Hon. Amelia M. Murray, a lady of supposable refinement, education, and of the highest social position in England; a lady whose daily bread was not dependent upon the immediate publication of her book; who had leisure and opportunity carefully to write, and to correct and revise what she had written.

We propose giving a few extracts to show what advance has been made upon American literature, by our aristocratic British sister. But before beginning, we wish to throw our glove in John Bull's face, and defy him to produce a greater, or even an equal amount of stupid twaddle, unrhetorical sentences, hap-hazard conclusions, petty, egotistical, uninteresting details, narrow-minded views, and utter want of talent, from between the covers of any American lady book yet published.

The political question discussed by "the Hon." authoress, we shall not meddle with further than to say, first, that her book contains not one new idea upon the subject; secondly, that her advocacy of a system which condemns a portion of her own sex to helpless, hopeless, brutal prostitution, reflects as little credit on her standard of what is lovely and of good report in woman, as does her book upon female English literature.

We quote the following specimens of Miss Murray's style:

"At the house of his sister I saw another work by the same artist: two children, the one as an angel leading the awakened soul of the other, with an inscription below; very pretty!"

Again.

Speaking of the cholera in Boston, and the practice of using hot vinegar there, as a disinfective, she says:

"I was told a carriage of this fumigated liquid had been driven through the streets; there are deaths here every day and some at Newport, but it is not believed to be contagious at present, only carrying off the profligate and the debilitated."

Again.

"Till my introduction to the Governor of New York I did not know that each State has a Governor. Governor Seymour lives at Albany. Some of those Governors are only elected for two years, and this gentleman does credit to popular choice."

So much for the Queen's English! Now for one or two specimens of her penetration. The first quotation we make will undoubtedly cause as much surprise to the very many benevolent associations in Boston (which are constantly deploring their inability to meet the voices of distress which cry, help us!), as it did to ourself:

"I never met a beggar in Boston, not even among the Irish, and ladies have told me that they could not find a family on which to exercise their benevolent feelings!"

Governor Seymour, Miss Murray's friend, will doubtless feel flattered by the following patronizing mention of him. And here we will say, that it would have been more politic in the Hon. Miss Amelia, when we consider England's late relations to Sebastopol, had she omitted to touch upon so ticklish a subject as British military discipline.

Speaking of Governor Seymour's review of the New York troops, on Evacuation Day, she says:

"Governor Seymour reviewed these troops in front of the City Hall with as much tranquillity of manner and simple dignity as might have been evinced by one of the most experienced of our public men!"

One more instance of Miss Murray's superior powers of observation:

"I have found out the reason why ladies, traveling alone in the United States, must be extravagantly dressed; without that precaution they meet with no attention, and little civility, decidedly much less than in any other country, so here it is not as women, but as ladies, they are cared for, and this in Democratic America!"

In the first place, every body but Miss Murray knows that an American lady never "travels expensively dressed." That there are females who do this, just as they walk our streets in a similar attire, and for a similar purpose, is undeniable; and that they receive from the opposite sex the "attentions" which they seek, is also true; but this, it seems to us, should hardly disturb the serenity of a "Maid of Honor!"

As an American woman, and proud of our birth-right, we resent from our British sister her imputation upon the proverbial chivalry of American gentlemen. We have traveled alone, and in threadbare garments, and we have never found these garments non-conductors of the respectful courtesy of American gentlemen; they have never prevented the coveted glass of water being proffered to our thirsty lips at the dépôt; the offer of the more eligible seat on the shady side of the cars; the offer of the beguiling newspaper, or book, or magazine; the kindly excluding of annoying dust or sun by means of obstinate blinds or windows, unmanageable by feminine fingers; the offer of camphor or cologne for headache or faintness, or one, or all, of the thousand attentions to which the chivalry of American gentlemen prompts them without regard to externals, and too often (shame on the recipients!) without the reward of the bright smile, or kindly "thank you," to which they are so surely entitled.

I could cite many instances in contradiction of Miss Murray's assertion that it is "not as women but as ladies," that American gentlemen care for the gentler sex in America. I will mention only two, out of many, which have come under my own personal observation.

Every body in New York must have noticed the decrepit old woman, with her basket of peanuts and apples, who sits on the steps near the corner of Canal-street (for how long a period the oldest inhabitant only knows). One day toward nightfall, when the execrable state of the crossings almost defied petticoat-dom, I saw her slowly gather up her decrepit limbs, and undiminished wares, and, leaning upon her stick, slowly totter homeward. She reached the point where she wished to cross; it was slippery, wet, and crowded with a Babel of carts and carriages.

She looked despondingly up and down with her faded eyes, and I was about to proffer her my assistance when a gentlemanly, handsome young man stepped to her side, and drawing her withered hand within his arm, safely guided her tottering footsteps across to the opposite sidewalk; then, with a bow, graceful and reverential enough to have satisfied even the cravings of the honorable and virginal Miss Murray, he left her. It was a holy and a beautiful sight, and by no means an uncommon one, "even in America."

Again. I was riding in an omnibus, when a woman, very unattractive in person and dress, got out, leaving a very common green vail upon the seat. A gentleman present sprang after her with it in his hand, ran two blocks, placed it in her possession, and returned to his place, not having received even a bow of thanks from the woman in whose service his nicely polished boots had been so plentifully mud-bespattered.

If "the honorable Miss Murray" came to this country with the expectation that a coach-and-six would be on hand to convey her from every dépôt to the hotel she was to honor with her aristocratic presence, or that gentlemen would remain with their heads uncovered, and their hands on the left side of their vests as she passed, in honor of the reflected effulgence of England's Queen (supposed to emanate from Miss Murray's very ordinary person), it is no marvel she was disappointed. We should like to be as sure, when we travel in England, of being (as a woman), as well and as courteously treated by John Bull as was the honorable Miss Amelia by Brother Jonathan in America.

That there may be men, "even in America," who measure out their nods, and bows, and wreathed smiles, by the wealth and position of the recipient, we do not doubt; for we have seen such, but would gently suggest to "the honorable Miss Amelia" that in the pockets of such men she will generally find—naturalization papers!

A HOUSE WITHOUT A BABY.

There was not a child in the house, not one; I was sure of it, when I first went in. Such a spick-and-span look as it had! Chairs—grown-up chairs, plastered straight up against the wall; books arranged by rule and compass; no dear little careless finger-marks on furniture, doors, or window-glass; no hoop, or ball, or doll, or mitten, or basket, or picture-book on the premises; not a pin, or a shred on the angles and squares of the immaculate carpet; the tassels of the window shades, at which baby-fingers always make such a dead set, as fresh as if just from the upholsterer's. I sat down at the well-polished window, and looked across the street. At the upper window of a wooden house opposite, I saw a little bald baby, tied into a high chair, speculating upon the panorama in the street, while its little fat hands frantically essayed to grab distant pedestrians on the sidewalk. Its mother sat sewing diligently by its side. Happy woman! she has a baby! She thought so, too; for by-and-by she threw down her work, untied the fettering handkerchief, took the child from its prison-house, and covered it with kisses. Ah! she had heard a step upon the stairs—thestep! And now there are two to kiss the baby; for John has come to his dinner, and giving both mother and child a kiss that made my lips work, he tosses the babe up in his strong arms, while its mother puts dinner on the table.

But, pshaw!—here come the old maids I was sent to see. I hear the rustle of their well-preserved silks in the entry. I feel proper all over. Vinegar and icicles! how shall I ever get through with it? Now the door opens. What a bloodless look they have?—how dictionary-ish they speak!—how carefully they lower themselves into their chairs, as if the cushions were stuffed with live kittens!—how smooth their ruffs and ribbons!

Bibs and pinafores! Give me the upper room in the wooden house, with kissing John and the bald baby!

GLANCES AT PHILADELPHIA.
NUMBER ONE.

And this is Philadelphia! All hail, Philadelphia! Where a lady's aching fingers may be reprieved from the New York thraldom of skirt-holding off dirty pavements; where the women have the good taste, in dress, to eschew the gaudy tulip and array themselves like the lily; where hoops are unknown, or at least so modified as to become debateable ground; where lady shop-keepers know how to be civil to their own sex, and do not keep you standing on one leg an hour after you hand them a bill, while with hawk eye and extended forefinger they peruse that nuisance called the "Counterfeit Detector." Where the goods, not better than in New York, save in their more quiet hue, are never crammed down a customer's unwilling throat; where omnibus-drivers do not expectorate into the coach-windows, or bang clouds of dust into your doomed eyes from the roof, thumping for your fare, or start their vehicles before female feet have taken leave of what has nearly proved to so many of us the finalstep! where the markets—but hold! they deserve a paragraph by themselves.

Ye gods! what butter! Shall I ever again swallow the abominable concoction called butter in New York? That I—Fanny Fern—should have lived to this time, and never known the bliss of tasting Philadelphia butter!—never seen those golden pounds, each separately folded in its fresh green leaf, reposing so temptingly, and crying, Eat me, so eloquently, from the snow-white tubs! What have the Philadelphians done that they should be fed on such crisp vegetables, such fresh fruits, and such creamy ice-creams? That their fish should come dripping to their mouths from their native element. That their meat should wait to be carried home, instead of crawling by itself? Why should the most circumscribed and frugal of housekeepers, who goes with her snowy basket to buy her husband's dinner, be able to daintyfy his table with a fragrant sixpenny bouquet? Why should the strawberries be so big, and dewy, and luscious? Why should the peas, and cauliflowers, and asparagus, and lettuce—Great Cæsar! what have the Philadelphians done that they should wallow in such high-stepping clover?

I have it!

It is the reward of virtue—It is the smile of Heaven on men who are too chivalric to puff tobacco-smoke in ladies' faces which beautify and brighten their streets. They deserve it—they deserve their lily-appareled wives and roly-poly, kissable, sensibly-dressed children. They deserve to walk up those undefiled marble-steps, into their blessed home sanctuaries, overshadowed by those grand, patriarchal trees. They deserve that their bright-eyed sons should be educated in a noble institution like "The Central High School," where pure ventilation and cheerfulness are considered of as much importance as mathematics, or Greek and Latin. Where the placid brow and winning smile of the Principal are more potent auxiliaries than ferules or frowns. Give me the teacher on whose desk blooms the bouquet, culled by a loving pupil's fingers; whose eye, magnetic with kindness—whose voice, electric with love for his calling, wakes up into untiring action all that is best and noblest in the sympathetic, fresh young hearts before him. A human teacher, who recognizes in every boy before him (be he poorly or richly clad—be he glorious in form and face as a young Apollo, or cramped and dwarfed into unshapeliness in the narrow cradle of poverty) an immortal soul, clamorous with its craving needs, seeking the light, throwing out its luxuriant tendrils for something strong and kindly to cling to, longing for the upper air of expansion and strength. God bless the human teacher who recognizes, and acts as if he recognized this! Heaven multiply such schools as "The Philadelphia High School," with its efficient Principal, its able Professors and teachers, and its graduates who number by scores the noble and honored of the land, and of the sea.

I love to linger in cemeteries. And so, in company with an editorial friend, Colonel Fitzgerald, of the Philadelphia City Item, to whose hospitality, with that of his lovely wife, I am much indebted, I visited

"Laurel Hill." The group "Old Mortality" at its entrance needs no praise of mine. The eye might linger long ere it wearied in gazing at it. I like cemeteries, but I like not elaborate monuments, or massive iron railings; a simple hedge—a simple head-stone (where the tiny bird alights, ere, like the parting spirit, it plumes its wings for a heavenward flight) for its inscription—the words to which the universal heart has responded, and will respond till time shall be no longer—till the graves give up their dead; "Mother"—"Husband"—"Wife"—"Child"—what epitaph can improve this? what language more eloquently measure the height and breadth, and length and depth of sorrow?

And so, as I read these simple words at "Laurel Hill," my heart sympathized with those unallied to me, save by the common bond of bereavement; and thus I passed on—until I came to an author's grave— no critic's pen again to sting that heart;—pulseless it must have been, not to have stirred with all the wealth of bud and blossom, waving tree and shining river, that lay bathed in the golden, summer sunlight above him. So, God willing, would I sleep at last; but not yet—not yet, my pen, till thou hast shouted again and again—Courage! Courage!—to earth's down-trodden and weary-hearted.

GLANCES AT PHILADELPHIA.
NUMBER TWO.

If you want to see unmasked human nature, keep your eyes open in railroad cars and on steamboats. See that man now, poring over a newspaper, while he is passing through scenery where the shifting lights and shadows make pictures every instant, more beautiful than an artist ever dreamed. See that woman, who has journeyed with her four children hundreds of miles alone—as I am proud to say women may safely journey in America (if they behave themselves)—travel-stained, care-worn and weary, listening to, and answering patiently and pleasantly the thousand and one questions of childhood; distributing to them, now a cracker, now a sip of water from the cask in the corner, brushing back the hair from their flushed brows, while her own is throbbing with the pain, of which she never speaks. In yonder corner are two Irish women, each with a little red-fretted baby, in the universal Erin uniform of yellow; their little heads bobbing helplessly about in the bumping cars, screaming lustily for the comfort they well know is close at hand, and which the public are notified they have at last found, by a ludicrously instantaneous suspension of their vociferous cries. Beautiful as bountiful provision of Nature! which, if there was no other proof of a God, would suffice for me.

There is a surly old fellow, who won't have the windows open, though the pale woman beside him mutely entreats it, with her smelling-salts to her nose. Yonder is an old bachelor, listening to a sweet little blue-eyed girl, who, with untasked faith in human nature, has crept from her mother's side, and selected him for an audience, to say—"that once there was a kid, with two little totty kids, and don't you believe that one night when the old mother kid was asleep," etc., etc. No wonder he stoops to kiss the little orator; no wonder he laughs at her naïve remarks; no wonder she has magnetised the watch from his pocket "to hear what it says;" no wonder he smooths back the curly locks from the frank, white brow; no wonder he presses again and again his bachelor lips to that rosy little mouth; no wonder, when the distant city nears us, and the lisping "good-by" is chirruped, and the little feet are out of sight and sound, that he sighs,—God and his own soul know why! Blessed childhood—thy shortest life, though but a span, hath yet its mission. The tiniest babe never laid its velvet cheek on the sod till it had delivered its Maker's message—heeded not then, perhaps—but coming to the wakeful ear in the silent night-watch, long after the little preacher was dust. Blessed childhood!

It is funny, as well as edifying, to watch hotel arrivals; to see the dusty, hungry, lack-luster-eyed travelers drag into the eating-room—take their allotted seats—enviously regard those consumers of dainties who have already had the good fortune, by rank of precedence, to get their hungry mouths filled; to see them at last "fall to," as Americans only know how. Heaven help the landlord! Beef-steak, chicken, omelette, mutton-chops, biscuit and coffee—at one fell swoop. Waiters, who it is to be hoped, have not been kept breakfastless since early daylight, looking on calm, but disgusted. Now, their appetites appeased, that respectable family yonder begin to notice that Mr. and Mrs. Fitzsnooks and Miss Fitzsnooks opposite, who are aristocratically delicate in their appetites, are shocked beyond the power of expression. They begin, as they wipe their satisfied lips with their table-napkins, and contemplate Miss Fitzsnooks's showy breakfast-robe, to bethink them of their dusty traveling-dresses; as if—foolish creatures—they were not in infinitely better taste, soiled as they are, than her gaudy finery at so early an hour—as if a man was not a man "for a' that"—ay, and a woman, too—as if there could be vulgarity without pretension—as if the greatest vulgarity was not ostentatious pretension.

"Fairmount," of which the Philadelphians are so justly proud, is no misnomer. He must be cynical, indeed, hopelessly weak in the understanding, who would grumble at the steep ascent by means of which so lovely a panorama is enjoyed. At every step some new beauty develops itself to the worshiper of nature. In the gray old rocks, festooned with the vivid green of the woodbine and ivy, considerately draping statues for eyes—I confess it, more prudish than mine. The placid Schuylkill flowing calmly below, with its emerald-fringed banks, nesting the homes of wealth and luxury; enjoyed less, perhaps, by their owners, than by the industrious artisan, who, reprieved from his day's toil, stands gazing at them with his wife and children, and inhaling the breeze, of which, God be thanked, the rich man has no monopoly.

Of course I visited Philadelphia "State-House;" of course I talked with the nice old gentleman who guards the country's relics; of course I stared —with my '76 blood at fever heat—upon the big bell which clanged forth so joyfully our American independence; of course I stared at the piece of stone-step, from which the news of our Independence was first announced; and of course I wondered how it was possible for it, under such circumstances, to remain stone. Of course I sat down in the venerable, high-backed leather chair, in which so many great men of that time, and so many little men of this have reposed. Of course I reverently touched the piece of a pew which formerly was part of "Christ Church," and in which Franklin and Washington had worshiped. Of course I inscribed my name, at the nice old gentleman's request, in the mammoth book for visitors. And of course I mounted to the Cupola of the State House to see "the view;" which, with due submission, I did not think worth (from that point) the strain on my ankles, or the confused state of my cranium, consequent upon repeated losses of my latitude and longitude, while pursuing my stifled and winding way.

"The Mint?" Oh—certainly, I saw the Mint! and wondered, as I looked at the shining heaps, that any of Uncle Sam's children should ever want a cent; also, I wondered if the workmen who fingered them, did not grow, by familiarity, indifferent to their value—and to their possession. I was told that not the minutest particle of the metal, whether fused or otherwise, could be abstracted without detection. I was glad, as I always am, in a fitting establishment, to see women employed in various offices —such as stamping the coin, etc., and more glad still, to learn that they had respectable wages. Heaven speed the time when a thousand other doors of virtuous labor shall be opened to them, and silence for ever the heart-rending "Song of the Shirt."

GLANCES AT PHILADELPHIA.
NUMBER THREE.

Always an if! If the Philadelphians would not barricade their pretty houses with those ugly wooden outside shutters, with those ugly iron hinges. I am sure my gypsy breath would draw hard behind one. And if the Philadelphians would not build such garrison-like walls about their beautiful gardens. Why not allow the passer-by to view what would give so much pleasure? certainly, we would hope, without abstracting any from the proprietors. Clinton avenue, as well as other streets in Brooklyn, is a beautiful example of this. Light, low iron railings about the well-kept lawns and gardens—sunset groups of families upon piazzas, and O—prettier yet—little children darting about like butterflies among the flowers. I missed this in Philadelphia. The balmy air of evening seemed only the signal for barring up each family securely within those jail-like shutters; behind which, I am sure, beat hearts as warm and friendly as any stranger could wish to meet, I must say I feel grateful to any householder who philanthropically refreshes the public eye with the vines and flowers he has wreathed about his home. I feel grateful to any woman I meet, who rests my rainbow-sated eye by a modest, tasteful costume. I thank every well-made man who passes me with well-knit limbs and expanded chest, encased in nice linen, and a coat he can breathe in; yes—why not? Do you purse up your mouth at this? do you say it was not proper for me to have said this? I hate the word proper. If you tell me a thing is not proper, I immediately feel the most rabid desire to go "neck and heels" into it. Proper! it is a fence behind which indelicacy is found hidden much oftener than in the open highway. Out upon proper! So I say again, I like to see a well-made man—made—not by the tailor—but by the Almighty. I glory in his luxuriant beard; in his firm step; in his deep, rich voice; in his bright, falcon eye. I thank him for being handsome, and letting me see him. We all yearn for the beautiful; the little child, who drew its first breath in a miserable cellar, and has known no better home, has yet its cracked mug or pitcher, with the treasured dandelion or clover blossoms. Be generous, ye householders, who have the means to gratify a taste to which God himself ministers, and hoard not your gardens and flowers for the palled eye of satiety. Let the little child, who, God knows, has few flowers enough in its earthly pathway, peep through the railing, and, if only for a brief moment, dream of paradise.

The Philadelphia Opera House, which I am told is a very fine one, I did not see, as I intended, as also many institutions which I hope yet to visit, when I can make a longer stay. Of one of the principal theaters I will say, that she must be a courageous woman who would dare to lean back against its poisonously dirty cushions. Ten minutes sufficed me to breathe an atmosphere that would have disgraced the "Five Points;" and to listen to tragic howlings only equaled in the drunken brawls of that locality. Upon my exit, I looked with new surprise upon the first pair of immaculate marble steps I encountered, and putting this and that together, gave up the vexed problem. New York streets may be dirty, but our places of amusement are clean.

At one public institution I visited, we were shown about by the most dignified and respectable of gray-haired old men; so much so, that I felt serious compunctions lest I should give trouble by asking questions which agitated my very inquiring mind. Bowing an adieu to him, with the reverence with which his appearance had inspired me, we were about to pass down the principal stairs to the main entrance, when he touched the gentleman who accompanied me on the shoulder, and said in an undertone, not intended for my ears, "Please don't offer me money, sir, in the presence of any one!" A minute after he had pocketed, with a bow, the neatly-extracted coin (which I should as soon have thought of offering to General Washington), and with a parting touch of his warning forefinger to his lip, intended for my companion, we found ourselves outside the building, doing justice to his generalship by explosive bursts of laughter. So finished was the performance, that we admiringly agreed to withhold the name of the venerable perpetrator.

We found the very best accommodations at the hotel where we were located, both as to the fare and attendance. I sent a dress to the laundry-room for a little re-touching, rendered necessary by my ride the day before. On ringing for its return, the summons was answered by a grenadier-looking fellow, with a world of whisker, who, as I opened the door, stood holding the gauzy nondescript at arm's length, between his thumb and finger, as he inquired of me, "Is this the item, mem?" Item! Had he searched the dictionary through, he could not have better hit it—or me. I have felt a contempt for the dress ever since.

Having had the misfortune to set the pitcher in my room down upon vacancy, instead of upon the wash-stand, and the natural consequence thereof being a crash and a flood, I reported the same, lest the chambermaid should suffer for my careless act. Of course, I found it charged in my bill, as I had intended, but with it the whole cost of the set to which it belonged! It never struck me, till I got home, that by right of proprietorship, I might have indulged in the little luxury of smashing the remainder—which I think of taking a special journey to Philadelphia to do!

GLANCES AT PHILADELPHIA.
NUMBER FOUR.

I wonder—I suppose a body may wonder—if the outward sweeping and garnishing one sees in Philadelphia is symbolical of its inward purity? If the calm placidity of its inhabitants covers up smoldering volcanoes? It is none of my business, as you say; for all that, the old proverb—"Still waters run deepest"—would occur to me, as I walked those lovely streets. An eye-witness to the constant verification of this truth, in the white-washed, saintly atmosphere of the city of Boston, may certainly be forgiven a doubt. Do the Philadelphia churches, like theirs, contain a sprinkling of those meek-faced Pharisees, who weary Heaven with their long prayers, and in the next breath blast their neighbor's character; who contribute large sums to be heard of men, and frown away from their doors their poverty-stricken relatives? Do those nun-like Philadelphia women ever gossip, "Caudle lecture" and pout? Do those correct-looking men know the taste of champagne, and have they latch-keys? Are their Quaker habits pulled off, when they come "on business" to this seething Sodom? Or—is it true of them, as Mackay says of Lady Jane—

"Her pulse is calm—milk-white her skin,She hath not blood enough to sin."

It is none of my business, as you say; but still I know that white raiment is worn alike by the rosy bride and the livid corpse.

Mischief take these microscopic spectacles of mine! mounted on my nose by the hypocrites I have known, who glide ever between my outstretched arms of love and those whom I would enfold. Avaunt! I like Philadelphia, and I like the Philadelphians, and I will believe in appearances once more before I die.

Like a cabinet picture in my memory, is lovely "Wissahickon;" with its tree-crowned summits—its velvety, star-blossomed mosses; its feathery ferns, and its sweet-breath'd wild flowers. If any one thinks an editor is not agreeable out of harness, let him enjoy it, as I did, with Mr. Fry of "The New York Tribune," whose early love it was in boyhood. In such an Eden, listening to the low whisper of the shivering trees, the dreamy ripple of the wave, and the subdued hum of insect life—well might the delicate artistic ear of song be attuned.

But "Wissahickon" boasts other lions than Fry—in the shape (if I may use a Hibernicism) of a couple of live bears—black, soft, round, treacherous, and catty; to be gazed upon at a distance, spite of their chains; to shiver at, spite of their owner's assurance, as they came as far as their limits through the trees to look at us, "that they wouldn't do nothing to nobody." It would be a speculation for some Broadway druggist to buy that one who stood upon his hind legs, and taking a bottle of Sarsaparilla Soda in his trained fore-paws, drained it standing with the gusto of a connoisseur.

Not one beggar did I see in Philadelphia. After witnessing the squalor which contrasts so painfully with New York luxury and extravagance, this was an untold relief.

Philadelphia, too, has what we so much need here—comfortable, cleanly, convenient, small houses for mechanics; comprising the not-to-be-computed luxury of a bath-room, and gas, at the attainable rent of seventy-five or a hundred dollars a year. No house ever yet was built, broad enough, wide enough, and high enough, to contain two families. Wars will arise over the disputed territory of front and back stairs, which lawless childhood—bless its trustful nature—will persist in believing common ground. But apart from the cozy pleasure of having a little snuggery of one's own—where one may cry, or laugh, or sneeze, without asking leave—this subject in its moral aspect is well worth the attention of humane New York capitalists—and I trust we have such.

IN THE DUMPS.

What does ail me? I'm as blue as indigo. Last night I was as gay as a bob-o'-link—perhaps that is the reason. Good gracious, hear that wind howl! Now low—now high—till it fairly shrieks; it excites me like the pained cry of a human. There's my pretty California flower—blue as a baby's eyes; all shut up—no wonder—I wish my eyes were shut up, too. What does ail me? I think it is that dose of a Boston paper I have just been reading (for want of something better to do), whose book critic calls "Jane Eyre" an "immoral book." Donkey! It is vain to hope that his life has been as pure and self-sacrificing as that of "Charlotte Bronte." There's the breakfast-bell—and there's Tom with that autumn-leaf colored vest on, that I so hate. Why don't men wear pretty vests? why can't they leave off those detestable stiff collars, stocks, and things, that make them all look like choked chickens, and which hide so many handsomely-turned throats, that a body never sees, unless a body is married, or unless a body happens to see a body's brothers while they are shaving. Talk of women's throats—you ought to see a whiskered throat I saw once——Gracious, how blue I am! Do you suppose it is the weather? I wish the sun would shine out and try me. See the inch-worms on that tree. That's because it is a pet of mine. Every thing I like goes just that way. If I have a nice easy dress that I can sneeze in, it is sure to wear out and leave me to the crucifying alternative of squeezing myself into one that is not broke into my figure. I hate new gowns—I hate new shoes—I hate new bonnets—I hate any thing new except new —spapers, and I was born reading them.

There's a lame boy—now why couldn't that boy have been straight? There's a rooster driving round a harem of hens; what do the foolish things run for? If they didn't run, he couldn't chase them—of course not. Now it's beginning to rain; every drop perforates my heart. I could cry tears enough to float a ship. Why need it rain?—patter—patter—skies as dull as lead—trees nestling up to each other in shivering sympathy; and that old cow—I hate cows—they always make a dive at me—I suppose it is because they are females; that old cow stands stock still, looking at that pump-handle just where, and as she did, when I went to bed last night. Do you suppose that a cow's tail ever gets tired lashing flies from her side; do you suppose her jaws ever ache with that eternal munching? If there is any place I like, it is a barn; I mean to go a journey this summer, not "to see Niagara"—but to see a barn. Oh, the visions I've had on haymows! oh, the tears I've shed there—oh, the golden sunlight that has streamed down on me through the chinks in the raftered roof—oh, the cheerful swallow-twitterings on the old cross-beams—oh, the cunning brown mice scampering over the floor—oh, the noble bay-horse with his flowing mane, and arching neck, and satin sides, and great human eyes. Strong as Achilles—gentle as a woman. Pshaw! women were never half so gentle to me. He never repulsed me when I laid my head against his neck for sympathy. Brute forsooth! I wish there were more such brutes. Poor Hunter—he's dead, of course, because I loved him;—the trunk-maker only knows what has become of his hide and my books. What of that? a hundred years hence and who'll care? I don't think I love any thing—or care for any thing to-day. I don't think I shall ever have any feeling again for any body or any thing. Why don't somebody turn that old rusty weather-cock, or play me a triumphant march, or bring me a dew-gemmed daisy?

There's funeral—a child's funeral! Oh—what a wretch I am! Come here —you whom I love—you who love me; closer—closer—let me twine my arms about you, and God forgive me for shutting my eyes to his sunshine.

PEEPS FROM UNDER A PARASOL.

People describe me, without saying "by your leave;" a little thought has just occurred to me that two can play at that game! I don't go about with my eyes shut—no tailor can "take a measure" quicker than I, as I pass along.

There are Drs. Chapin and Bethune, whose well-to-do appearance in this world quite neutralizes their Sunday exhortations to "set one's affections on a better." There's Greeley—but why describe the town pump? he has been handle-d enough to keep him from Rust-ing. There's that Epicurean Rip-lie, critic of the "New York Tribune;" if I have spelt his name wrong, it was because I was thinking of the unmitigated fibs he has told in his book reviews! There's Colonel Fuller, editor of the "New York Evening Mirror," handsome, witty, and saucy. There's Mr. Young, editor of "The Albion," who looks too much like a gentlemen to have abused, in so wholesale a manner, the lady writers of America. There's Blank-Blank, Esq., editor of the "New York Blank," who always reminds me of what the Scotch parson said to his wife, whom he noticed asleep in church: "Jennie! Jennie! you have no beauty, as all the congregation may see, and if you have no grace, I have made but a poor bargain of it!" There's Richard Storrs Willis, or, Storrs Richard Willis, or, Willis Richard Storrs (it is a way that family have to keep changing their names), editor of the "Musical World," not a bad paper either. Richard has a fine profile, a trim, tight figure, always unexceptionably arrayed, and has a gravity of mien most edifying to one who has eat bread and molasses out of the same plate with him.

Behind that beard coming down street in that night-gown overcoat, is Mr. Charles A. Dana, of the "New York Tribune," who is ready to say, "Now lettest thou thy servant depart in peace," when he shall have made the "New York Tribune" like unto the "London Times;" Charles should remember that the motto of the "London Times" is "Fair Play"—not the appearance of fair play. And here is Philander Doesticks, of the "New York Picayune," and "New York Tribune," a delightful specimen of healthy manhood, in a day whose boys at sixteen look as though they had exhausted life; may his wit continue as keen as his eyes, his heart as fresh as his complexion, and his fancy as luxuriant as his beard. There's Bayard Taylor, "the Oriental Bayard." Now I don't suppose Bayard is to blame for being a pretty man, or for looking so nice and bandbox-y. But if some public benefactor would tumble his hair and shirt collar, and tie his cravat in a loose sailor knot, and if Bayard himself would open that little three-cent piece mouth of his a l-i-t-t-l-e wider when he lectures, it would take a load off my mind! I write this, in full view of his interest in the Almighty "Tribune," and also set up before him certain "Leaves" for a target, by way of reprisal.

And there is George P. Morris—General George Morris—and Briga-dear General at that, with an eye like a star; and more vitality in him than there is in half the young men who might call him father. May Time, who has dealt so gently with "The Woodman," long delay to cut him down.

One day, after my arrival in New York, I met a man striding down street, in the face of a pin-and-needle wind, that was blowing his long hair away from his bloodshot eyes, and forcing him to compress his lips, to keep what breath he had—inside—to warm him; tall and lank, he clutched his rough blanket shawl about him like a brigand. Fearing he might be an escaped lunatic, I gave him a wide berth on the sidewalk. Each day, in my walks, I met him, till at last I learned to watch for the wearied, haggard-looking face; I think the demonism of it magnetized me. After looking at the kidded dandies, who flourished their perfumed handkerchiefs past, the sight of him was as refreshing as a grand, black thunder cloud, looming up in the horizon, after the oppressive hum-drum-ness of a sultry day. One night I was at the opera; and amid its blaze, and glitter, and glare, was that haggard face, looking tenfold more satanic than ever. Grisi charmed him not, nor Mario either.

Ah—that strain! who could resist it? A luminous smile in an instant transforms Lucifer—was that the same haggard face, upon which, but one moment ago, every passing hour had seemed to set its seal of care, and sorrow, and disappointment?

What was that smile like?

It was like the glorious outbursting of the sun on bud and tree, and blossom, when the thunder cloud has rolled away. It was like the sudden flashing of light through a crystal vase, revealing the delicate tracery of His fingers who made man originally "but little lower than the angels."

And so when I hear Mr. Fry, the musical thunderer of the "Tribune," called "gaunt" and "ugly"—I shake my head incredulously; and when I read in the "Tribune" a biting article from his caustic pen, dissecting poor Napoleon (who certainly expiated all his sins, even that wretched divorce, when he fretted his eagle soul away at St. Helena, beating his strong, but powerless wings, heavily against his English prison bars); when I read Mr. Fry's vulture-like dissection of Napoleon, I recall that luminous music-born smile, and rejoice that in every man's heart is an oasis which the Simoon-breath of worldly care, and worldly toil and ambition has no power to blight!

And here comes Barnum—poor Barnum! late so riant and rosy. Kick not the prostrate lion, ye crowing changelings; you may yet feel his paws in your faces; Mammon grant it! not for the love I bear to "woolly horses," but for the hate I bear to pharisaical summer friends.

Ah! here comes Count Gurowski; Mars of the "Tribune." Oh! the knowledge buttoned up in that shaggy black overcoat! Oh! the prophet eyes hid by those ugly green goggles! Not a move on the European checker-board escapes their notice; but no film of patriotism can cloud to their Russian owner the fall of Sebastopol; and while we gladly welcome rare foreign talent like his to our shores, our cry still must be, "Down with tyranny and tyrants."

And there is Briggs; whilome editor of "Putnam's Monthly," now factotum of the "New York Times," a most able writer and indefatigable worker. People judge him to be unamiable because his pen has a sharp nib. Fudge! one knows what to expect from a torpedo, but who can count on an eel? I trust no malicious person will twist this question to the disparagement of Briggs's editorial coadjutor.

And here, by the rood, comes Fanny Fern! Fanny is a woman. For that she is not to blame; though since she first found it out, she has never ceased to deplore it. She might be prettier; she might be younger. She might be older; she might be uglier. She might be better; she might be worse. She has been both over-praised and over-abused, and those who have abused her worst, have imitated and copied her most.

One thing may be said in favor of Fanny: she was NOT, thank Providence, born in the beautiful, backbiting, sanctimonious, slandering, clean, contumelious, pharisaical, phiddle-de-dee, peck-measure city—of Boston!

Look!

Which? How? Where?

Why there; don't you see? there's Potiphar Curtis.

Potiphar Curtis! Ye gods, what a name! Pity my ignorance, reader, I had not then heard of the great "Howadji"—the only Potiphar I knew of being that much-abused ancient who—but never mind him; suffice it to say, I had not heard of "Howadji;" and while I stood transfixed with his ridiculous cognomen, his coat tails, like his namesake's rival's, were disappearing in the distance. So I can not describe him for you; but I give you my word, should I ever see him, to do him justice to the tips of his boots, which, I understand, are of immaculate polish. I have read his

"Papers" though, and to speak in the style of the patronizing critics who review lady-books, they are very well—for a man.

I was sauntering along one sunny day last week, when I saw before me a young girl, hooped, flounced, fringed, laced, bugled, and ribboned, regardless of cost. Her mantilla, whether of the "Eugenie" or "Victoria" pattern I am too ignorant to inform you, was of black, and had more trimming than I could have believed the most ingenious of dressmakers could pile on one mantilla, though backed by every dry goods merchant in New York. Venus! what a figure it was hung on! Short, flat-chested, narrow-shouldered, angular, and stick-like! her bonnet was a marvel of Lilliputianism, lightness, and lilacs. Raphael! what a face was under it! Watery, yellow, black eyes, a sallow, unwholesome skin, and— Bardolph! what a nose! Imagine a spotted "Seckle pear"—imagine a gnarled bulb-root—imagine a vanquished prize-fighter's proboscis, and you have it! That such a female, with such repulsive features, living in a Christian country, where there were looking-glasses, should strain back from the roots what little hair she had, as if her face were beautiful in its outline—it was incredible.

Who, or what, was she? One of those poor, bedizened unfortunates who hang out signal "Barkis" flags? The poor thing had no capital, even for that miserable market; nobody would have bid for her, but a pawnbroker.

While I speculated and wondered, she slowly lifted her kidded forefinger. I was all eyes and ears! A footman in livery sprang forward, and obsequiously let down the steps of a superb carriage, in waiting, on whose panels was emblazoned a coat-of-arms. The bundle of millinery— the stick-like figure inside the hoops—the gay little bonnet, and the Bardolphian nose, took possession of it. The liveried footman mounted behind, the liveried coachman cracked his whip on the box, the sleek, shiny horses arched their necks, the silver-mounted harness glistened in the sunlight, and the vision was gone. F-a-n-n-y F-e-r-n! is there no limit to your ignorance? You had been commiserating— actually commiserating—one of the élite of New York!

All-compensating nature! tossing money-bags to twisted features, and divorcing beauty from brains; unfortunate they, whom in thy hurry thou hast overlooked, bestowing neither beauty, brains, nor money!

That was not all I saw from under my parasol, on that sunny morning. I saw a young girl—bonnetless, shawlless—beautiful as God often makes the poor—struggling in the grasp of two sturdy policemen. Tears streamed from her eyes, while with clasped hands, as she shrank away from their rough gripe, she plead for release. What was her sin I know not. It might have been the first downward step in a life of unfriended and terrible temptation; for the agony in that young face could not have been feigned; or—she might have been seized only on suspicion; but in vain she begged, and prayed, and wept. Boys shouted; men, whose souls were leprous with sin, jeered; and heartless, scornful women "passed by on the other side."

The poor young creature (none the less to be pitied, had she sinned) goaded to madness by the gathering crowd, seized her long trailing tresses, and tossing them up like a veil over her shame-flushed and beautiful face, resigned herself to her fate.

Many will think any expression of sympathy for this poor unfortunate, uncalled for. There are enough to defend that side of the question, and to them I willingly leave it; there are others, who, with myself, could wish that young girls thus (it may be innocently) accused, should not, before trial, be dragged roughly through the public streets, like shameless, hardened offenders. There are those who, like myself, as they look upon the faces of their own fair young daughters, and think of the long life of happiness or misery before them, will wish that the sword of the law might be tempered with more mercy.

The two scenes above recorded, are not all that I saw from under my parasol, on that sunny morning. I passed the great bow-windows of the St. Nicholas—those favorite lounging-places for male guests, and other gentlemen, well pleased to criticise lady pedestrians, who, thanks to the inventor of parasols, can dodge their battery of glances at will.

Not so, the gentlemen; who weary with travel and sight-seeing, unthinkingly fall asleep in those luxurious arm-chairs, in full view of the public, with their heels on the window-sill, their heads hanging on one side, and their wide-open mouths so suggestive of the——snore—that I fancy I hear. Heaven forgive these comical-looking sleepers the cachinatory sideaches they have often given me!

Was there ever any thing uglier than a man asleep? Single women who have traveled in railroad cars, need not be too modest to answer!

One of the first things I noticed in New York, was the sharp, shrill, squeaking, unrefined, vixenish, uneducated voices of its women. How inevitably such disenchanting discord, breaks the spell of beauty!

Fair New Yorkers, keep your mouths shut, if you would conquer.

By what magnetism has our mention of voices conjured up the form of Dr. Lowell Mason? And yet, there he is, as majestic as Old Hundred—as popular—and apparently as indestructible by Time. I would like to see a pupil of his who does not love him. I defy any one to look at this noble, patriarchal chorister (as he leads the congregational singing on the Sabbath, in Dr. Alexander's church) with an unmoistened eye. How fitting his position—and oh! how befitting God's temple, the praise of "all the people." Should some conquering hero, whose blood had been shed, free as water, for us and ours, revisit our shores, oh, who, as his triumphal chariot wheels rolled by, would pass over to his neighbor for expression the tumultuous gratitude with which his own heart was swelling?

That the mantle of the father should have fallen on the son, is not surprising; and they who have listened delightedly at Mr. William Mason's "Musical Matinée's" must bear witness how this inherited gift has been enriched by assiduous culture. Nature in giving him the ear and genius for a pianist, has also finished off his hands with such nicety, that, as they dart over the keys, they look to the observer like little snow-white scampering mice.

Ah—here is Dr. Skinner! no misnomer that: but what a logician—what an orator! Not an unmeaning sentence—not a superfluous word—not an unpolished period escapes him. In these day of superficial, botched, evangelical apprentice-work, it is a treat to welcome a master workman. Thank Providence, all the talent is not on the side of Beelzebub!

Vinegar cruets and vestry meetings! here come a group of Bostonians! Mark their puckered, spick-and-span self-complaisance! Mark that scornful gathering up of their skirts as they sidle away from that gorgeous Magdalen who, God pity and help her, may repent in her robes of unwomanly shame, but they in their "mint and anise," whitewashed garments—never!

I close with a little quotation, not that it has any thing to do with my subject, but that it is merely a poetical finish to my article. Some people have a weakness for poetry; I have; it is from the pen of the cant-hating Hood.

"A pride there is of rank—a pride of birth,A pride of learning, and a pride of purse,A London pride—in short, there be on earthA host of prides, some better, and some worse;But of all prides, since Lucifer's attaint,The proudest swells a self-elected saint.

To picture that cold pride, so harsh and hard,Fancy a peacock, in a poultry-yard;Behold him in conceited circles sail,Strutting and dancing, and planted stiffIn all his pomp and pageantry, as ifHe felt "the eyes of Europe" on his tail!"

THE CONFESSION BOX.

I confess to being nervous. I don't admire the individual who places a foot upon the rounds of the chair on which I am sitting; or beats a prolonged tattoo with his fingers on the table; or stands with his hands on a creaking door, moving it backward and forward, while he performs an interminable leave-taking; or spins napkin-rings, while he waits for the dessert; or tips his chair back on its hind legs, in the warmth of debate; or tells jokes as old as Noah's ark; or levels volleys of puns at me when I am not in the laughing mood.

Yes, I'm nervous. I would rather not hear a dog bark more than half the night. The scissors-grinder's eternal bell-tinkle, and the soap-fat man's long-drawn whoop, send me out of my chair like a pop-gun. I break down under the best minister, after "forty-ninthly;" and am prepared to scream at any minute after every seat in a street car is filled, and every body is holding somebody in their laps; and somebody is treading on every body's toes in the aisle; and every door and window is shut; and onions and musk, and tobacco and jockey-club, and whisky, and patchouli are mingling their sweets; and the unconscionable conductor continues to beckon to misguided females upon the sidewalk, with whole families of babies (every one of whom is sucking oranges or sugar-candy), to crowd in, and add the last drop of agony to my brimming cup.

Yes, I think I may say I am nervous. I prefer, when the windows of an omnibus are open, and the wind "sets that way," that the driver should not ex-spit-orate any oftener than is necessary. If the skirt of my dress must be torn from my belt by hasty feet upon the sidewalk, I prefer it to be done by a man's boot rather than a woman's un-apologizing slipper; if the fringe of my mantle is foreordained "to catch," the gods grant it may be in a surtout button rather than on a feminine watch-chain. If women shopkeepers were less lavish of cross looks, and crossed sixpences, I might have more faith in the predicted "millennium." I don't wish the Irish woman any harm who tortures me by grinding on her accordeon in the cars, but, if I thought she had settled her little reckoning with the priest, I should be happy to peruse her obituary. I had rather not exchange a pleasant parlor circle for the company of a huge bundle of "proof, to be called for by seven o'clock the next morning;" and I had rather not have the pianos, in five different houses near, each playing different tunes while I am revising it. I don't wish to interfere with infant boys who are fond of bonfires, but if they could make them of something beside dried leaves, it would be a saving to my bronchial apparatus. If people who address me would spell "Fanny" with two ns, I should be more likely to answer their letters. If the little cherub, in jacket and trowsers, who blows the organ of a Sunday, would stand behind a screen, it would materially assist my devotions. If all the men in New York had as handsome a beard as the editor of the ——, I would not object to see them h—air 'em. I should rather the New Yorker would not say that such and such a paragraph would "go all over," instead of "everywhere." I should rather the Connecticuter, when he does not comprehend me, would not startle me out of my chair with a sharp Which? I should rather the Yankee would not say "he was going to wash him," or speak of the "backside of the church." And, lastly, if all the people who are born with seven fingers on one hand, or feet minus toes, or two noses, would not select me in the street to inspect their monstrosities, my epitaph might possibly be deferred a while longer.

A WORD TO PARENTS AND TEACHERS.

I have before me a simple but imploring letter from a little child, begging me "to write her a composition." I could number scores of such which I have received. I allude to it for the sake of calling the attention of parents and teachers to this cruel bugbear of childhood, with which I can fully sympathize, although it never had terrors for me. The multiplication table was the rock on which I was scholastically wrecked; my total inability to ascertain "if John had ten apples, and Thomas took away three, how many John would have left," having often caused me to wish that all the Johns in creation were—well, never mind that, now. I have learned to like Johns since!

But to return to the subject. Just so long as themes like "The Nature of Evil," or "Hydrostatics," or "Moral Science," and kindred subjects, are given out to poor bewildered children, to bite their nails and grit their teeth over, while the ink dries on the nip of their upheld pens, just so long will "composition day" dawn on them full of terrors. Such themes are bad enough, but when you add the order to write three pages at a mark, you simply invite them to diffuse unmeaning repetitions, as subversive of good habits of composition as the command is tyrannical, stupid, and ridiculous. You also tempt to duplicity, for a child, cornered in this way, has strong temptations to pass off for its own what is the product of the brains of another; and this of itself, as a matter of principle, should receive serious consideration at the hands of these child-tormentors. A child should never be allowed, much less compelled to write words without ideas. Never be guilty of such a piece of stupidity as to return a child's composition to him with the remark, "It is very good, but it is too short." If he has said all he has to say, what more would you have? what more can you get but repetition? Tell him to stop when he gets through if it is at the end of the first line— a lesson which many an adult has yet to learn.

In the first place, give a child no theme above his comprehension and capacity; or, better still, allow him to make his own selection, and always consider one line, intelligibly and concisely expressed, better than pages of wordy bombast. In this way only can he be taught to write well, sincerely, and fluently. Nature teaches you this: The little bird at first takes but short flights to the nearest twig or tree. By-and-by, as his strength and confidence grow, they are voluntarily and pleasurably lengthened, till at last you can scarce follow him, as he pierces the clouds. This forcing nature—pushing the little fledgeling rudely out of the nest, can result only in total incapacity, or, at best, but crippled flights. In the name of the children, I enter my earnest protest against it, and beg teachers and parents to think of and remedy this evil.

BREAKFAST.

Let the world fly off its axle any hour in the twenty-four, save the breakfast hour. Ruffle me not then, and I promise to out-Socrates Socrates, though it should rain tribulations all the rest of the day. If I am to have but one glimpse of sunshine until nightfall, let it be then. A plague on him or her who sits down to coffee (all hail coffee!) with a doleful phiz. The witches fly away with that female who presents herself in curl-papers, or introduces herself with a yawn. Unassoiled be that grocer, who offends my proboscis with a doubtful egg; garroted be that dairyman who waters my milk; kneaded be that fat podge of a baker who is tardy with his hot rolls.

Tell me no disagreeables—be not argumentative over our Mocha; discourse not of horrid murders, nor yet dabble in the black sea of politics. Tell me not the price of any article I am eating, neither inquire of me prematurely what I will have for my dinner. Let thy "Good-morning" have heart in it, and touch thy lips to my eyelids as thou passest to thy seat. If thou hast a clover-blossom, or a babe, set it before me; and dream not, because my heart's incense rises silently as its perfumed breath, that I praise not God for the sweet morning.

GREENWOOD AND MOUNT AUBURN.

I have seen Greenwood. With Mount Auburn for my ideal of what a cemetery should be, I was prepared for disappointment. But the two are not comparable. Greenwood is the larger, and more indebted to the hand of art; the gigantic trees of Mount Auburn are the growth of half a century; but then Greenwood has its ocean view, which, paradoxical as it may seem, is not to be overlooked. The entrance to Mount Auburn I think the finer. Its tall army of stately pines stand guard over its silent sleepers, and strew their fragrant leaves on the pathway, as if to deaden the sound of the carriage wheels, which, at each revolution, crush out their aromatic incense, sweet as the box of spikenard which kneeling Mary broke at Jesus' feet.

Greenwood has the greater monumental variety, attributable, perhaps (more than to design), to the motley population of New York; the proprietors of each tomb, or grave, carrying out their national ideas of sepulture. This is an advantage. Mount Auburn sometimes wearies the eye with its monumental monotony. Mount Auburn, too, had (for he long since laid down in its lovely shade), a gray-haired old gate-keeper, courteous and dignified: "a man of sorrows," whose bald, uncovered head, many will remember, who have stood waiting at the portal to bear in their dead. Many a bouquet, simple but sweet, of my favorite flowers have I taken from his palsied hand; and many a sympathizing look, treasured up in my heart from him whom Death had also bereft of all. Greenwood has, at least if my afternoon visit was a fair exponent, its jocund grave-diggers, who, with careless poise, and indecent foot, of haste stumble on with the unvarnished coffin of the poor, and exchange over the fresh and narrow mound, the comrade's time-worn jest. Money has its value, for it purchases gentler handling and better manners.

Let those who will, linger before the marble statue, or chiseled urn of the rich; dearer to me is the grave of the poor man's child, where the tiny, half-worn shoe, is sad and fitting monument. Dearer to me, the moldy toys, the whip, the cap, the doll, the faded locks of hair, on which countless suns have risen and set, and countless showers have shed their kindly tears. And yet for the infant army who slumber there, I can not weep; for I bethink me of the weary toil and strife; the wrecks that strew the life-coast; the plaint of the weary-hearted, unheard in life's fierce clamor; the remorseless, iron heel of strength, on the quivering heart of weakness; the swift-winged, poisoned arrow of cruel slander; the hearts that are near of kin as void of love; and I thank God that the little shoes were laid aside, and the dreary path untrod.

And yet, not all drear, for, as I pass along, I read, in graven lines, of those who periled life to save life; who parted raging billows and forked flames, at woman's wild, despairing shriek, and childhood's helpless wail. Honor to such dauntless spirits, while there are eyes to moisten and hearts to feel!

Beautiful Greenwood! with thy feathery swaying willows, thy silver-voiced fountains and glassy lakes: with thy grassy knolls and shady dells; with thy "Battle Hill," whose sod of yore was nourished by brave men's blood. The sailor here rests him well, in sound of old Ocean's roar; the fireman heeds nor booming bell, nor earthly trump, nor hurried tramp of anxious feet; the pilot's bark is moored and voyage o'er; the school-boy's lesson conned; beauty's lid uncloses not, though rarest flowers bloom above her; no husband's hand is outstretched to her who stoops with jealous care to pluck the obtrusive weed which hides the name she, lonely, bears; no piping, bird-like voice, answers the anguished cry, "My child, my child!" but, still the mourners come, and sods fall dull and heavy on loved and loving hearts, and the busy spade heeds never the dropping tears; and for her who writes, and for them who read—ere long —tears in their turn shall fall. God help us all.

GETTING UP THE WRONG WAY.

It was an unlucky day; every body has known such. I got up just one hour too late, and spent the whole day vainly trying to make it up. It was useless. Things were predestined to go wrong. I felt it. Hooks and eyes, strings and buttons were in the maddening conspiracy. Shoes and stockings were mis-mated; there was a pin in the towel on which I wiped my face; my hair-brush and comb had absconded, and my tooth-brush and nail-brush had gone to keep them company. I ate a hurried breakfast, salting my coffee and sugaring my beefsteak: for I recollected that I had pressing business down town which required a cool head and punctual feet. As I looked at my watch, I saw that it was already time that I was on my way. I wound it up with a jerk, snapping the crystal, and dislocating a spring. Now my boot laces knotted and twisted, and defied every attempt to coerce them into duty; and what was worse, upon looking for the MS. (the product of hours and days of labor), I found that I had burned it, in my absent state of mind, along with some waste paper! and I recollected with agony how indifferently I had watched the last sparkling fragment, as the hated wind merrily whistled it up the chimney.

I held my head for one distracted minute! Was it possible to recall it as it was originally written? Even suppose I could? think of all that lost labor (on heavenly days, too, when the pleasant sunlight wooed me out-of-doors), and think of all that jog-trot punctuating to be gone over again. For me, who hate stops—who believe only in an exclamation point and a dash! I, who turn my back disdainfully upon an interrogation point, who despise coal-on (save in January), who religiously believe that a writer should no more be expected to fritter away his brains on stupid stops, than that an artist should be required to manufacture with his own hands the wooden frames used for his pictures.

Well, the MS. was gone—stops and all—past praying for. I had not even time to whine about it; I must go directly down town. I had the misfortune to be boarding, so every drawer, closet, and cupboard must be locked before starting; for locking one's room door is a mere farce while there are duplicate keys in the house. Yes, I locked them, and unlocked them, too, twenty times or more, as I recollected some handkerchief, collar or purse, which I had forgotten to take out.

All right now, said I, dolorously, as I put the rattling keys in my pocket, descended the interminable hotel stairs, and gained the street. I had passed two blocks when I discovered that the pair of gloves I had brought were both for one hand; the thermometer was at nipping point and I had left my muff behind! I thrust one bare hand into my shawl, shut my teeth together, and exclaimed, as I looked Fate full in the face—now, do your worst.

And so it did!

Down came the snow; had I taken my umbrella, not a flake would have fallen; every body knows that. I looked at the omnibusses; they were all full—full of great, lazy, black-coated men. I hate a black coat; I don't know why a man, unless he has received "the right hand of fellowship," should button himself up in one. Yes, there they sat, as solemn as so many parsons, with their hats slouched over their faces, thinking to save time (while they ruined their eye-sight) by reading the morning papers as they joggled along to their offices. Meanwhile down came the pitiless snow, as I plodded along. Plodded, for every wheel-barrow, box, bale, cask, cart, and wagon, got purposely across my track; and not for the life of me could I remember a sentence of that ascension MS.

I tried not to meet any body, but I met every body, and every body would speak to me: beggars stopped me, country folks singled me out to inquire the way—me!why me? with a street full of people? Did I direct them wrong? Let them learn to ask somebody next time who does not mourn a lost MS.; somebody whose life is not spent in locking up things and losing the keys; somebody who is not required to write an article with a stupid chambermaid flying in and out every ten minutes, leaving your door ajar, whirling your papers across the room, and scattering your ideas to the remorseless winds; somebody whose meals are not always not to be had, when type and printers wait for no woman.

This is a digression. I reached the goal at last; simply and only because one who keeps moving must inevitably fetch up somewhere. I performed my errand, or thought I had, till I had got half-way home, when I recollected an important fact omitted—n'importe. I was desperate now. Guns and pistols could not have turned my steps back again. How it blew! how it snowed! I did not hurry one step; I took a savage pleasure in thinking of my spoiled bonnet-ribbon, wet feet, and ice-ermined skirts. I even stopped, as I observed some umbrella-shielded pedestrian looking wonderingly at me, and gazed with affected delight at the miserable feminine kick-shaws in the shop windows, just to show my sublime indifference to the warring elements.

I reached my room, by dint of climbing the obnoxious stairs. I turned the key, as I fondly hoped, on all my species.

Rat, tat, rat, tat!

Shall I hear it?

Not I!

Rat, tat, tat, rat, tat!

It is of no use; I shall go mad with that thumping. I had rather face Cloven Foot himself than hear it. I open the door; it is my washerwoman. She has a huge pile of clothes to be counted, and sorted, and paid for, too! She dumps them down on the floor, just as if every minute was not to me so much gold-dust until that MS. was resurrectionized. I look around for my list of the clothes. It is not in the big dictionary, no, nor in the Bible, no, nor in the pocket of my blue, red, gray, green, or plaid dress.

Bother! I exclaim, I can't find it. I dare say you have them all right; so I commence taking them out, and counting the pieces with an eye to her pay. What's that? A dickey, two shirts, and a vest! I hold them up to the light with the tips of my fingers.

Woman alive! what need has a female of such garments?

She had made a mistake. She had brought me Mr. ——'s clothes—I will not expose him by telling his name, for they were wretchedly ragged; but as I turned the key again on them and her, I squeezed this drop of comfort out of my misery—Thank heaven, I have not to mend those clothes!

Rat, tat, tat! Merciful man! what now?

163

A bundle of proofs, big as my head, to read and return by the bearer immediately, and quick at that.

I sat down. So did the devil. I began to read, pen in hand. I could not remember, with my bewildered brain, whether "stet" stood for "let it be," or "take it out;" or what "d" signified in a typesetter's alphabet. I read on. Could it be possible that I ever wrote such a disconnected sentence as this? No, they have left out an entire line; and forgot to send the MS. copy, too!

Devil take it! I exclaim; and so he does (the literal infernal!) and is out of sight before I can explain that the unorthodox exclamation was wrung out of me by the last drop in my brimming cup on that unlucky day.

A HOT DAY.

Sissing fry-pans, and collapsed flapjacks—what a hot day! Not a breath of air stirring, and mine almost gone. Fans enough, but no nerve to wield 'em. Food enough, but no strength to chew it. Chairs hot; sofa hotter; beds hottest. Sun on the back stoop; sun on the front stoop; and hot neighbors on both sides. Kittens mewing; red-nosed babies crying; poor little Hot-ten-tots! dogs dragging about with protruding tongues and inquiring tails; cockerels feebly essaying to crow. Every thing sticky, and flabby, and limpsy. Can't read; can't sew; can't write; can't talk; can't walk; can't even sleep; hate every body who passes through the room to make it hotter.

Now, just see that fly. If I have knocked her off my nose once, I have done it forty times; nothing will serve her but the bridge of my nose. I say her, because I am sure it is a female, on account of its extraordinary and spiteful persistence.

"Will I have any thing to drink?" No. Wine heats me; lemonade sours me; water perspires me. "Will I have the blinds closed?" No. "Will I have 'em open?" No. "What will I have?" Well—if there's an old maid to be had, for heaven's sake, walk her through this room to cool it. "What will I have for dinner?" Now, isn't that the last drop in my brimming cup? Dinner, indeed! Soup hot; fish hot; beef hot; mutton hot; chicken hot;—ugh! Hot potatoes; hot squash; hot peas; hot pudding; hot children;—ugh! Tell that butcher to make his will, or get out of my kitchen. "Lady down stairs wishes to see me?" In the name of Adam and Eve, take all my dresses off the pegs and show her—but never believe I'd be so mad as to get into them for any body living.

FUNERAL NOTES.

Was there ever any thing like these insensate New Yorkers? Peep with me into that undertaker's shop, sandwiched between a millinery establishment and an oyster saloon. See the coffins, Behemoth and Lilliputian, pyramided in corners, spread out in rows, challenging in platoons, on the sidewalk, the passers-by; while in the windows are corpse-caps, stiffly starched and plaited, with white ribbon strings, ready to be tied under your chin, or mine.

See the jolly owner, seated on a chair in the middle of his shop, with his legs crossed, his hat on the back of his head, nonchalantly smoking, with his children about his knee; as if the destroying angel had charge to pass unvisited his blood-besprinkled door-post; as if eyes now bright with hope were never to weep themselves dim over those narrow houses.

Now a customer comes in; a young man, whose swollen lids tell their own sorrowful tale. The jolly undertaker, wide awake, throws away his cigar stump, hands a chair to the new comer, exchanges a few words with him, draws pencil and paper from his pocket, and taking an infant's coffin into his lap for a writing desk, commences scribbling down directions. Meanwhile, a hearse rattles up to the door; none of your poor-house hearses, in rusty black, with "seedy" driver, and hang-dog looking horses; but a smart, sonsie, gay-looking New York turn-out—fit for a turtle-consuming, turtle-consumed mayor; with nine huge ostrich feathers, black and white, nodding patronizingly to the a-gape urchins, who stand around the door, who are almost willing to get into a coffin to have a ride with them—with two spanking white horses, equal to Dan Rice's "Excelsior," with ostrich feathers in either ear, flowing as their well-combed tails, which whisk gracefully over the black velvet pall and trappings, as if Life were a holiday and Death its Momus.

Now the young man staggers out, shuddering as he passes the hearse, and screening his swollen lids from curious gazers and the obtrusive sunshine, to whom broken hearts are an every-day story. The jolly undertaker rubs his hands, for death is busy and business is brisk. The young man has made no bargain with him beforehand as to prices; how could he? his heart was full of the widowed sister he left behind, and her newly-made orphans; he only remarked, as he left the street and number, "to do what is customary;" and custom requires that carriages shall be provided for all the "friends and acquaintances" who may wish to go. So "friends and acquaintances" gather (when the funeral hour arrives). Why not? The day is fine and a ride to the out-of-town cemetery pleasant, and (to them) inexpensive; they whose eyes scarce rested with interest on the living form, gaze ceremoniously and curiously on the dead; the widow's tears are counted, the mourning dresses of herself and children scrutinized; the prayer that always falls so immeasurably short of what critical ears demand, is said; a great silence—then a rustling—bustling—whispering—then the coffin is borne past the widow, who sees it through a mist of tears; and then the long procession winds its way through harlequin Broadway, with its brass bands, and military companies, its thundering omnibusses, its bedizened courtezans, its laughing pedestrians, and astonished, simple-hearted country-folk. Wheels lock, milk carts and market wagons join the procession; Barnum's band pipes from out the Museum balcony merry "Yankee Doodle," and amid curses and shouts, laughter and tears, the mournful cavalcade moves on.

And now the incongruous showy farce is over, and the "friends and acquaintances" alighting at their respective houses, re-cross their unblighted thresholds, and the widow and children return to their desolate hearth-stone (how desolate, God and themselves only know); while poverty, strange and unbidden guest, creeps stealthily after them, and takes the empty chair.

O clamorous tyrant, Custom! O thoughtless, unfriendly friends, who can mourn for the dead only in carriages, that swallow up the little legacy left for the living, by the dead for whom you profess to grieve!

Beautiful the calm faith of Swedenborg, turning its hopeful eye away from such childish sackcloth mummery; anchoring where no wave of earthly trouble rolls; gliding through the accustomed life-paths, not lonely, not hopeless; feeling still the warm life-clasp, hearing still the loved voices, breaking the bread, or blessing the meat.

THE "FAVORITE" CHILD.

Why will parents use that expression? What right have you to have a favorite child? The All-Father maketh his sun to shine alike upon the daisy and the rose. Where would you be, were His care measured by your merits or deserts? Is your child none the less your child, that nature has denied him a fluent tongue, or forgotten her cunning, when, in careless mood, she fashioned his limbs? Because beauty beams not from the eye, is there no intelligence there? Because the rosy flush mantles not the pale cheek, does the blood never tingle at your coldness or neglect? Because the passive arms are not wound about your neck, has the soul no passionate yearnings for parental love? O, how often does God, more merciful than you, passing by the Josephs of your household, stoop in his pity and touch those quivering lips with a live coal from off the altar? How often does this neglected one, burst from out the chrysalis in which your criminal coldness has enveloped him, and soaring far above your wildest parental imaginings, compel from your ambition, what he could not gain from your love?

How often does he replenish with liberal hand the coffers which the "favorite child," in the selfishness which you fostered, has drained of their last fraction. "He that is first shall be last, and the last shall be first." Let parents write this on their heart tablets. Let them remember it when they repulse the little clinging arms, or turn a deaf ear to the childish tale of sorrow. O, gather up those clinging tendrils of affection with gentlest touch; trample them not with the foot of haste or insensibility rudely in the dust.

"And they, in the darkest of days, shall beGreenness, and beauty, and strength to thee."

A QUESTION, AND ITS ANSWER.

To Mary M., who desires a frank expression of opinion from the undersigned, with regard to her marrying an old bachelor.

Answer. Don't do it. A man who for so long a period has had nobody but himself to think of, who knows where the finest oysters and venison steaks are to be found, and who has for years indulged in these and every other little selfish inclination unchecked, will, you may be sure (without punning), make a most miserable help-meat. When you have tea, he will wish it were coffee; when you have coffee, he will wish it were tea; when you have both, he will desire chocolate; and when you have all, he will tell you that they are made much better at his favorite restaurant. His shirts never will be ironed to suit him, his cravats will be laid in the drawer the wrong way, and his pocket-handkerchiefs marked in the wrong corner. He will always be happy to wait upon you, provided your way is his way; but an extra walk round a block will put him out of humor for a week. He will be as unbending as a church-steeple—as exacting as a Grand Turk, and as impossible to please as a teething baby. Take my advice, Mary; give the old fossil the mitten, and choose a male specimen who is in the transition state, and capable of receiving impressions.

WINTER.

Hoary-headed old Winter, I have had enough of you! Not that I shrink from facing your rough breath, in a ten-mile walk, on the coldest day on which you ever made icicles; for I am no fair-weather sailor, not I; I have no thousand-dollar dress to spoil, and I am not afraid to increase the dimensions of my ankle by a never-to-be-sufficiently-adored India-rubber boot. I am dependent neither upon cars nor omnibusses, though I am, like other mortals, sometimes brought up short for want of a ferry-boat; but I am tired of frozen ground. I am tired of denuded trees, and leafless vines and branches, scraping against walls and fences, in the vain attempt to frictionize a little warmth into their stiffened limbs. I am tired of gray skies, and the mournful wailing of the winter wind; the stars have a steel-like glitter, and the moonbeams on the snow petrify me like the ghost of a smile on the face of a wire-drawn old maid. I long, like a prisoned bird, for a flight into green fields—I can not sing without the blossoming flowers. I would go to sleep with them, nor wake till the soft spring sheds warm, joyful tears, to call forth her hidden treasures.

And yet, old Winter, I have liked thee less well than now; when the hungry fire devoured the last remaining faggot, and Nature's frozen face was but typical of the faces that my adverse fortune had petrified; but who cares for thee or them? So surely as prosperity brought back their sycophantic smiles, so surely shall thy stiff neck be bowed before the bounty-laden Spring. "Hope on—hope ever;" and yet how meaningless fall these words upon the ear of the poor widow, who but a stone's throw from my window, sits watching beside her dead husband, heeding neither the wailing cry of the babe at her breast, nor the wilder wail of the winter wind, as it drifts the snow against the door.

"Hope on—hope ever." She looks at you with a vacant stare, and then at the lifeless form before her, as if that were her mute answer. You tell her to trust in God, when it is her bitterest sorrow that the voice of her rebellious heart is, "Ye have taken away my idol, and what have I left?"

"Left?" poor mourner. O, so much, that you can not see until those falling tears have cleared your vision and eased your pain. "Left?" the sweet memory of unclouded earthly love, of which not even death can rob you; tones and looks which you will count over, when no human eye sees you, as the miser tells his hoarded gold.

"Left?" his child and yours, who, with the blessed baptism of holy tears, you will call God's. "Left?" O, many a household, whose inmates pressing their anguished brows under living sorrows, would bless God for the sweet memories of earthly love that you cling to in your pain. "Left?" tearful mourner; a crown to win, sweeter for the wearing, when thorns have pressed the brow.

"Left?" a cross to bear, but O, so light to carry, when heaven is the goal!

"One by one thy griefs shall meet thee,Do not fear an armed band;One will fade as others greet thee,Shadows passing through the land.

"Do not look at life's long sorrow,See how small each moment's pain;God will help thee for to-morrow,Every day begin again."

A GAUNTLET FOR THE MEN.

I maintain it: all the heroism of the present day is to be found among women. I say it to your beards. I am sick of such remarks as these: "Poor fellow! he was unfortunate in business, and so he took to drinking;" or —"poor fellow! he had a bad wife, and lost all heart." What does a woman do who is unfortunate in business, I would like to know? Why —she tries again, of course, and keeps on trying to the end of the chapter, notwithstanding the pitiful remuneration man bestows upon her labor, notwithstanding his oft-repeated attempts to cheat her out of it when she has earned it! What does a woman do, who has a bad, improvident husband? Works all the harder, to be sure, to make up his deficiencies to her household; works day and night; smiles when her heart and back are both breaking; speaks hopeful words when her very soul is dying within her; denies herself the needed morsel to increase her children's portion, and crushed neither by the iron gripe of poverty, nor allured by the Judas-smile of temptation, hopefully puts her trust in Him who feedeth the sparrows.

She "the weaker sex?" Out on your pusillanimous manhood! "Took to drinking because he was unhappy!" Bless—his—big—Spartan—soul! How I admire him! Couldn't live a minute without he had every thing to his mind; never had the slightest idea of walking round an obstacle, or jumping over it; never practiced that sort of philosophical gymnastics— couldn't grit his teeth at fate, and defy it to do its worst, because they chattered so;—poor fellow! Wanted buttered toast, and had to eat dry bread; liked "2.40," and had to go a-foot; fond of wine, and had to drink Croton; couldn't smoke, though his stove-pipe did; rushed out of the world, and left his wife and children to battle with the fate that his coward soul was afraid to meet. Brave, magnanimous fellow!

Again—we are constantly hearing that the extravagance of women debars young men from the bliss of matrimony. Poor things! they can't select a wife from out the frivolous circle of fashion; there are no refined, well-educated, lady-like, practical girls and women, whom any man, with a man's soul, might be proud to call wife, nobly struggling for an honest maintenance as writers, governesses, teachers, semptresses, and milliners. They never read such an advertisement as this in the papers:

"Wanted, by a young girl, a situation as governess. She can teach the English branches, French and Italian; and is willing to accept a small remuneration, to secure a respectable home."

Fudge! None so blind as they who won't see. The truth is, most of the young men of the present day are selfish to the backbone. "Poor," too— very poor!—never go to Shelby's or Delmonico's for a nice little game supper, washed down with champagne at $2 a bottle; never smoke dozens of cigars a day, at six cents a piece; never invite—themselves to go to concerts, the opera, or the theater! Wish they could afford to get married, but can't, at least not till, as they elegantly express it, "they meet a pretty girl who has the tin."

SOLILOQUY OF A LITERARY HOUSEKEEPER.

"Spring cleaning!" Oh misery! Ceilings to be whitewashed, walls to be cleaned, paint to be scoured, carpets to be taken up, shaken, and put down again; scrubbing women, painters, and whitewashers, all engaged for months a-head, or beginning on your house to secure the job, and then running off a day to somebody else's to secure another. Yes, spring cleaning to be done; closets, bags, and baskets to be disemboweled; furs and woolens to be packed away; children's last summer clothes to be inspected (not a garment that will fit—all grown up like Jack's bean-stalk); spring cleaning, sure enough. I might spring my feet off and not get all that done. When is that book of mine to get written, I'd like to know? It's Ma'am, will you have this? and Ma'am, will you have that? and Ma'am, will you have the other thing? May I be kissed if I hadn't more time to write when I lived in an attic on salt and potatoes, and scrubbed the floor myself. Must I turn my house topsy-turvy, and inside out, once a year, because my grandmother did, and send my MSS. flying to the four winds, for this traditionary "spring cleaning." Spring fiddlestick! Must I buy up all Broadway to be made into dresses, because all New York women go fashion-mad? What's the use of having a house, if you can't do as you like in it? What's the use of being an authoress, if you can't indulge in the luxury of a shabby bonnet, or a comfortable old dress? What's the use of dressing when your cook can outshine you? What is the use of dragging brocade and velvet through ferry-boats and omnibusses, to serve as mats for market-baskets and dirty boots? "There goes Lily Larkspur, the authoress, in that everlasting old black silk." Well—what's the use of being well off, if you can't wear old clothes. If I was poor, as I was once, I couldn't afford it. Do you suppose I'm going to wrinkle up my face, scowling at unhappy little boys for treading on a five-hundred-dollar silk? or fret myself into a fever because some gentleman throws a cigar-stump on its lustrous trailing folds? no, no; life is too short for that, and much too earnest. Give me good health —the morning for writing, and no interruptions, plenty of fresh air afterwards, and an old gown to enjoy it in, and you may mince along in your peacock dry-goods till your soul is as shriveled as your body.

A BREAKFAST-TABLE REVERIE.

I looked up—they were laughing at me—I am accustomed to be laughed at—so it neither moved nor astonished me. They had been laughing because I had been reading so long, and so intently, the advertising page of my daily paper. And why not? when it is often to me the most interesting part of it. To be sure, I look at it with a pair of eyes that have not always been undimmed with tears; I think sometimes of the unwritten tragedy there may be in a four-line advertisement which scarce arrests the careless, laughing eye. I think of the days and nights of misery it took, the suffering and privation, to goad the sensitive heart up to its first appeal to the public ear—the trembling fingers which may have penned it—the tears which well-nigh obliterated it—the leaden feet which bore it, almost helplessly, to its destination.

No, I was not vexed that they laughed at me, for how should they, whose life-path had been always flower-bestrown, think of these sad things?

I had been reading what follows. Listen

"A young lady, suddenly thrown upon her own resources for support, desires a situation as Governess. She can teach all the English branches, understands French, German, and Italian, and would be willing to accept even the smallest compensation."

I saw her! homeless—friendless—heart-broken; willing to accept the most humiliating, grinding conditions for a safe and immediate shelter for her innocence. I saw the cold, calculating eye of some lady fashionist fasten upon the touching appeal. I saw her place the young girl's pressing necessities in one scale, and her avarice in the other. I saw her include, in her acceptance of the post of governess, that of lace-laundress and nursery-maid; and I saw the poor young creature meekly, even thankfully, accept the conditions, while her wealthy patroness questioned her qualifications, depreciated her services, and secretly rejoiced at securing such a prize, at such an economical rate of compensation.

I saw another young girl similarly situated, but even less fortunate than the one of whom I have spoken. I saw the libidinous eye of a wretch who reads the advertising sheet with an eye to "young governesses," fasten upon her advertisement. I saw him engage her, as he has others, for some fictitious family, in some fictitious place, constituting himself the head of it, and her escort on the way—only to turn, alas! her sweet innocent trust into the bitter channel of a life-long and unavailing remorse.

I took up the paper and read again:

"Who wants a boy?—A widower, with six children, will dispose of an infant to some family inclined to receive it."

That a widower might possibly be so situated as to render such a measure necessary, I could conceive, but that a father could pen such a brusque, hilarious, jocular—"halloa-there"—announcement of the fact, rather stunned me.

"Who wants a boy?"

As if it were a colt, or a calf, or a six-weeks young pup—or any thing under heaven but his own flesh and blood! as if the little innocent had never lain beneath the loving heart of her whose last throb was for its sweet helplessness—last prayer for its vailed future.

Shade of the mother hover over that child!

I read again:

"Information wanted of a little girl, who, at the age of five years, was placed, ten years ago, in —— alms-house."

I thought of her cheerless childhood (as I looked around my own bright hearthstone at my own happy children). I saw her yearning vainly for the sweet ties of kindred. I followed her from thence out into the world, where all but herself, even the humblest, seem to have some human tie to make life sweet; I saw her wandering hither and thither, like Noah's weary dove, without finding the heart's resting-place; wondering, when she had time to wonder (for the heavy burden of daily toil which her slender shoulders bent beneath), if one heart yet beats on God's green earth, through which her own life-tide flows.

I think of this—I wonder who it is who "wants information" concerning her. I wonder is it some remorseful relative, some brother, some sister, some father whose heart is at length touched with pity for the unrecognized little exile—ay—such things have been!

"Clerks out of employment."

Need it be? With acres of fertile earth lying fair in the broad sunshine, waiting only the touch of their sinewy muscles, to throw out uncounted embryo treasures, while ruddy Health stands smiling at the plow!

Then I read of starving seamstresses, with no stock in trade but their needle; nothing but that too often, God help them! between their souls and perdition; and, then, in the very face of my womanly instincts, I say, let them lecture—let them preach—let them even be doctors, if they will (provided they keep their hands off me!)

Then I read, alas! advertisements, which promise youth and purity to lead them through the scorching fires of sin unharmed, unscathed, which say that the penalty annexed by a just God to his violated laws (even in this world), they will turn aside; that a man can take fire into his bosom and not be burned. And then I think that the editor who for paltry gain, throws such firebrands into pure and happy homes should look well that the blight fall not on his own.

But there is comedy as well as tragedy in an advertising sheet. I am fond of poetry; my eye catches a favorite extract from Longfellow, or Bryant, or Percival, or Morris; I read it over with renewed pleasure, blessing the author in my heart the while. I am decoyed into the building to which it serves as a fairy vestibule. Where do I find myself?

By Parnassus! in a carpet-warehouse—in a sausage-shop—in a druggist's—shoemaker's—tailor's—or hatter's establishment.

Who shall circumscribe American ingenuity where dollars and cents are concerned?

Answer me, great Barnum!

A GLANCE AT A CHAMELEON SUBJECT.

"Tell you what are the fashions?" I, who am sick of the very word fashion? who could shake hands with every rustic I meet, for very delight at his napless hat, and ark-like coat?

You should be surfeited, as I am, with harlequin costumes; disgusted, as I am, with troops of women, strutting, like peacocks, to show their plumage; but who, less sensible than peacocks, never shed their feathers. You should see brocades, and silk velvets, fit only for carriage or dinner dresses, daily mopping up the tobacco pools on these unmitigatedly nasty sidewalks. You should see the gay little bonnets, and oh! you should see the vapid, expression-less, soul-less faces beneath them. You should see the carriages, with their liveried servants, in our republican streets, and the faces, seamed with ennui and discontent, which peer through the windows, from beneath folds of lace and satin.

You should see how this dress furore infects every class and circle. You should see the young apprentice girl who can afford but one bonnet, buying a flimsy dress-hat, to be worn in all weathers; securing for Sunday, a showy silk dress and gilt bracelet, when she has hardly a decent chemise, or petticoat, and owns, perhaps, but one handkerchief, and a couple of pairs of stockings. You should see the wife of the young mechanic, with her embroidered pocket-handkerchief, and flaunting pink parasol, while she can number but one pair of sheets, and one table-cloth. You should see her children, with their plumed hats, while parti-colored, dilapidated petticoats peep from beneath their dresses, and they are shivering for the want of warm flannels. You should see the servant-girl, with her greasy flounces, and soiled artificial flowers. You should see young men, with staring diamond pins stuck on their coarse shirt-bosoms, with shabby velvet vests, and mock chains looped over them.

You should go into the "furnishing stores for ladies' and children's garments;" and see how impossible it is to find plain, substantial articles of clothing for either—two thirds, at least, of the cost of every article being for elaborate trimming, and ruffling, and useless embroidery. You should go into the "ladies' cloak stores," and see these garments loaded indeed with gay trimmings, but miserably thin, and ill-adapted for winter wear; hence the stories of garments you frequently notice on New York ladies (as winter intensifies), as if one good, sensible, thickly-wadded, old-fashioned, outside garment, could, by any possibility, be more awkward and ugly than such an "arrangement," and as if it were not a million degrees more comfortable, and less troublesome; but, then— Fashion says, No!

"Tell you the fashions?"

Excuse my rambling. Well; here they are, as near as I can find out:

Puff your hair and your skirts. Lace your lungs and your handkerchief. Put on the most stunning dress you can find; wear it of a stumbling length, because Queen Victoria's royal ankles are thick.

Take a handful of artificial roses, each of a different color, half a dozen yards of ribbon ditto, lace ditto. Secure them, for a bonnet, to your bump of amativeness, with two long pins. Then sprinkle the contents of a jeweler's shop promiscuously over your person; and by no means, before you go out, omit drawing on a pair of bright yellow gloves; that sine quâ non of a New York woman's toilette.

"Tell you the fashions?" Take a walk down Broadway, and see for yourself. If you have a particle of sense, it will cure you of your absorbing interest in that question during your natural life, though your name be written "Methuselah."

FACTS FOR UNJUST CRITICS.

A few scraps from the "Life of Charlotte Bronte," that I would like to see pasted up in editorial offices throughout the length and breadth of the land:

"She, Miss Bronte, especially disliked the lowering of the standard by which to judge a work of fiction if it proceeded from a feminine pen; and praise, mingled withpseudo-gallant allusions to her sex, mortified her far more than actual blame.

"Come what will," she says, "I can not, when I write, think always of myself, and of what is elegant and charming in femininity; it is not on these terms, or with such ideas, that I ever took pen in hand, and if it is only on these terms my writing will be tolerated, I shall pass away from the public and trouble it no more.

"I wish all reviewers believed me to be a man; they would be more just to me. They will, I know, keep measuring me by some standard of what they deem becoming to my sex; where I am not what they consider graceful, they will condemn me.

"No matter—whether known or unknown—misjudged or the contrary—I am resolved not to write otherwise. I shall bend as my powers tend. The two human beings who understood me are gone; I have some who love me yet, and whom I love, without expecting or having a right to expect they shall perfectly understand me. I am satisfied, but I must have my own way in the matter of writing."

Speaking of some attacks on Miss Bronte, her biographer says:

"Flippancy takes a graver name, when directed against an author by an anonymous writer; we then call it cowardly insolence."

She also says:

"It is well that the thoughtless critics, who spoke of the sad and gloomy views of life presented by the Brontes in their tales, should know how such words were wrung out of them by the living recollection of the long agony they suffered. It is well, too, that they who have objected to the representation of coarseness, and shrank from it with repugnance, as if such conception arose out of the writers, should learn, that not from the imagination, not from internal conception—but from the hard cruel facts, pressed down, by an external life upon their very senses, for long months and years together, did they write out what they saw, obeying the stern dictates of their consciences. They might be mistaken. They might err in writing at all, when their afflictions were so great that they could not write otherwise than as they did of life. It is possible that it would have been better to have described good and pleasant people, doing only good and pleasant things (in which case they could hardly have written at any time): all I say is, that never, I believe, did women possessed of such wonderful gifts exercise them with a fuller feeling of responsibility for their use."

A friend of Miss Bronte says:

"The world heartily, greedily enjoyed the fruits of Miss Bronte's labors, and then found out she was much to blame for possessing such faculties."

Mrs. Gaskell says:

"So utterly unconscious was Miss Bronte of what was by some esteemed 'coarse' in her writings, that on one occasion, when the conversation turned upon women's writing fiction—she said, in her grave, earnest way, 'I hope God will take away from me whatever power of invention, or expression I may have, before he lets me become blind to the sense of what is fitting, or unfitting to be said.'"

Fanny Fern says:

I would that all who critically finger women's books, would read and ponder these extracts. I would that reviewers had a more fitting sense of their responsibility, in giving their verdicts to the public; permitting themselves to be swayed neither by personal friendship, nor private pique; speaking honestly, by all means, but remembering their own sisters, when they would point a flippant, smart article by disrespectful mention of a lady writer; or by an unmanly, brutal persistence in tearing from her face the mask of incognito-ship, which she has, if she pleases, an undoubted right to wear. I would that they would speak respectfully of those whose pure, self-denying life, has been through trials and temptations under which their strong natures would have succumbed; and who tremblingly await the public issue of days and nights of single-handed, single-hearted weariness and toil. Not that a woman's book should be praised because it is a woman's, nor, on the contrary, condemned for that reason. But as you would shrink from seeing a ruffian's hand laid upon your sister's gentle shoulder, deal honestly, but, I pray you, courteously, with those whose necessities have forced them out from the blessed shelter of the home circle, into jostling contact with rougher natures.

TRY AGAIN.

"No woman ever produced a great painting or statue."—Ex.

On the contrary, she has produced a great many "statues," who may be seen any sunshiny day, walking Broadway, in kid gloves and perfumed broadcloth, while "Lawrence" lies in ashes.

"No woman ever wrote a great drama."—Ex.

Ay—but they have lived one; and when worn out with suffering at hands which should have shielded them, have died without a murmur on their martyr lips.

"No woman ever composed a great piece of music."—Ex.

What do you call a baby?

"No woman was ever a great cook!"—Ex.

True—it takes a man to get up a broil.

"Women have invented nothing outside of millinery since the world began."—Ex.

How can they? when they are so hooped in?

"Women have written clever letters, tolerable novels, and intolerable epics."—Ex.

Indeed! It strikes me, though, that we have furnished you the material for yours; just tell me what your "letters," your "novels," your "epics," would have amounted to, without the inspiring theme—woman. When the world furnishes us heroes, perhaps we shall write splendid novels, and splendid epics. Pharaoh once required bricks to be made "without straw."

"Letters?" No man, since the world began, could pen a letter equal to a woman. Look at the abortions dignified by that name in men-novels; stiltified—unnatural—stiff—pedantic, or else coarse. You can no more do it than an elephant can waltz. The veriest school girl can surpass you at it. I have often heard men confess it (when off their guard). One thing at least we know enough to do, viz.: when we wish to make one of your sex our eternal and unchangeable friend we always allow him to beat us in an argument.

FAIR PLAY.
OR, BOTH SIDES OF THE STORY.

"It is too bad," said a lady to me, not long since, "it is too bad; I am almost tired to death." She had been to York on a shopping expedition; and, having finished her purchases, and returned, laden with them to the ferry, found two thirds of the seats in the ladies' cabin of the ferry-boat occupied by men, while she and several other ladies were compelled to stand till the boat reached the pier. "It is too bad," she repeated; "they have no right to occupy the ladies' cabin, when ladies are standing. Give them a dig, Fanny, won't you?"

"Of course I will," said I; "the case, to my mind, is clearly against the coat-tails; more especially, as, when the boat touches the pier, they rush past the ladies, and by right of their pantaloons leap over the chain (which femininity must wait to see unhooked), in order to monopolize all the seats in the street cars, to the exclusion of the aforesaid dismayed and weary ladies. Most certainly I will give them a dig, my dear; it is an exhibition of 'grab' which is quite disgusting."

But stay—have the ladies no sins to answer for? May it not be just possible that the men are at last getting weary of rendering civilities to women who receive them as a matter of right, without even an acknowledging smile, or "Thank you?" May they not have tired of creeping, with an abject air, into cars and omnibusses, and gradually and circumspectly lowering themselves amid such billows of hoops and flounces? May they not at last have become disgusted at the absurd selfishness which ladies manifest on these occasions? the "sit closer, ladies," of the conductors and drivers being met with a pouting frown, or, at best, the emigration of the sixteenth part of an inch to the right or left. And is it not a shame, that a deprecating blush should crimson a gentleman's forehead because he ventures to seat himself, in a public conveyance, in the proximity of these abominable, limb-disguising, uncomfortable, monopolizing hoops? Women who are blessed with hips, should most certainly discard these nuisances, and women who are not, should know that narrow shoulders, and a bolster conformation, look more ramrod-y still, in contrast with this artificial voluminousness of the lower story.

And then the little girls! The idea of hunting under these humbugs of hoops, for little fairy girls, whose antelope motions are thus circumscribed, their graceful limbs hidden, and their gleeful sports checked—the monstrosity of making hideous their perfect proportions, and rendering them a laughing-stock to every jeering boy whom they meet; and—worse than all—the irreparable moral wrong of teaching them that comfort and decency must be sacrificed to Fashion! Bah!—I have no patience to think of it. I turn my pained eyes for relief to the little ragged romps who run round the streets, with one thin garment, swaying artistically to the motion of their unfettered limbs. I rush into the sculptor's studio, and feast my eyes on limbs which have no drapery at all.

Yes, it is trying to feminine ankles and patience, to have gentlemen occupy ladies' places in the "ladies' cabin," and gentlemen who do this will please consider themselves rebuked for it; but it is also disgusting, that women have not fortitude sufficient to discard the universal and absurd custom of wearing hoops. Nay, more, I affirm that any woman who has not faith enough in her Maker's taste and wisdom, to prefer her own bones to a whale's, deserves the fate of Jonah—minus the ejectment.

TO GENTLEMEN.
A CALL TO BE A HUSBAND.

Yes, I did say that "it is not every man who has a call to be a husband;" and I am not going to back out of it.

Has that man a call to be a husband, who, having wasted his youth in excesses, looks around him at the eleventh hour for a "virtuous young girl" (such men have the effrontery to be very particular on this point), to nurse up his damaged constitution, and perpetuate it in their offspring?

Has that man a call to be a husband, who, believing that the more the immortal within us is developed in this world, the higher we shall rank with heavenly intelligences in the next, yet deprecates for a wife a woman of thought and intellect, lest a marriage with such should peril the seasoning of his favorite pudding, or lest she might presume in any of her opinions to be aught else than his echo?

Has that man a call to be a husband, who, when the rosy maiden he married is transformed by too early an introduction to the cares and trials of maternity, into a feeble, confirmed invalid, turns impatiently from the restless wife's sick-room, to sun himself in the perfidious smile of one whom he would blush to name in that wife's pure ears?

Has he any call to be a husband, who adds to his wife's manifold cares that of selecting and providing the household stores, and inquires of her, at that, how she spent the surplus shilling of yesterday's appropriation?

Has he any call to be a husband, who permits his own relatives, in his hearing, to speak disrespectfully or censoriously of his wife?

Has he any call to be a husband, who reads the newspaper from beginning to end, giving notice of his presence to the weary wife, who is patiently mending his old coat, only by an occasional "Jupiter!" which may mean, to the harrowed listener, that we have a President worth standing in a driving rain, at the tail of a three-mile procession, to vote for, or—the contrary? and who, after having extracted every particle of news the paper contains, coolly puts it in one of his many mysterious pockets, and goes to sleep in his chair?

Has he a call to be a husband, who carries a letter, intended for his wife, in his pocket for six weeks, and expects any thing short of "gunpowder tea" for his supper that night?

Has he a call to be a husband, who leaves his wife to blow out the lamp, and stub her precious little toes while she is navigating for the bed-post?

Has he a call to be a husband, who tells his wife "to walk on a couple of blocks and he will overtake her," and then joins in a hot political discussion with an opponent, after which, in a fit of absence of mind, he walks off home, leaving his wife transformed by his perfidy into "a pillar of salt?"

Has he any call to be a husband, who sits down on his wife's best bonnet, or puts her shawl over her shoulders upside down, or wrong side out at the Opera?

Has he any call to be a husband, who goes "unbeknown" to his wife, to some wretch of a barber, and parts, for twenty-five cents, with a beard which she has coaxed from its first infantile sprout, to luxuriant, full-grown, magnificent, unsurpassable hirsuteness, and then comes home to her horrified vision a pocket edition of Moses?

Has he any call to be a husband, who kisses his wife only on Saturday night, when he winds up the clock and pays the grocer, and who never notices, day by day, the neat dress, and shining bands of hair arranged to please his stupid milk-and-water-ship?

TO THE LADIES.
A CALL TO BE A WIFE.

Has that woman a call to be a wife, who thinks more of her silk dress than of her children, and visits her nursery no oftener than once a day?

Has that woman a call to be a wife, who cries for a cashmere shawl when her husband's notes are being protested?

Has that woman a call to be a wife, who sits reading the last new novel, while her husband stands before the glass, vainly trying to pin together a buttonless shirt-bosom?

Has that woman a call to be a wife, who expects her husband to swallow diluted coffee, soggy bread, smoky tea, and watery potatoes, six days out of seven?

Has she a call to be a wife, who keeps her husband standing on one leg a full hour in the street, while she is saying that interminable "last word" to some female acquaintance?

Has she a call to be a wife, who flirts with every man she meets, and reserves her frowns for the home fireside?

Has she a call to be a wife, who comes down to breakfast in abominable curl-papers, a soiled dressing-gown, and shoes down at the heel?

Has she a call to be a wife, who bores her husband, when he comes into the house, with the history of a broken tea-cup, or the possible whereabouts of a missing broom-handle?

Has she a call to be a wife, whose husband's love weighs naught in the balance with her next door neighbor's damask curtains, or velvet carpet?

Has she a call to be a wife, who would take advantage of a moment of conjugal weakness, to extort money or exact a promise?

Has she a call to be a wife, who "has the headache" whenever her husband wants her to walk with him, but willingly wears out her gaiter boots promenading with his gentlemen friends?

Has she a call to be a wife, who takes a journey for pleasure, leaving her husband to toil in a close office, and "have an eye, when at home, to the servants and children?"

Has she a call to be a wife, who values an unrumpled collar or crinoline more than a conjugal kiss?

Has she a call to be a wife, to whom a good husband's society is not the greatest of earthly blessings, and a house full of rosy children its best furnishing, and prettiest adornment?

MATRIMONIAL ADVERTISEMENTS.

That prurient young men, and broken-down old ones, should seek amusement in matrimonial advertisements, is not so much a matter of surprise; but that respectable papers should lend such a voice in their columns, is, I confess, astonishing. I do not say that a virtuous woman has never answered such an advertisement; but I do say, that the virtue of a woman who would do so is not invincible. There is no necessity for an attractive, or, to use a hateful phrase, a "marketable" woman, to take such a degrading step to obtain what, alas! under legitimate circumstances, often proves, when secured, but a Dead Sea apple. It is undesirable, damaged, and unsaleable goods that are oftenest offered at auction. A woman must first have ignored the sweetest attributes of womanhood, have overstepped the last barrier of self-respect, who would parley with a stranger on such a topic. You tell me that marriage has sometimes been the result. Granted: but has a woman who has effected it in this way, bettered her condition, how uncongenial soever it might have been? Few husbands (and the longer I observe, the more I am convinced of the truth of what I am about say, and I make no exception in favor of education or station) have the magnanimity to use justly, generously, the power which the law puts in their hands. But what if a wife's helplessness be aggravated by the reflection that she has abjectly solicited her wretched fate? How many men, think you, are there, who, when out of humor, would hesitate tauntingly to use this drawn sword which you have foolishly placed in their hands?

Our sex has need of all the barriers, all the defenses, which nature has given us. No—never let woman be the wooer, save as the flowers woo, with their sweetness—save as the stars woo, with their brightness—save as the summer wind woos—silently unfolding the rose's heart.

A SABLE SUBJECT.

Every day, in my walks, I pass a large bow window on the corner of two streets, in which is displayed the agreeable spectacle of big and little coffins of all sorts and shapes, piled up and standing on end. This is in bad taste enough; but yesterday, through the ostentatious glass-windows of the shop, I saw a little rosy baby crawling over and around them, while the elder children were using them for play-houses for their dolls! Now such a sight may strike other people agreeably, or they may pass it every day with entire indifference; unfortunately for my peace of mind, I can do neither one nor the other, for by a sort of horrid fascination my eyes are attracted to that detestable window, and familiarity but increases my disgust.

Now I know I shall need a coffin some day or other; but to-day the blue sky arches over my head, the fresh wind fans my temples, and every blade of grass, and new-blown violet, makes me childishly happy; now what right has that ghoul of an undertaker to nudge me in my healthy ribs as I pass, check my springing step, send the blood from my cheek back to my heart, change my singing to sighing, and turn this bright glorious earth into one vast charnel-house? In the name of cheerfulness, I indict him, and his co-fellows, for unmitigated nuisances.

And while I am upon this subject I would like to ask why the New York sextons, for I believe it is peculiar to them, should have the exclusive privilege of advertising their business on the outer church-walls, any more than the silversmith who furnishes the communion-plate; or the upholsterer who makes the pulpit and pew-cushions; or the bookseller who furnishes the hymn-books; or the dry-goods merchant who sells the black silk to make the clergyman's robe? It strikes me that it is a monopoly, and a very repulsive one. In my opinion, this whole funeral business needs reforming. Much of the shrinking horror with which death is invested even to good Christians, is traceable to these repulsive, early associations, of which they can not, by any exercise of faith, rid themselves in after years. These unnecessary, ostentatious, long-drawn-out paraphernalia of woe; these gloomy sable garments, which all should unite in abolishing; these horrible pompous funerals, with their pompous undertakers, where people who scarce ever glanced at the living face congregate to sniffle hypocritical tears over the dead one; these stereotyped round-about prayers that mean so little, and which the mourner never hears; this public counting of scalding tears by careless gazers at the grave-yard or the tomb; it is all horrible—it need not be—for the sake of childhood, often, through fear of death, all its life-time subject to bondage, it ought not to be. Even the "heathen," so called, have the advantage of us in the cheerfulness with which they wisely invest a transition, from which flesh and blood, with its imperfect spiritualization, instinctively shrinks.

NEW YORK.

"There is no night there," though spoken of a place the opposite of New York, is nevertheless true of Gotham; for by the time the ennuied pleasure seekers have yawned out the evening at the theater or opera, and supped at Taylor's, or danced themselves lame at some private ball, a more humble but much more useful portion of the community are rubbing open their eyelids, and creeping by the waning light of the street lamps, and the gray dawn, to another brave day of ill-requited toil; while in many an attic, by the glimmer of a handful of lighted shavings, tear-stained faces resume the coarse garment left unfinished the night before. At this early hour, too, stunted, prematurely-old little boys may be seen, staggering under the weight of heavy shop window shutters, and young girls, with faded eyes and shawls, crawl to their prisoning workshops; while lean, over-tasked omnibus horses, commence anew their never-ceasing, treadmill rounds. God help them all! my heart is with the oppressed, be it man or beast.

The poet says there are "sermons in stones." I endorse it. The most eloquent sermons I ever heard were from "A. Stone;" (but that is a theme

I am not going to dwell upon now.) I maintain that there are sermons in horses.

Crash—crash—crash!

I turned my head. Directly behind me, in Broadway, was a full-freighted omnibus. One of the horses attached had kicked out both his hind legs, snapped the whiffle-tree to the winds, and planting his hoofs into the end window, under the driver's seat, had shivered the glass in countless fragments, into the faces of the astonished passengers, plunging and rearing with the most '76-y spirit. Ladies screamed, and scrambled with what haste they might, out on to the pavement; gentlemen dropped their morning papers, and uttering angry imprecations as they brushed the glass splinters from their broadcloth, followed them; while the driver cursed and lashed in vain at the infuriated hoofs, which abated not a jot of their fury at all his cursing and lashing.

"Vicious beast!" exclaimed one bystander. "Ought to be shot instanter!" said a second. "I'd like to lash his hide raw!" exclaimed a third Nero.

Ah! my good friends, thought I, as I went laughing on my way, not so fast with your anathemas. The cause of that apparently malicious and unprovoked attack, dates a long way back. Count, if you please, the undeserved lashings, the goadings, and spurings, that noble creature has borne, while doing a horse's best to please! Think of the scanty feed, the miserable stable, the badly-fiting, irritating harness; the slippery pavements, where he has so often been whipped for stumbling; the melting dog-days with their stinging bottle-flies and burning sun-rays, when he has plodded wearily up and down those interminable avenues, sweating and panting under the yoke of cruel task-masters.

'Tis the last ounce which breaks the camel's back; 'tis the last atom which balances the undulating scales. Why should that noble horse bear all this? He of the flashing eye, arching neck, and dilating nostril? He of the horny hoof and sinewy limb? He!—good for a score of his oppressors, if he would only think so!—Up go his hoofs! As a Bunker Hill descendant, I can not call that horse—a jackass.

AIRY COSTUMES.

Are the New York children to be frozen this winter, I want to know? Are their legs to be bared from the knee to the tip of their little white socks, just above the ankle, to please some foolish mother, who would rather her child were a martyr to neuralgia and rheumatism, its natural life, than to be out of fashion? Are sneezing babes to face the winter wind in embroidered muslin caps, lined with silk, the costly lace borders of which are supposed to atone for the premature loss of their eye-sight? Are little girls to shiver in cambric pantalettes, and skirts lifted high in the air by infantile hoops? Are their mothers to tiptoe through the all-abounding "slosh" of New York streets, in paper-soled gaiters, and rose-colored silk stockings? And yet one scarcely cares about the latter, because the sooner such "mothers of families" tiptoe themselves into their graves, the better for coming generations; but for the children, one can but sigh, and shiver too; and inquire, as did an old-fashioned physician of a little undressed victim, "If cloth was so dear that her mother could not afford to cover her knees?" It is a comfort to look at the men, who, whatever follies they may be guilty of (and no human arithmetic can compute them), have yet sense enough to wear thick-soled boots, and wadded wrappers in the proper season. One looks at their comfortable garments and heaves a sigh for breeze and mud-defying pantaloondom; for with the most sensible arrangements for skirts, they are an unabated and intolerable nuisance in walking; and yet those horrid Bloomers! those neutral, yet "strong-minded" Miss Nancys! with their baggy stuff-trowsers, flaping fly-aways, and cork-screw stringlets. I could get up a costume! but alas! the brass necessary to wear it! I see now, with my mind's eye, the jaunty little cap, the well-fitting, graceful pants, the half-jacket, half-blouse—the snow-white collar, and pretty fancy neck-tie—the ravishing boot—the nicely fitting wrist-band, with its gold sleeve-buttons; but why awake the jealousy of the other "sect?" Why drive the tailors to commit suicide in the midst of their well-stocked warehouses? Why send little boys grinning round corners? Why make the parson forget his prayers, and the lawyer his clients? Why drive distracted the feminine owners of big feet and thick ankles? Why force women to mend the holes in the heels of their stockings? Why leave to scavengers the pleasant task of mopping up dirty streets and sidewalks? Why drive "M. Ds." to take down their signs, and take up "de shovel and de hoe?" I'll be magnanimous. I won't do it.

A PEEP AT THE OPERA.

I was at the opera last night. It was all gas-glare, gilding and girls. Oh, the unspeakably tiresome fix-up-ativeness of New York women! The elaborate hair-twistings and braidings; the studied display of bracelets and rings; the rolling-up of eyes, and casting-down of eye-lashes; the simperings and smirkings; the gettings-up and sittings-down, ere the fortunate attitude is fixed upon; the line at which a shawl must be dropped to show a bust; the ermine sheets, worn without reference to lily or leopard complexions; the fat damsels who affect Madonna-ism; the lean women, whaleboned to "Peter Schemel"-ism; the tinsel-y head-dresses; the gaudy opera-cloaks; the pray-do-look-at-me air; the utter absence of simplicity, and of that beautiful self-forgetfulness which is the greatest charm of woman. It is a relief to see some honest country people stray in, simply cloaked and bonneted (and old-fashioned and homely at that,) who, ignorant of the mighty difference between "point" and cotton-lace, ermine and cat-skin, drop into a seat, ignore their artificial neighbors, and lose themselves in the illusions of the stage.

Mark Grisi! What perfection of grace in attitude, what simplicity and appropriateness in costume, what a regal head, what massive white shoulders, what a queenly tread. How could such an imperial creature ever love that effeminate little pocket-edition—Mario? A pretty man! with his silky locks parted in the middle, and a little dot of an imperial under his little red lip! Antidote me his effeminacy, oh memory, with the recollection of Daniel Webster's unfathomable eyes and Lucifer-ish frown;—something grand—something noble—something homely if you like, but for Heaven's sake, something manly.

HARD TIMES.

"Is me velvet j-a-c-k-e-t ready to try on?" drawled a lady, dropping her elegant cashmere from one shoulder, as she sauntered into Mme. ——'s dress-making saloon.

"It is not," replied the young girl in waiting.

"Ve'y extraordinary—ve'y surprising; madame promised it, without fail, this morning."

"Madame has been unexpectedly called out," replied the girl, coolly rehearsing the stereotyped fib.

"Ve'y perplexing," muttered the lady; "ve'y ridiculous—pray, when will she see me?" she asked (unwilling to trust the draping of her aristocratic limbs to less practiced hands).

"This afternoon at five," answered the girl, fibbing a second time, knowing very well that it was part of madame's tactics to keep her saloon daily filled with just such anxious expectants, up to the last endurable point of procrastination. And there they sat, poor imbeciles! grouped about the room, pulling over the last fashion prints, overhauling gayly-colored paper dress patterns, discussing modes, robes, basques, and trimmings, with the most ludicrously-grave earnestness, ordering ruinous quantities of point lace and velvet, with the most reckless abandon, and vying which should make themselves look most hideously-Babylonish and rainbow-like; while their husbands and fathers, in another part of the city, were hurrying from banks to counting-houses, sweating and fretting over "protested notes," care, meanwhile, anticipating old Time in seaming their brows, and plowing their cheeks with wrinkles.

In an unfashionable, obscure part of the city, in the basement of a small two-story house, sat a woman of twenty-seven years, the mother of ten children, who were swarming about her like a hive of bees—fat, clean, rosy, noisy, merry, and happy. They had little space for their gymnastics, it is true, the little room dignified as "the parlor" being only twelve feet square; back of this was a dark bedroom, leading to a small kitchen, filled with the usual variety of culinary utensils. The pot of potatoes for their simple dinner, was boiling over the kitchen fire; the happy mother of this little family was putting the last touches to a silk dress for a lady in the neighborhood; and the baby was sleeping as sweetly, as though its brothers and sisters were not using their lungs and limbs, as God intended children's lungs and limbs should be used. On a small table in the corner lay a pile of medical books—for the father of these ten children was absent at a medical lecture, preparatory to a physician's practice.

"Poor George!" said the prolific young mother, with a laugh—"all these big books yet to be crammed into his curly head; never mind—I had rather do all my own work, take in dress-making, and support the family two years longer, than that he should be disappointed in his favorite wish of becoming a doctor. There he comes!" said she, dropping her needle, as a dark-eyed, intelligent-looking, mercurial little fellow bounced into the room—snatched the baby from the cradle—jumped pell-mell into the laughing group of little boys and girls, and kissed his wife's forehead, as he helped her to draw out the dinner-table.

Ah, thought I, as I contrasted this with the scene at Madame B——'s saloon, better is a dinner of potatoes where love is, than a stalled ox and a protested note therewith!

COUNTER IRRITATION.

"That is all clerks are fit for," said a heartless woman, who had been diverting herself with turning a store full of goods topsy-turvy.

Is it?

Is the situation of a clerk always a congenial one? Have those who occupy it never a soul above ribbons and laces? Are they as frivolous, and mindless as many of the ladies upon whom they are often obliged to wait? Is their future bounded by the counter to which necessity has chained them?

Not at all.

Look into our library reading-rooms of an evening. See them joining the French, Spanish, German, and Italian classes. See them, unconscious of the flight of time, devouring with avidity works of history, biography, and books of travel. See the eye sparkle, and the brow flush, as they read how a Greeley shut his teeth on discouragement, and hewed out with his unaided arm a path to honor and usefulness. Ah! has the clerk no noble, hopes or aspirations for the future, which the grinding, treadmill round of his daily toil can neither smother nor crush out? Is there no far-off home from which he is an unwilling exile? No mother, no sister, whom he must make proud of son and brother? No bright-eyed, winsome young girl, whose image enshrined in his heart is at once a talisman against evil, and a spur to unremitting exertion? the hope of whose love sweetens and dignifies his unpretending labor, nerves him to bear uncomplainingly, unresentfully, the overbearing and undeserved rebuke of arrogant assumption?

You shake your head, and cite sad instances to the contrary. You tell me of dishonest, dissolute, improvident clerks, lost to every just, generous, and noble feeling; who look not beyond the present hour either for soul or body.

True.

But what if, when they entered upon their clerkship they stood alone in the world, uncared for, irresponsible, held in check by no saving home influences, adrift upon the great human life tide? What if their employers looked upon them merely as tools and machines, not as human beings? What if they ground them down to the lowest possible rate of compensation. What if never by look, act, word, or tone, they manifested a kindly parental interest in their future, cared not what company they kept, or what influences surrounded them in their leisure hours? What if these young men returned at night, after their day's meagerly rewarded toil, to a small, dreary, desolate, comfortless, lodging room, where there was nothing to cheer the eye or rest the heart? What if the syren voice of sin softly whispered those youthful, restless, craving hearts away?

What then?

Oh! if employers sometimes thought of this! Sometimes stopped the Juggernaut wheels of Mammon to look at the victims which lay crushed beneath, for want of a little human love, and care, and sympathy! Sometimes thought, while looking with fond pride upon their own young sons, that fortune's wheel, in some of its thousand revolutions, might whirl them through the same fiery ordeal, and that their now unclouded sun might go down while it was yet day.

You, who are employers, think of it!

Youth hungers for appreciation—sympathy—must have it—ought to have it—will have it. Oh, give it an occasional thought whether the source from whence it is obtained be good or evil, pure or impure! Speak kindly to them.

Oh, the saving power there is in feeling that there is one human being who cares whether we stand or fall!

SUNDAY IN GOTHAM.

'Tis Sabbath morning in Now York. You are wakened by children's voices, pitched in every variety of key, vying which shall shout the loudest: "Her'ld—Dispatch—Sun'y Times—Sunny Atlas"—parenthetized by an occasional street-fight between the sturdy little merchants, when one encroaches on the other's "beat." You have scarce recovered from their ear-splitting chorus, before the air is rent by a sound like ten thousand Indian war-whoops, and an engine thunders by, joined by every little ragamuffin whose legs are old enough to follow. Close upon the heels of this comes the milk-man, who sits philosophically on his cart, and glancing up at the windows, utters a succession of sounds, the like of which never was heard in heaven above, or earth beneath, or in the waters under the earth.

Now, saloons and cigar stores open half a shutter each, and apple-stalls multiply at street corners. Then the bells ring for church, and, with head and heart distracted, you obey the summons. On your way you pass troops of people bound to Hoboken, Jersey, Williamsburg—anywhere, but to the house of God. Groups of idle young men, with their best beavers cocked over one eye, stand smoking and swearing at the street corners; and now Yankee Doodle strikes on your ear, for the dead is left to his dreamless sleep, and the world jogs on to a merrier measure.

You enter the church porch. The portly sexton, with his thumbs in the arm-holes of his vest, meets you at the door. He glances at you: your hat and coat are new, so he graciously escorts you to an eligible seat in the broad aisle. Close behind you follows a poor, meek, plainly-clad seamstress, reprieved from her treadmill round, to think one day in seven of the Immortal. The sexton is struck with a sudden blindness. She stands one embarrassed moment, then, as the truth dawns upon her, retraces her steps, and, with a crimson blush, recrosses the threshold, which she had profaned with her plebeian foot.

Now the worshipers one after another glide in; silks rustle; plumes wave; satins glisten; diamonds glitter; and scores of forty-dollar handkerchiefs shake out their perfumed odors.

What an absurdity to preach the gospel of the lowly Nazarite to such a set! The clergyman knows better than to do so. He values his fat salary and his handsome parsonage too highly. So with a velvet-y tread he walks round the ten commandments, places the downiest of pillows under the dying profligate's head, and ushers him with seraphic hymning into an upper-ten heaven.

From this disgusting farce let me take you to the lecture-room of the Rev. Dr. Tyng. It is the first Sunday afternoon of the month (when he regularly meets the children of his parish, who are mostly members of his Sabbath-school). It would seem an easy thing to address a company of children. Let him who thinks so, try it! Let him be familiar without being flat; let him be instructive, and at the same time entertaining; let him fix roving eyes; let him nail skittish ears; let him stop just at the moment when a child's mental appetite has lost its digestive power. All this requires a—Dr. Tyng.

See—group after group of bright faces gather around him, and take their seats; not one is afraid of "the minister." He has a smile of love and a word of kindness for all. He has closed his church purposely to meet them, and given the grown-folks to understand, that the soul of a child is as priceless as an adult's, and that he has a message from God for each little one, as well as for father and mother and uncle John. He asks some question aloud. Instantly a score of little voices hasten to reply, as fearlessly as if they were by their own fire-side. He wishes to fix some important idea in their mind: he illustrates it by an anecdote, which straightway discloses rows of little pearly teeth about him. He holds up no reproving finger when some lawless, gleeful little two-year-older rings out a laugh musical as a robin's carol. He calls on "John," and "Susy," and "Fanny," and "Mary," with the most parental familiarity and freedom. He asks their opinion on some point (children like that!), he repeats little things they have said to him (their minister has time to remember what even a little child says!) He takes his hymn-book and reads a few sweet, simple verses; he pitches the tune himself, and, at a wave of his hand, the bright-eyed cherubs join him.

Look around. There is a little Fifth Avenue pet, glossy haired, velvet skinned—her dainty limbs clad in silk and velvet. Close by her side, sits a sturdy, freckled, red-fisted little Erin-ite, scantily clad enough for November, but as happy, and as unconscious of the deficiency as his tiny elbow neighbor; on the same seat is a little African, whose shiny eye-balls and glittering teeth, say as plainly as if he gave utterance to it, we are all equal, all welcome here.

Oh, this is Christianity—this is the Sabbath—this is millennial. Look around that room, listen to those voices, if you can, without a tear in your eye, a prayer in your heart, and Christ's sweet words upon your lips: "Feed my Lambs."

ANNIVERSARY TIME.
MR. GOUGH AT THE OPERA HOUSE.

Funny, isn't it? Country ministers, with their wives and daughters, in the unhallowed precincts of an Opera House! I trust they crossed themselves on the threshold, by way of exorcising Beelzebub. Observe their furtive glances at the naked little dimplednesses perched upon yonder wooden pillars. How legibly is—Saints and angels! where are those children's trowsers? written upon the elongated corners of their evangelical mouths. R-a-t-h-e-r different, I confess, from the Snagtown "meetin'-house," with its slam-down seats, its swallow-nested roof, and its shirt-sleeved chorister; but, my strait-laced friends, if you strain at a harmless marble Cupid, how could you swallow an electric flesh-and-blood ballet-dancer? Such as we are wont to see in this house? I have tried to educate myself up to it, but may I be pinched this minute if I do not catch myself diligently perusing the play-bill, whenever they execute one of their astounding rotary pas. I can't stand it; and yet my friends, at the risk of being excommunicated, allow me to say, that I would rather stand a ballet-dancer's chance of getting to heaven, than that of many a vinegar-visaged saint of high repute in your churches.

But this is a digression. Just see those women seating themselves on the stage. Saucy as I am, I could not do that; nor, if I did, would I put my feet upon the rounds of a chair in front of me—and the audience. How patriarchal Solon Robinson looks, with his clear, calm face, and his long, snow-white beard! He is quite a picture. What a pity he ever burned his fingers with "Hot Corn." But let him throw the first stone who has never by one well-meant, but mistaken act of his life, called forth the regretful "what a pity!" The river which never overflows its banks may never

195

devastate, nor—does it ever freshen the distant and arid Sahara. Many a poor man has blessed, and will bless, the name of Solon Robinson; and many a hard-toiling woman, too, whom he has instructed how to procure the most nutriment for her starving children from an old bone or a couple of onions. Let those who make wry mouths at "Hot Corn," taste his "poor man's soup," and do justice to the active brain and philanthropic heart of its originator.

I used to think the "New York Tribune," of which Solon is agricultural editor, a great institution, until I discovered two things: first, the number of able, talented, practical men employed in its getting up; secondly, that a bull's head is kept constantly seething in the machine boiler to impart a wholesome ferocity to its paragraphs!

Hush! here comes the speaker of the evening—John B. Gough, supported by Dr. Tyng (who believes in preaching to dear little children, as well as to their fathers and mothers). John says, "Ladies and gentlemen" (not— Gentlemen and ladies, as do some ungallant orators). "Ladies and gentlemen, when the admission tickets are twenty-five cents I feel doubtful of giving you your money's worth; judge then how a fifty cent ticket embarrasses me." A very politic preface, John; but ere you had spoken five consecutive sentences, I knew it was mock-modesty. You know very well that no man understands better how to sway a crowd; you know that many an audience, who yawn through addresses that are squared, rounded, and plumb-ed by nicest rules of rhetoric, will sit spell-bound unconscious hours, and laugh and cry at your magnetic will. John, you are a good and a great institution, and right glad am I that the noble cause in which your eloquence is enlisted, has so pleasing and indomitable a defender.

But John—it is not all in you. Double-edged is the sword wielded in a just cause; and not a man, woman, or child has listened to your burning words to-night who did not know and feel that you spoke God's truth.

Success to the Temperance cause, and all its apostles, both great and small; and above all, never let woman's lip baptize the bowl, which, for aught she can tell, may sepulcher her dearest hopes this side heaven.

WAYSIDE WORDS.

I wonder is there a country on the face of the earth, where the Almighty is oftener called upon to send to perdition the souls of those who offend its inhabitants? Everywhere that horrid imprecation, so familiar that it is unnecessary to shock you by writing it, meets the pained ear. I say pained, because I, for one, can not abhor it less on account of its frequency, or consider it less disgusting, because it filters through aristocratic lips. Everywhere it pursues me; in crowded streets, on ferry boats, inomnibusses, and, I am sorry to say, in ladies' parlors, which should afford a refuge from this disgusting habit.

From old men—whose toothless lips mumble it almost inarticulately; from those who would resent to the death any question of their claim to the title of gentlemen; from young men, glorious else, in the strength and vigor of youth; and sadder still—from little children, who have caught the trick, and bandy curses at their sports. An oath from a child's lips! One would as soon expect a thunderbolt from out the heart of a rose. And yet, there are those who deliberately teach little children to swear, and think it sport, when the rosy lips, with childish grace, lisp the demoniac lesson.

An oath from a woman's lips! With shuddering horror we shrink away, and ask, what bitter cup of wrong, suffering, and despair, man has doomed her to drink to the dregs, ere she could so belie her beautiful womanhood.

One lovely moonlight night, I was returning late from the opera, with a gentleman friend, the delicious tones I had heard still floating through my charmed brain. Suddenly from out a dark angle in a building we passed, issued a woman; old, not in years, but in misery, for her long, brown hair curtained a face whose beauty had been its owner's direst curse. To my dying day I shall never forget the horrid oaths of that wretched woman as she faced the moonlight and me. Perhaps I had evoked some vision of happier days, when she, too, had a protecting arm to lean upon; sure I am, could she have read my heart, she would not have cursed me. But oh, the wide gulf between what she must have been and what she was! Oh, the dreadful reckoning to be required at the hands of him who defaced this temple of the living God, and left it a shapeless, blackened ruin!

CHARLOTTE BRONTE.

Who has not read "Jane Eyre?" and who has not longed to know the personal history of its gifted author? At last we have it. Poor Charlotte Bronte! So have I seen a little bird trying bravely with outspread wings to soar, and as often beaten back by the gathering storm-cloud—not discouraged—biding its time for another trial—singing feebly its quivering notes as if to keep up its courage—growing bolder in each essay till the eye ached in watching its triumphant progress—up—up— into the clear blue of heaven.

Noble Charlotte Bronte! worthy to receive the baptism of fire which is sent to purify earth's gifted. I see her on the gloomy moors of Haworth, in the damp parsonage-house—skirted by the grave-yard, sickening with its unwholesome exhalations, crushing down, at the stern bidding of duty, her gloomy thoughts and aspirations; tending patiently the irritable sick, performing cheerfully the most menial household offices; the days "passing in a slow and dead march;" cheered by no mother's loving smile, or rewarding kiss; waiting patiently upon the hard, selfish, unsympathizing father, who saw, one by one, his gifted daughters sink into untimely graves, for want of the love, and sympathy, and companionship for which their yearning hearts were aching.

I see these sisters at night, released from toil, when their father had retired to rest, denied the cheerful candle-light, pacing up and down, in utter darkness, the dreary little sitting-room, talking of the vacant past and present, and trying vainly to pierce the impenetrable future for one glimmering ray of hope; and as years passed on, and vision after vision faded away—alas! with those who wove them—I see Charlotte, the last survivor of that little group, pacing alone that desolate sitting-room; while the winds that swept over the bleak moor, and through the church-yard, and howled about the windows, seemed to the excited imagination of the lonely, feeble watcher, like the voices of her sisters shrieking to be again enfolded in her warm, sisterly embrace. Alone—all alone!—no shoulder to weep upon—no loving sister's hand to creep about her waist —the voices of her soul crying eternally, unceasingly, vainly, Give, give —and he who gave her life, sleeping, eating, drinking, as stoically as if ten thousand deaths were not compressed, to that feeble girl, into each agonized moment.

One smiles now, when the praise of "Jane Eyre" is on every tongue, at the weary way the author's thumbed manuscript traveled from publisher to publisher, seeking a resting-place, and finding none; and when at length it did appear in book form—the caution of the sapient book-dissecting "London Athenæum" containing only "very qualified admissions of the power of the author"—also of "The Literary Gazette," which "considered it unsafe to pronounce upon an unknown author;" also at "The Daily News," which "did not review novels"—but found time soon afterward to notice others. Mistaken gentlemen! you were yet, like some others of your class, to take off your publishing and editorial hats to the little woman who was destined to a world-wide fame, but—and if ye have manly hearts they must have ached ere now to think of it—not until the bitter cup of privation and sorrow had been so nearly drained to the dregs by those quivering lips, that the laurel wreath, so bravely, hardly won, was twined with the cypress vine.

Literary fame! alas—what is it to a loving woman's heart, save that it lifts her out of the miry pit of poverty and toil? To have one's glowing thoughts handled, twisted, and distorted by coarse fingers; to shed scalding tears over the gravest charge which can be untruthfully brought against a woman's pen; to bear it, writhing in silence, and have that silence misconstrued, or speak in your own defense, and be called unwomanly; to be a target for slander, envy, and misrepresentation, by those of both sexes who can not look upon a shining garment without a wish to defile it—all this, a man's shoulders may be broad enough to bear, but she must be a strong woman who does not stagger under it.

I see Charlotte Bronte in the little parsonage parlor, at Haworth, draperied, hung with pictures, furnished, at last, with books from the proceeds of her own pen; and upon the vacant chairs upon which should have sat the toiling, gifted sisters, over whom the grave had closed, I see inscribed, Too late—Too late! and I look at its delicate and only inmate, and trace the blue veins on her transparent temples, and say, Too late!— even for thee—Too late! Happiness is not happiness if it be not shared— it turns to misery. But, thank God, at last came the delirious draught of love, even for so brief a space, to those thirsting lips—but which, incredible as it may seem, the father, in his selfishness, would have dashed aside; relenting at last, he gave up this tender, shrinking flower to more appreciative keeping; but the blast had been too keen that had gone before—the storms too rough—the sky too inclement. We read of a wedding, the happiness of which the selfish father must cloud at the last moment, by refusing, for some inexplicable reason, or no reason at all, to give away the bride in person according to episcopal usage—we read of a short bridal tour—of a return to a love-beautified, love-sanctified home —we read of a pleasant walk of the happy pair—of a slight cold taken on that occasion—of a speedy delirium—of a conscious moment, in which the new-made bride opened wide her astonished eyes upon her kneeling husband, pleading with God to spare her precious life; and we read the heart-rending exclamation of the latter as the truth flashed upon her clouded intellect—"O! I am not to die now?—when we have been so happy?" and with streaming eyes we turn away from the corpse of Charlotte Bronte.

THE END

www.ingramcontent.com/pod-product-compliance
Lightning Source LLC
LaVergne TN
LVHW010948040525
810355LV00009B/900